MISS SOUTHEAST

MISS SOUTHEAST

ESSAYS

ELIZABETH LINDSEY ROGERS

Curbstone Books / Northwestern University Press
Evanston, Illinois

Curbstone Books
Northwestern University Press
www.nupress.northwestern.edu

Printed in the United States of America

10 9 8 7 6 5 4 3 2 1

Library of Congress Cataloging-in-Publication Data

Names: Rogers, Elizabeth Lindsey, 1985– author.
Title: Miss Southeast : essays / Elizabeth Lindsey Rogers.
Description: Evanston, Illinois : Curbstone Books/Northwestern University Press,
    2024.
Identifiers: LCCN 2024015082 | ISBN 9780810147720 (paperback) |
    ISBN 9780810147737 (ebook)
Subjects: LCSH: Rogers, Elizabeth Lindsey, 1985– | Authors, American—21st
    century—Biography. | Lesbians—United States—Biography. | Women—
    United States—Social conditions. | LCGFT: Autobiographies. | Essays.
Classification: LCC PS3618.O4577 M57 2024 | DDC 824.92—dc23/
    eng/20240408
LC record available at https://lccn.loc.gov/2024015082

CONTENTS

A BEARING

When my father and I first find my car—what will soon be known as the Wing—it's parked in front of the Shell station on Mount Hope Church Road, a For Sale sign taped to the passenger's-side window. It's August in Guilford County, where heat rises off the bleached road in sinuous, hallucinogenic waves. The world smells like hogs and chicken shit and gasoline. Gas is still cheap, $1.20 a gallon. This is rural North Carolina: the land of failing tobacco, megachurches, and Jesse Helms. Gas is cheaper out here than it is Greensboro proper, and it's cheaper in Greensboro than pretty much everywhere else.

This is good news for us, because other than driving around, there isn't much to do. After school lets out for the day, teenagers hang out at the nearby Amoco station. Red is a popular car color in my peer group, making everyone look like a NASCAR driver or firefighter. On any given day, some kid cranks up his stereo bass and swaggers inside to buy chips and a twenty-four-ounce Mountain Dew. A group of girls stand with their sedans at the periphery, their eyes raccooned in makeup. They wear tank tops cropped just above the navel, their bellybuttons pierced with rhinestones: souvenirs from unchaperoned weekends down at Myrtle Beach.

I have just gotten my driver's license, proof of being able to straight line back, do a three-point turn, and use my blinker when changing lanes. The person giving my test, a middle-aged woman in a blue uniform, finished the exam by instructing me to pull into one of the DMV's diagonal parking spaces: the easiest of all maneuvers, even for bad parkers. The North Carolina test does not involve parallel parking, for which the occasion, given where we live, is infrequent. I won't learn to parallel park until I'm twenty-six years old, a decade from now. I've grown up on a dead-end road at the rural border of a subdivision: two-story houses on one side, cows and horses and brick ranches on the other. There are curing cabins in the woods east of the house, holdouts from the land's tobacco heyday. Southeastern Guilford County, at least to me, feels mostly like empty space. We are far enough outside the city limits to be forgotten by most everyone; it's a place where there is no noise except insects and the occasional car zooming past.

Having a car is a cultural mandate where we live, even for teenagers. You can't walk anywhere. There aren't sidewalks. Bikes are for the kids in the driveway, dirt paths circling the ponds, or maybe the cul-de-sac if you live in one of the subdivision neighborhoods that are cropping up around the farms. Even the poorest kids all seem to get cars, either as gifts or by saving their minimum-wage earnings: lifeguarding at Emerald Pointe, driving farm machinery, bagging at Winn-Dixie. It's common to pass one of the trailer parks and find two or three newer-looking cars parked in front of each unit. And the enormous high school blacktop is always full of that glamorous, new-car shine: candy red, coastal blue.

But the Wing's exterior is white: a color reserved for grandmothers' cars, Oldsmobiles, or my mother's Buick Skylark back in 1985. Nine months pregnant in one photo, she poses in front of the Skylark, a car so long and so white that it might as well be a polyester pantsuit on *Dynasty*. The Wing itself is also dated, a 1989 Volvo 240—one of those long, boxy sedans, a living room on wheels. European cars are not common at my high school, where anything "foreign" is regarded with deep suspicion. There are only two or three other Volvos in the parking-lot sea of Fords and Dodges. These Volvos are wagons, mostly recycled middle-class-mom mobiles. My father explains to me, in his best diamond-seller voice, "A Volvo is forever." His own 240 wagon has clocked nearly three hundred thousand miles, and he doesn't plan on getting rid of it anytime soon.

The Volvos make us look like geeks, frankly. It is a signal to my classmates that there is something weird about me, even if my family looks relatively normal on the surface. No one has told us that, in the rest of America, the Volvo is the liberal family's trademark, the older models a marker of a kind of faux bohemianism. But my father, an ex–farm kid with a strong North Carolina accent, bought his first Volvo in 1988 because of a bad wreck on I-40. He'd totaled my mom's old blue Mustang in a multicar pileup, smashing his nose, jawbone, and some teeth in the process. He watched everyone's cars crinkle up like accordions. Somehow he was alive, but my mom's Mustang was history.

From there, my father researched the least dangerous vehicle to drive, and his Volvo commitment was born. Buying that first used one in the late eighties—and the second, third, fourth, and fifth— wasn't about my father being a bohemian or countercultural. This is a guy who, back in the day, voted twice for Reagan, and then twice for George H. W. Bush. The Volvo was supposed to be a conservative measure. It was a gesture toward reliability and security. Driving, after all, is the most dangerous thing we do on a daily basis. Life in southeastern Guilford County doesn't come with that many hazards, at least not ones that are visible.

∴ ∴ ∴

After some negotiation, my dad and I buy the Wing for around three thousand dollars from a guy in McLeansville who hangs doors for a living. At Swedish Auto Works in Greensboro, the only place that will touch a Volvo, we replace the air-conditioning fluid, the brake pads, one belt. The car probably needs new shocks, but those are expensive and will have to wait. For now, the back of the car flies up over railroad tracks and the country potholes, like a dog trying to run with a bum leg. A crack begins to creep up from the right-hand side of the windshield, bifurcating the profuse green landscape as I drive. I have adjusted the seat all the way forward, a setting my father calls "M," for midget. He buys me an old-lady cushion, a step up from the phone book I sat on to learn to drive. I'm only four foot eleven, still mostly looking and feeling like a little kid. The Wing is tall and big boned, as if designed for ancient Swedes.

Each morning I ease into my assigned parking space at school. Southeast Guilford High is a drab, one-story cracker box of a building. My parents actually met here in 1972 during study hall, a phenomenon that no longer exists there. My father was "a kind and mild-mannered hick," my mother tells me, but also a guy who owned a blue Barracuda, the result of working the second shift at a mattress factory and saving everything. My mother, on the other hand, was a Raleigh-raised middle-class girl—Southern through and through but more of a suburbanite—who'd been uprooted to Guilford County halfway through her junior year. She drove the baby-blue Mustang back then, a showy gift for her sixteenth birthday. Her father, as a joke, had presented the car to her in an enormous gift box that he built in their driveway.

In my time, the high school is poor kids, farm kids, people who are trying to become suburbanites but have the rural Piedmont in their blood. Lots of people are related to one another: The most common last names are Garrett and Causey. With my sisters at college and my cousins living down in Charlotte, my friend Hope is the only other person at school who has my last name. She is dark skinned, wears glasses, and feels like a freak because she gets such good grades; Black and nerd don't sync at our school. I'm red haired and freckled, my skin so white that people are always telling me to go get a tan. Hope and I don't look related at all, but our standing joke is that we are sisters because we have the same last name. We keep telling people that, although no one believes us.

Hope sits behind me in trigonometry, our first class of the day. The mowers hum outside the low windows, the cinderblock room drowsy with sunlight. Our teacher, a big woman with a lilting voice, is teaching us sine, cosine, and tangent. "Did you ever hear the legend of SOH CAH TOA?" she asks, holding her marker like a baton. No one answers. She writes SOH CAH TOA on the whiteboard. "SOH CAH TOA was the only child of a great Indian chief," the teacher says. "And she was a *very bright* Indian girl. She was especially good at math."

I can feel Hope rolling her eyes behind me. "Oh sweet Jesus," she whispers in my ear. "Is this the part when all the white people learn that the earth is round?" I stifle my laugh.

"One day, SOH CAH TOA climbed a very tall tree." The teacher draws a tree in three swipes of the marker and then a stick figure with two long lines on the sides of her head, maybe braids. "SOH CAH TOA's father asks her if she can calculate the sine of the sacred theta tree. She is confused and asks the chief for a hint. He says, 'Think about the name I gave you, daughter.'" The teacher points to the letters on the board again, our eyes glazing over their scramble. "SOH CAH TOA remembers the *H* in her name stands for 'hypotenuse.'" Well, now we see where this is going. "She thinks to herself, well, I remember that sine = O/H, cosine = A/H, and tangent = O/A." The teacher feigns thinking. Someone sneezes, as if the sacred theta tree were producing pollen.

"Bless you! SOH CAH TOA takes her measuring rope and drops it from the top of the theta tree to measure its height. That gives her the length of O, opposite the angle theta. Then, she throws the rope from the top of the tree to where the tree's shadow ends on the grass." The teacher draws a square where the tree meets the ground to represent its right-angledness. *Aha.* This problem has been solved with the help of a made-up story about Native peoples as collateral damage. Never mind that all the terminology in this lesson is Greek.

"Was that really necessary?" Hope whispers to me. "I mean, can't she come up with *anything* else?" I glance around the room, but no one seems to be paying attention. Two years from now, Hope will be at MIT, the first person from our school to go. No one in Guilford County has even heard of MIT. Hope will find herself depressed and overwhelmed from the culture shock; it will take her a long time to figure things out in Boston.

I look down at the loose leaf in my binder, filled with notes and symbols and numbers. For me, just in that past year, math is finally beginning to make sense. Not in the sense of SOH CAH TOA, but in the way that I am starting to trust math, this abstract process of moving toward what I can't see right away. As a child, math was stressful to me: the word problems, the trial-and-error methods, the timed tests, the one-mistake-might-destroy-everything computations. If you are an anxious child, as I was, always worrying about checking your work and the clicking clock, Mylanta ends up being part of a complete breakfast before a math test. Later, when I was a freshman, my geometry teacher was frustrated because I couldn't picture the straight dotted line from the base of the pyramid to its point, couldn't see the faces of a prism that weren't drawn out on the page. "You have no imagination," he told me, an accusation I internalized.

But the more complex the math gets, the more I feel I am delving into some other realm, one where you can't always see or understand everything right away. There's a satisfaction in knowing that if I start with letters and degree marks, the Greek symbols and the parentheses, and work according to the formulas I've been given, the answers emerge after many steps. Math is becoming almost mystical, although I cannot voice that yet. I am fascinated by the hyperbola, how its two arms stretch out forever, coming close to those dotted asymptotes (God?) but never touching them completely. The first time I graphed a sine on my calculator, I almost couldn't believe the beauty of the wave that emerged. It snaked on and on: like radio waves or electricity, not unlike the uphill and downhill of one of Guilford County's country roads.

At school, you get your assigned parking space by seniority but also, unofficially, what kinds of grades you make. It's a kind of shaming technique, I suppose. The highest-achieving seniors, the ones taking Advanced Placement classes, park right in front of the main entrance, their cars lined up like an octave of shiny piano keys. It is the exact opposite of the classroom, where the teachers are always trying to get kids with low grades out of the back row and toward the front of the classroom, where they can be watched and forced to pay attention. Although I'm only a junior, my parking space is also pretty good: right by the cafeteria door. It's so close to building that rain barely touches me before I'm at the car.

But the first morning that I get caught behind a tractor on the way to school, pulling the Wing into the parking lot later than usual, I find someone else's car in my parking space. I've never seen it before. It's a Ford Escort, two-door hatchback, cherry colored, shiny as a prom dress. It's pretty much the opposite of my 1989 Volvo sedan. I'm forced to park in one of the empty gravel spaces, way over by the baseball diamond.

I leave a passive-aggressive Post-it note on the windshield of the offending car. "This is my assigned space. Thanks."

But the car is back again just a few days later.

"Please"—I write on my next Post-it note—"park elsewhere. You're in the wrong space. B.R."

My space stays open for the next few days. But the red car returns by the first week of September.

It doesn't take long to discover the culprit. She's in that tough group of girls who are always taking up the stalls with their not-so-covert smoking, scattering ashes across the seats, leaving the rest of us still desperate to pee when the bell starts ringing. She's older than I am, a senior, a gruff country girl with bleached-blond hair and very black eyeliner. Across the lot, I hear someone calling her. *Shannon.*

Shannon puts her key in the ignition of that mean little Ford, a car that seems about a third of the length of the Wing. On the other side of the tinted windshield, she fiddles with some knob—air-conditioning, probably—and then gets out again to yell something across the parking lot.

"Excuse me," I say, approaching her.

Shannon doesn't turn around. She's still yelling at her friends, throwing up her hands in a dramatic way. She gives one of them the finger and then laughs.

"Hey!" I say again. "Shannon!"

She whips around, confused that I know her name. We've never spoken before. Despite the distance between us, she already seems to be looming over me. I'm beginning to feel like an eighth grader who has wandered over from the middle school next door.

"Hey, so, this is my parking space," I tell her, as if maybe she didn't know that already. The round headlights of her Ford seem to stare me down. Shannon rolls her eyes, saying nothing, like I'm speaking with a weird accent and she can't be bothered to listen.

"Just move your car," I warn her, "or I'm going to say something to the office."

Shannon looks amused for a second, smirking. I know that I've made a mistake. I turn toward the gravel lot, hoisting my heavy backpack as I go. I've got my purse on one arm, my lunch bag crumbled under the other. The bag is argyle print, like the dweeby socks of a grandfather.

"Go ahead and tell on me, you stupid ho," Shannon yells at my back, finally acknowledging what I've said. The word *ho* is a catch-all insult for girls in Guilford County, even for those of us who can count the number of people we've kissed on one hand. *Don't react.* *Don't react.* I keep my eyes fixed on the gravel lot, seeing the Wing in the distance.

Shannon yells over the roar of all the cars trying to get out of the lot. "Go ahead. See what happens next. Just wait. I'll kick your ass!"

The last time someone threatened to beat me up was in the seventh grade, and I'm not enjoying the feeling again. It's a reminder that no amount of following rules seems to matter in the high school social order. It seems like whoever can be meanest and loudest holds the keys to everything.

I chicken out and don't follow up on my threat to tell the school office what's going on. Instead, I take matters into my own hands, employ a more passive-aggressive method: I make sure I get to school before Shannon does. That next week, I roll in early each day, finding my two white lines like a landing strip in morning fog.

But by Friday after school, I find one of my old Post-its, now tucked under *my* windshield wiper. I study it, confused at first. Underneath my own serial-killer scrawl—the most unfeminine, inconsistent handwriting of any girl I know—there's a response from Shannon. *Whatever bitch* it reads in bloated, curly letters. UR *car is so* UGLY! And, underneath: *PS Get a life. You need to learn to park straight.*

I circle around to look at the rear of the Wing. Shannon is right. The tires are a little skewed to the right: the result, I know, of pulling into the space too late and too close, the wheel overly revolved in the process. The long nose of the car sits in the space's right-hand corner while the back left wheel almost grazes the line. My face stings with embarrassment. So this is what my father means when he says I've "overcorrected." I sigh, letting my load of books drop onto the Wing's enormous back seat.

∴ ∴ ∴

The first full week after Labor Day, I wake from a ghostly dream. I was wandering aimlessly in the school hallway, hearing students' voices but not seeing any bodies. I sit up in bed, the sheets balled up at my waist. I've got a bad feeling in my stomach as I head into the week, my intuition sending signals I don't understand.

I eat some cereal and take Mylanta. My father, who has never been a morning person, goes off to work, half-asleep in his Volvo. My mother, noticing my silence, asks if I'm OK. "I just have this weird feeling," I say to her, shuffling down the basement steps to leave for school.

She pauses. "Be careful," she says, not knowing how else to help.

All the way to school, I'm dreading the parking lot. Instead of her red car, I imagine Shannon herself taking up my parking space, her body suddenly huge and towering between the two parallel lines. When I get to school, though, my parking spot is still open. I hurry into the building before anyone can see me. The sky over the parking lot is a pregnant gray: unusual for September.

We're currently reviewing for our first unit test in trigonometry. The hour and a half passes quickly as the clock in the classroom moves, almost unseen, toward the small angle of 10 A.M., what will mark the second block of my school day: AP US History. It rains. We scuttle under the walkway between the two school buildings. In the afternoon, I take US 421 northbound to the commuter arts school in Greensboro where a couple of friends and I now take intermediate guitar class, no longer offered at my high school due to recent budget cuts. The school is downtown, right near the Woolworth's where the lunch counter sit-ins happened in 1960. The old Woolworth's building will eventually become a civil rights museum, but in 2001, the project is still stalled due to lack of funds. The storefronts on that row are all empty, waiting for some sort of revival.

The rain has stopped and the sun is out. The air coming in the windows is steam. In the tobacco fields I pass before the city limits, the remaining leaves have turned yellow, wilting: harvest time. We have been talking in US History about the Virginia Colony and how Europe wanted North Carolina only for more tobacco and cotton and lumber and ports. We have been reminded that the *Mayflower* got caught in northerly winds, that the Pilgrims were supposed to be much farther south than where they ended up. We've reviewed the facts of Sir Raleigh and his colony on the coast, which vanished inexplicably. Sometimes I get the feeling that North Carolina is entirely about the past, as if there's nothing here that's even real.

I turn on the car's terrible radio. No good music. No real news. Donald Rumsfeld is declaring war on Pentagon bureaucracy, whatever that means. Venus has beaten Serena in the US Open. Like a ball bouncing back and forth, the radio din switches between the Wing's left and right speakers, refusing to come out of both at once. The Wing's enormous rear flies up over the railroad tracks, making the guitar in the back seat knock against the door. I can't relax, even after rolling the windows down. At the edge of town, I bear west.

My clearest memory of the next morning is what I wear to school: flared jeans, a green tank top. An old plaid shirt rolled up to the elbows, which I bought with my guitar friends on my first thrift-store trip in Greensboro. It's the first day since the age of twelve that I've decided to go to school without a bra on. Rural North Carolina culture is one in which a small chest like mine is subjected to a push-up bra. Under the plaid shirt, without any bra, my breasts seem to disappear. I walk around feeling new, unarmed, afraid and unafraid in alternating measures.

We're finishing our trigonometry test when another teacher appears at our door, her expression blank with shock. There have been three plane crashes in the last hour, I hear her say in a hushed tone. Eager for an interruption, ears prick up all over the classroom, although my own pencil hardly lifts from the page. I can't make sense of anything larger than the problem that's right in front of me.

But I soon know something is wrong because Ms. K isn't doing her usual raucous corralling as we scuttle into her room after the class change. Ms. K is our US history teacher, a loudmouth from upstate New York, which might as well be another planet. When someone sasses her or another student, she just throws them out of class. She's ruthless: normally, we're quizzed every day, in the first ten minutes of class, on the reading the night before.

But when we get to her classroom that day, she doesn't mention the quiz or try to hustle people into their seats. Instead, she turns the TV on. All the stations are showing shots of New York. Manhattan. One tower at the World Trade Center has already burned into collapse, a column of dust in its place.

If you're a kid in the South, you most likely don't have the skyline of New York memorized. To most of us, New York is rich people, Wall Street, suits, giant Christmas trees and ice skating, *Home Alone 2*. We've never been to New York. We've got no sense of what a plane crash in the middle of Manhattan might mean—politically, symbolically, or otherwise—for the whole of the United States. We've never been through any kind of disaster except for hurricanes coming inland, drowning the rivers in shit and hogs and snapping trees in half. But disasters in cities are different. I've never been inside a skyscraper. I have flown on two airplanes in my lifetime. For most of my classmates, that number is zero.

But we have heard of the World Trade Center. Like the Capitol or the White House, it is supposed to be a metaphor for our country—or something. How it represents us, we're not exactly sure. All we know is that people are inside a burning building, and there's nothing we can do. Twenty minutes into our class period, we're still watching the northern tower, with its top engulfed in smoke. For a moment, the long radio mast on its top, erect as an arrow, is intact. I feel myself holding my breath, as if I know what will happen next.

"Shit," Hope says. "Shitshitshit."

It's when the tower's radio mast begins to slide down the screen, still completely vertical—like a rocket launch but in reverse—that we gasp out loud. The trusses have given out. The second building is collapsing. That two-dimensional needle drags from the top to the bottom of the TV, then disappears behind the smoke plume: three dimensional, coming right toward us. Just like that, the northern tower vanishes. A pole point of reference erases itself in front of us, though we don't understand why it's a point of reference to begin with.

∴ ∴ ∴

After history class, the school hallway feels weird, like it's leading to some other dimension. The pipes run the length of the ceiling like an abandoned railroad track. There's very little sound. I hear the custodian emptying the trash cans, the crumbled loose-leaf paper crunching inside the bags: refuse from our small, unimportant lives. Death is on the brain. By now, we've learned that thousands of people had been trapped inside that burning building. That the people flying the planes seemed to have done this on purpose. "True evil," the teachers are telling us, shaking their heads. "There's no other way to look at it." This doesn't make sense to me. The precision of the coordinated planes, someone's willingness to die to make this happen. So much planning.

We move slowly, more like particles or atoms than people. I cross between the math-science-history building, known as the Annex, and the main building, shuffling under the ramp. The sky is that otherworldly blue of early fall. Not knowing what else to do, I leave early

for my guitar class downtown. No one seems to notice. The interior
of the Wing is sweltering. I take off the plaid shirt, the greenhouse
heat pressing my bare shoulders. My flip phone, sitting in the passenger's seat, shows two missed calls on its neon screen. Both are from
my mother. She knows I'm in school, that my phone is in my car for
emergencies.

I turn on the radio, spinning the dial, searching for a clear signal.
When I get to the news, the pitch of the voices alarms me. *Terrorist
attack*, they are saying. We have to *band together*, they are saying.
Others are saying, *war*. I think right away of the uniformed recruiters
who show up at our high school every spring, setting up their table
near the front double doors. How many seniors will they enlist this
year? For many of my classmates, the military is the best option after
high school, the easiest way toward a respectable future. In the coming years, some of my classmates will go on to defend causes that we
barely comprehend.

In our cow-dotted pocket of the county, it seems that we teenagers
are unequipped to make sense of a disaster like this one. Our understanding of the world is based only on how our own oversimplified
factions grate against one another: Black versus white. Boys versus
girls. Poor versus almost-poor versus smugly middle class. (No one at
our school is rich the way we imagine people are in New York.) Those
of us who follow the rules versus those who feel like the rules were
made without taking them into account. People like me, parking
my clunky old Volvo in the parking lot, going through the motions
of school because I'm too ashamed to do otherwise. Some of us feel
like all or none of these things at different times, the strict categories
blurred. And there are the Shannons of the world, ready to fight tooth
and nail for whatever small space there is to claim.

Before I head downtown, I pass the Amoco station. As if someone
had predicted a hurricane or an ice storm, all the pumps are occupied in the middle of the afternoon: a red Ford 150 pickup, a black
Ford Explorer, a Dodge Caravan that's painted the light blue everyone calls Carolina blue because it's worn by UNC teams. When I
ease onto US 421, I accelerate to fifty miles per hour, then fifty-five.

At the first major pothole, I lose the sound coming from my front left speaker, and the right one sounds garbled. I slap the left one. The sound returns for a second, then goes out again. When I've given up on the radio, I become hyperaware of how fast I'm moving. I lift my sandaled foot off the gas, hearing the motor start to descend in pitch, but the Wing's interior is quiet and unchanged, a living room on wheels.

A living room with wings. That's how my dad's friend, who flies small planes, once described the static feeling of being on a commercial jet. But I know from all those problems in trig class that big planes move ten times as fast as I am moving right now. *A plane flies at six hundred miles per hour at eighty-one degrees west of south*, I hear in my head, the rhythm of the math problem familiar, almost innate. But then: *it turns due north, crashes into a tower, and burns up.*

Squinting into the Volvo's bisected windshield, I feel September's green-and-blue glare, the afternoon sun bearing down on the white car from the left side. A floater hovers in the corner of my left eye that is the same color and thickness—about the width of a pencil lead—as the windshield crack. I now know that this is a string of cells in my retina that appears when I am exhausted or have been looking too long at something too bright. But back then, it's inexplicable, a translucent wave that comes at times I don't understand. I can feel Guilford County receding behind me.

That morning's trigonometry review, just before our test, had been filled with bearing problems: nameless boats and planes and bicycles headed out at thirty degrees or two hundred degrees away from true north. We were asked to calculate the number of nautical miles directly from the shore to the boat or how long it would take to get there. Our teacher filled the whiteboard with blue and green vertical lines labeled *N*, which, in the case of these problems, is supreme, unquestionable. As a child, I'd always held that north was a mystical idea, a place where it snowed all the time, where the world eventually doubled back on itself. In reality, *N* was just a line pointing toward the ceiling. From where we stood, with our limited frame of reference, it was impossible for this *N* it to be anything more than imaginary.

As I approach my usual turns toward the other school, I feel a strong urge to cut class—even though it's music, the best of all—and keep going forward. Through the clusters of government housing and the nearly abandoned rail yard, up and past to the blocks where Greensboro's few tall buildings stand in that small, dark, glass heart of downtown. And past that, out to the airport, toward the state line, toward Virginia and New York, and whatever else comes after that. Due north—if there is such a thing—and forward and up, as if following that strange and vertical aperture in my windshield. If I had looked up into the sky, I would have noticed there were no planes flying that day.

∴ ∴ ∴

Earlier that day, just after history class and the towers' collapse, I'd headed into the girls' bathroom. As I was coming out of the stall, I looked over to the sinks, and I froze.

There was Shannon, standing alone. Her back was to me. She stared at herself in the mirror, her ponytail like a bundle of blond straw on the nape of her neck. She rubbed under her eyes with a tissue, holding a chubby black eyeliner pencil in the other hand. The empty bathroom, with its mustard-colored tiles and slit of frosted window, suddenly felt cavernous. If I were to have said anything, I don't know how loud or echoing it might have sounded. Shannon must have felt me standing there because I saw her expression change in the mirror. Her face hardened.

I braced myself. I'd seen girls shove each other against the wall when one stole the other's boyfriend. Maybe the same rules applied to parking spaces. *You stupid ho*, I remembered her calling me, the phrase an earworm.

Shannon continued lining her right eye with the pencil, started redrawing the border underneath her left. *Liner on your lower lid is trashy!* I could hear my math-major sister saying mockingly. But Shannon kept drawing with deep concentration. Her eyes were small and brown. From how she layered the lines on top of each other, I sensed that she was after something, that she wanted to make some part of herself visible. As we stood there, not speaking, I felt something vulnerable from Shannon, maybe even fear. It didn't quite make sense. It could have been the aftershocks of the day's tragedy, I guess: events relayed to us from somewhere so far from our understanding that we didn't know what to do with them.

Still, I wasn't sure that Shannon wouldn't jump me right then, finally giving me what she thought I deserved. Adrenaline flooded my body. I decided to make a run for it. When I was almost halfway to the door, Shannon turned suddenly from the mirror and exited just ahead of me, cutting me off. Our eyes didn't meet, partially because her head was down. But I realized, as she zoomed ahead of me, that she was almost as short as I was. The hem of her jeans dragged a bit on the tiles and into the hallway. She turned right. She might've been going to her next class. Or she might have decided to cut it, going straight for the school's back entrance and out to the parking lot, onward toward the rest of her life, a mystery to me. I knew only that my conflict with her, as real as it had felt, wasn't the whole story.

I hadn't seen Shannon's car in a while. I wondered where she was parking these days. Did she have a designated space somewhere else? It is, I realized, weirdly unfair, the way the school assigned them. Shannon is a senior, a full year ahead of me. Maybe I should just give it up. *In the end,* I thought to myself, *she wants that space more than I do. Let her park there if she got to school first.* Whatever claim I'd thought I had to the spot was imaginary, anyway. It wasn't worth fighting over.

I don't see Shannon, or her car, for the rest of the year. For a while, I wonder whether she's dropped out of school. But I spot her at the high school's graduation in the spring, a whooping-and-cowbell-ringing event that takes place at the Coliseum in Greensboro's downtown. Since my grade-point average is high for my class—I'm ranked below only the obnoxious fifteen-year-old genius and Hope—I am part of the group of juniors made to lead the senior class's procession. We wear black dresses; the boys black suits. We are draped with black and white sashes that make us look like pageant contestants or debutantes. Despite my complaints, my mom snaps a picture of me in the driveway before I head to the ceremony, as she had done for both of my sisters.

At the ceremony, in the sea of names called to the stage, I hear the principal say Shannon's. Her middle name turns out to be Elizabeth—the same as my first, although it's only the name I use on paper. For a moment, I'm caught up in this coincidence, this small overlap in our circumstances. The principal makes a point of mentioning people's future plans. She doesn't say anything after she says Shannon's name. I wonder if this means Shannon will go to work full-time now, as many graduating seniors do. Maybe she'll have a baby within the next couple years, as many will. Maybe she'll live with her mom for a while and take community college classes, her little red car shuttling her back and forth to Greensboro or Burlington or Asheboro, a student parking permit sticker on the back windshield. Maybe the military is in her future, although I can't picture her there.

I shift inside my high heels, uncomfortable from standing up for so long. From my post beside the raised platform, I watch Shannon climb up, her blond hair fanning out of the bottom of her black graduation hat. She flashes a beauty-queen smile to the crowd when she passes. She doesn't look at me and has probably forgotten who I am by now, my face receding in the sea of others.

Shannon doesn't wear any special cords around her neck. In her plain black polyester robe, she files quickly through the diploma line, climbs down from the platform. From here, she will head back to wherever she's been sitting, a number of rows back. The floor, with its endless lines of collapsible chairs, suddenly feels a lot like the high school parking lot. Soon, I can't see Shannon anymore. As the rest of the names are called, I'm trying to get my bearings, still looking for her. I'm still trying to tease her small figure out from the long black arrow of students—and then, from the rows that black arrow breaks into, what fills this wide space in front of me.

MISS SOUTHEAST

Late February in North Carolina: hormonal, daffodil-spewing days alternate with days of cold, slobbering rain. All winter long, the white girls have made regular visits to the tanning bed. The backless dresses hang in closets, waiting. At our rural county high school, this time of year brings out the worst in everyone—not so much because of the weather, but because it's beauty pageant season.

"It's *not* a beauty pageant," the Treasurer tells me for the umpteenth time. "It's a scholarship competition."

We are having a student officer meeting in Condo #2, one of the trailer classrooms behind the school building. The Treasurer has just agreed to direct this spring's pageant, which means that the rest of us, thank the Lord, are mostly off the hook. She actually won when she competed last year, so we reason that she'll be able to anticipate everything about the pageant before it even happens.

I think back to the Treasurer's winning performance. Between the typical pop-song renditions and flashy dance numbers, she had emerged onstage wearing a peasant blouse and a long skirt, a white kerchief tied around her head. Her voice, normally small and nasal, seemed to have grown overnight, carrying Sojourner Truth's famous convention speech to the back of the auditorium. "I have as much muscle as any man," she proclaimed, pulling back her sleeve and flexing her bicep in an exaggerated, jokey way. The audience laughed. "You need not be afraid to give us our rights," the Treasurer insisted, "for fear we will take too much." Every so often, she threw her hand on her hip, punctuating her speech with a refrain: "And ain't I a woman?" she asked the crowd, her voice trumpeting through the dark.

As I watched her perform, I wasn't thinking so much about women as I was about how the Treasurer was a Black girl and how Sojourner Truth was born a slave. How our classmate, Brandon, had recently been sent home for wearing a Confederate-flag belt buckle to school. How Hailey—a white girl on the cheerleading squad with the Treasurer—had recently told me that her father was, of course, completely fine with her having a Black best friend, but that he'd bury her alive in the yard if she ever got engaged to a Black boy. These things made me ashamed. I made a resolution then to try to go as far north as possible to college, as if bigotry doesn't exist outside the South.

In the last moments of the pageant, the Treasurer stood posed in her backless silver dress, not fully cognizant that her name had just been called. Despite her popularity at school, you could tell by the odd, unpracticed motions of her face that she wasn't expecting to win. But the crowd was cheering. She hesitated as she started her victory walk down the runway. No one said it out loud, but it was probably the first year in school history that the pageant winner wasn't a white girl. At the runway's end, she stopped and smiled demurely, looking down at all the hands raised around her.

This year I'm the vice president of student government, the officer with the vaguest responsibilities. In truth, it's the second half of junior year, and I'm now starting to feel apathetic toward most school activities, although I'm brave enough to pretend I don't care at all. It is in this spirit, perhaps, that I am involved with this year's pageant: as a distant sort of "ceremonial leader," which, as we learned in US History class, is what you call your executive when she needs to show up for nameless moral or social reasons but not to actually do anything useful.

When I arrive at the dress and tech rehearsal, the plywood runway still looks pretty rickety. Some boys are working to reinforce it. My friend Maya is with them, an actual hammer hanging from the carpenter's loop of her overalls, her spiky brown head bobbing up and down as she surveys her progress. She's not even on student government. "Who enlisted Maya?" I ask the Treasurer, my verb choice revealing my true feelings.

The Treasurer, who is working on last-minute choreography with the girls, looks at me suspiciously. "Maya said *you* were stressed out about all this," she replies. My ambiguous stance on this pageant is not a secret to the Treasurer, and neither is the fact that I've done very little to help with the efforts. "She says she is here to help you out."

I shrug. I might've complained to Maya about the pageant earlier that week. We have guitar class together: our elective that used to serve only metalhead boys and the occasional uptight Baptist kid who wanted to learn how to play his Christian rock power ballads. Now, though, girls are slowly finding their way into the class. Outside of school, Maya has taken it upon herself to introduce me to important music from decades past—Fleetwood Mac, Prince, Queen, Heart, the Police—which we blare from the Discman-plugged-into-cigarette-lighter setup in her Ford Aspire. When Maya drops me off at home, I often find myself lingering in her front seat until the song finishes.

From across the auditorium, I see Maya pick up the staple gun, working to attach fabric and a long garland to the edge of the plywood. The runway is transforming into a gaudy sheet cake. It stretches over the stage pit and the first few rows of the auditorium, sacrificing a few center seats.

I sidestep toward Maya through one of the auditorium rows. "Hey," I say. "I didn't know you were helping with all of this."

"Oh." Maya smiles sheepishly, swaggers a little. "Yeah, no big deal." She runs her hand through the back of her hair, which is about an inch long. Since last year, I've watched her go through a slow revolution, ditching that paperback Bible she used to carry at all times, replacing her contact lenses with black-rimmed glasses and her ponytail with shorter and shorter cuts. I loved the haircut before this one—a funky-artsy bob, all sass—but her current haircut, which seems to ignore the standards of beauty entirely, makes me sort of nervous in a way I can't explain.

"How are you holding up?" she asks me, as if I'd recently experienced a tragedy.

I motion toward the stage, where the girls keep getting confused about the choreography, intercepting one another like frightened gazelles. "Whatever, I guess. There are still some things to work out," I add unnecessarily.

"SMILE!" the Treasurer shouts at the girls from the auditorium. "YOU'RE SUPPOSED TO LOOK LIKE YOU'RE HAVING FUN." The cheerleader quality has disappeared from her voice. Now she just sounds mean.

The pageant always has a theme. This year, it's Egypt. I don't know whose idea this was. The Treasurer chose the costumes and the songs, along with the choreography. The contestants are wearing their group dance costumes for the first time: shiny gold leotards, black sarongs, bangle bracelets. The leotards are flimsy and unforgiving for anyone who wears larger than a B cup or isn't thin. Luckily, most of the dance moves are stiff poses. Beneath the sarongs, they wear nude-colored pantyhose (to simulate bare-leggedness, if your skin is light beige?), which look alien on almost everyone. White canvas sneakers detract from the overall Egyptian look, but the stage floor is full of splinters. This costume can best be described as middle-aged pool partier meets child's tap recital. The low budget may be partially to blame.

When the music starts again—a midtempo, electronic beat—they lean from side to side, punctuating their sways with poses from "Walk Like an Egyptian," with one arm forward, one arm behind. The girls start to move laterally in flocklike formations, as if trying to give the impression of two-dimensional hieroglyphs. *I know I may be young*, Britney Spears begins to narrate. *But I have feelings too. And I need to do what I feel like doing.* Occasionally, the girls hug their own bodies and face the phantom audience dead-on, confronting the empty auditorium with images of being trapped. The song they are dancing to is Britney's "I'm a Slave 4 U." This was the Treasurer's choice.

It is hard to imagine how this can fly. These are the years before college—before *cultural appropriation, Orientalism*, or even *anti-semitic* enter my vocabulary. I don't have language yet for so many of the things I see and feel. Still, I know just enough to guess at all the ways this dance number might be wrong. I watch the scene in horror, wondering what there is to be done.

Maya watches them, trying not to laugh. I study the side of her face. There is a makeup line near her jawbone, a small cluster of blemishes just below the surface. "You know," she says over the music, "you should have entered this year. You might have even won. They give you money, right?" She turns to me. "You could have danced, yeah? Or played guitar? *That* would have been a first for them."

I feel my eyebrows go up. Despite our distance from the stage, this scene feels too close for comfort: campy pose after pose, bodies shifting inside those identical leotards. But they are all up there: the cheerleaders, the debate champion, the girl-power athletes, and a few girls who are usually quite reserved. There is even the one goth kid, shocking us all.

We stand like this for a few minutes. I am flushed, as if I am also under the stage lights. The song fades out. Britney's slinky voice evaporates into the dark. In the quiet, I am holding back something else that I can't name. Maya is just behind me. She's standing so close that her shirt sleeve, soft cotton, occasionally brushes the back of my arm.

∴ ∴ ∴

Thankfully, it would probably be against the law for us to include a swimsuit competition. It's 2002, and this is high school, not the Miss America pageant. Still, in preparation for the dance numbers and low-backed evening gowns, all the paler girls have perfected their tans. How anyone gets used to this process, I'll never know. I recall my one try at the tanning salon, a few years back, with my older sisters, when I couldn't stay inside the tanning bed due to panic. I felt like a freckled vampire frying in a fluorescent coffin.

This pageant night is the rainy, not-quite-spring-yet variety. In the art classroom, the girls are busy transforming themselves into Guilford County Cleopatras with blue eye shadow and liquid eyeliner. The tables normally used for drawing are littered with lipstick tubes, tubs of glitter, good-luck notes, and flowers—some grocery-bought carnations and a few extravagant rose bouquets from parents or the boyfriend who got the clue. Dress hangers are wedged between the low ceiling tiles, the evening gowns hanging like gaudy Christmas decorations. The terrible leotards are on; the pantyhose runs are thwarted by clear nail polish.

"You look nice," Maya says to me. For my ceremonial duties, I'm dressed in a gray angora turtleneck, black skirt, black pantyhose, modestly high heels: an ensemble slightly more edgy than a missionary. Maya's in her overalls again. Next to her, I feel like I'm in costume, maybe in drag. "I'll be in the back," she tells me, motioning to the rear of the theater.

The auditorium is filling with coughs and wet umbrellas. I sit down near the judges' table with a pen and strips of small paper, thinking up a few more last-minute questions for the final round. "Ask them about the war on terror!" my loudmouth history teacher says, almost sadistically, when she comes up to say hello. She's a fixture, though a cultural outsider: "Maybe it's because I'm a Roman Catholic?" she once proposed to me, "And, you know, a carpetbagger of sorts." I consider what she says about the war. I admit there's some part of me wanting a final question with more substance, one that might show us which girls can actually think for themselves. I write down the question and toss it in the fishbowl.

When the lights finally dim, I stand huddled on the wooden step below the stage with the president and the secretary, waiting to be introduced. The Treasurer walks on wearing last year's evening gown and tiara, the crowd whooping and calling her name. There's nothing uncalculated about her this year: she speaks firmly, sticking to her script. She thanks our sponsors, the girls, and the student government. We climb up onto the lip of the stage, giving our obligatory wave to the community: *ceremonial leader.* I stare out into the charged space between me and the exit signs, getting a brief glimpse of what it might be like to perform in these girl Olympics. I feel exposed.

I have to admit that I've never seen the auditorium so packed. Not for our guitar concerts. Not for any school play I've seen. Not for the speech we'd gotten about how poorly we were doing on the SAT, for which our school's scores, as well as our whole state's, were lower than average. You know, as if that were our fault somehow.

Tonight is a scholarship competition, I tell myself, trying to get with the program, literally and figuratively. Almost every seat is filled, people's jackets and bags spilling into the aisles. At the back of the auditorium, I recognize Maya's tall, spiky figure shadowing the space near the door.

The girls take their places for the opening number, Britney's beats filling the air. The sexy pulse has the audience hooting before anything has even happened. The dancing starts, limbs and gold flashes everywhere. *All you people look at me like I'm a little girl . . .* The crowd works themselves into a roar. "Go Megan!" someone yells from the back. And then, someone else, for the whole team: "You go, girls!" I turn to our glittery Treasurer, who looks mildly pleased. She's been working on this all spring.

Every contestant gets to perform in the talent portion, a democratizing force. But the range of activities is narrow. There are canned songs with dramatic hand-gesture accompaniment plus a few dance numbers: watered-down ballet or tap mixed with MTV-inspired moves. Some acts have religious themes. This year, to mix it up, there is one Shakespeare recitation from the goth girl, complete in period attire. The night's most painful moment is a shrill rendition of "Summertime," the girl's hand shaking under the microphone and creating untended vibrato. She's more or less on key, but her timbre is too angular to be pleasing and too timid to be like, say, Janis Joplin. As someone whose hands usually shake before any guitar performance, I feel for this girl trying so hard to be something other than who she is the rest of the time.

Being music nerds, Maya and I are mostly rooting for Jamie-Ann Appleton, a lanky, freckled blonde who is playing a trombone prelude. There has never been a brass player, we guess, in the history of the pageant. We watch her face inflate, her bare arm flex as she grips the trombone slide. Somehow, she manages to make this look graceful, standing up there in her silver evening gown. But during an interlude from her piano accompanist, we catch Jamie-Ann emptying the spit out of her trombone valve, letting it leak onto the floor behind the piano. "That was awesome," Maya whispers.

Ultimately, Jamie-Ann is chosen for the final round. Goth girl has also advanced unexpectedly. The last couple of girls are called. There is a terrible moment just before the curtain goes down for intermission when you can see the losing girls fully receded into the background, their smiles starting to slip.

At intermission, I duck backstage, grabbing a few bottles of water for the judges. Everything smells muggy, a mix of flowers and hairspray and sweat. I'm startled by Allison—my closest friend in kindergarten and first grade—with mascara running muddily down her face, a pageant cliché. She has just lost. I barely recognize her at first. She is strangely compelling to me in her song-and-dance, Judy Garland cross-dressing getup: a fedora, men's shirt, and tie, an outfit in which she wouldn't be caught dead in normal life. Her long ponytail coming out of the back of the hat gives her away.

Even more surprising is that her mom is standing beside her like an indignant ice-skating coach. "I can't *believe* this," I hear her saying in protest to the pageant results. I'm embarrassed for both of them. There are no other parents backstage. It's true that Allison's rendition of "The Man That Got Away" was just as good, probably even better, than the other songs. But she's a jock, spends most of her time playing soccer and running track. You wouldn't think she would care about something as stupid as a pageant. But no one enters a pageant without hoping—believing, even—that she might win. Every girl here wants something.

I'm starting to sweat, my legs sticking to my pantyhose. The rain has stopped by the time Maya and I step outside to the lit area on the cafeteria loading dock. Nearby, some of the younger-looking parents, looking like high schoolers themselves, are gossiping about their daughters. This is also where everyone has come to smoke, even though it's technically banned on campus. The ban is ironic, seeing that our school is built at the edge of what used to be a very large tobacco field.

Maya leans against the brick exterior. "It's going fine," she reassures me.

"I know," I say. "I can't, like, wait until this is over."

"But you've got to admit, it is sort of fun," she says, "seeing everyone do their thing. Right?" She pauses, considering, touching her hands to her face. "I should have sucked it up and entered," she says.

I snort. "Are you serious?"

"It's just one night," she points out. "I could really use that scholarship money." I try to picture Maya in a rhinestone evening gown, but it is the Maya I remember from last year: long hair, eye shadow, carrying the Bible in her purse. I feel a twinge of jealousy for her willingness to change every year, to not care what others think every time she reinvents her image.

I tug at the pantyhose wrinkle at my knee and stare out into the parking lot, which is almost eclipsed by the fog. "There's always next year," I say.

Maya changes the subject. "I really think Jamie-Ann's going to win," she says. "Everyone likes her."

"She played *trombone*," I pointed out.

"True," she says. "She also looks really good in that dress, though."

I shift uncomfortably in my heels. One of the smoking women has turned to us and is studying Maya, perplexed.

With her short-short hair and dark-rimmed glasses, Maya looks decidedly older, stranger than our school's usual "just turned seventeen." Maya has been getting a whole lot of looks lately. Once, a few weeks back, when we stopped for pizza with some music people on the way home from a concert, the waitress had referred to Maya as "sir." The mistake had offended me, but Maya just grinned. "Did you just hear that?" Maya had asked me. "Yeah," I said. I heard her. I was pretending to look for something in my purse.

When the curtain reopens, the glass fishbowl appears: a messy, paper-filled oracle, filled with final questions for the contestants. Maya and I don't take seats but instead stand in the back, noncommittal. The Treasurer pulls out the early questions: the standard ones about problems facing American youth and grand proposals for the future of our world. At last, she looks at one of the slips of paper and hesitates. She frowns a little.

"What do you feel is our country's responsibility," she asks the contestant, "when it comes to the war in Afghanistan?" My heart jumps at the sound of my own words being read aloud.

The crowd mutters. It's been less than a week since the United States officially invaded, the events of 9/11 only a few months behind us. Every house between here and town is hung with an American flag. But it's unusual for anyone in high school to ask a political question or even expect anyone to be aware of political events. I realize that I know very little myself, less than I should know. I have only listened to radio snippets driving back and forth to school. My stomach flips.

Carly, a prepubescent freshman, steps forward. She's wearing a pale-pink dress with sequins. My oldest sister used to babysit for her. Carly doesn't look much older now than she did then. She's drawn the lowest number, has to respond first to this one. "Can you repeat the question?" she asks, her voice wavering and small. But then she changes her mind right away and starts to speak.

"I believe that . . ." Carly begins, but stops. Her body sharpens. It's terrible to watch: this girl trying to transform the panic flickering inside her brain into something we can recognize. "The responsibility would be that . . ." She stops again and glances over her shoulder for a second, as if looking for someone to lead her. Then she puts her hand up next to her face, obscuring her mouth.

"I'm sorry," she says finally. Silence from the audience. Carly passes the microphone back to the Treasurer and politely exits the stage.

I don't smirk the way I'd imagined I would in this moment. Instead, I feel awful. Cruel.

"This is my fault," I whisper to Maya. "Totally my fault."

"What do you mean?" Maya asks.

"I'm the one who put this question in."

Even the Treasurer looks bewildered, her eyes trying to avoid the space where Carly just was. After a moment, the Treasurer composes herself, asks the same question to Tiffany, a blond sophomore in a white halter dress. "What do you feel is our country's responsibility," she begins again, "when it comes to the war in Afghanistan?"

It is a terribly vague question, I think to myself. Like something made up on a standardized test to trick someone into choosing the wrong answer. Badly worded. What does *our* even mean? Who is the *our*? Why *feel* and not *think*?

Lucky for all of us, I guess, Tiffany doesn't flinch, acts as if she's been waiting her whole life to speak out on the subject. "Nothing's more important than protecting *our* country," she answers triumphantly, gesturing at the audience for community emphasis. "I'm proud. I'm proud of our military. The most important thing . . . I mean, the thing to remember is . . ." she trails off for a microsecond. "United, we stand!" Tiffany smirks a little, the year's most popular national slogan ringing through the auditorium. The crowd explodes, cheers moving through the rows like the ripples in a giant American flag.

There is some waving from the judges' section. They flag down the Treasurer for a quick conference. Whispering, hand gestures. Finally, it is announced that Carly's attempt at the question will be thrown out and not counted against her. They don't give their reasons. I smooth the back of my skirt absently, feeling my face go hot again.

Carly is brought back out, visibly shaken, but the crowd claps lightly for encouragement. They don't want her to freak out again. She is asked a question about cloning—a question I didn't write, thank god—which she firmly believes is wrong. She vaguely mentions the Bible's teachings. An easy sell. She's been redeemed.

The goth girl, whose real name is Meredith, also responds to this one. She pauses for a long time, gathering her thoughts.

"Every person has a soul," she says, deliberately. "And of course you can clone a body. But you can't clone a person's soul."

Her voice haunts me in the dark auditorium. I remember a poem of hers from English class: verses about wandering through our local Winn-Dixie, her lines filled with images of cracked linoleum, garish toy machines. What I remember best is the descriptions of everyone's shoes. "Sometimes I think mine are the ugliest," she had written. "Dirty white leather and stained laces." Although she's made it this far, we know she'll likely be eliminated after this round. She is too strange, wearing elbow-length black gloves with her black-and-red lacy gown and noticeably heavier than the girls around her. Despite her colorless, stringy hair and pasty skin, she has a kind of beauty: almost like something from another century.

Like someone you'd see in a painting, I say inside my head, but then want to correct myself. This, too, feels like the wrong thing to think for some reason, or at least an unoriginal thought.

I wonder if her boyfriend is in the audience. He's a year older than us, and I don't know his name. But he is recognizable: even in the hot months, he usually wears a cape to school. If only I had such courage.

The judges have made their final decisions. Jamie-Ann is the runner-up and named Miss Congeniality. There's a pregnant pause before the winner is announced: the second girl to respond to the Afghanistan question. Realizing that she's won, Tiffany—whose talent performance was a mediocre rendition of Mariah Carey's "And Then a Hero Comes Along"—opens her mouth in an exaggerated, elastic fashion: "Oh my gosh. Oh my gosh."

I clap numbly, realizing that any small hopes for an oddball winner were unfounded. The Treasurer mechanically removes the tiara from her head, signaling her return to normal life. Her hair is sticking up a little from where she pulled the crown off. The Treasurer has to stretch a little to bobby pin the crown on this new, much-taller Miss Southeast, who has just shimmied into her satin sash.

Tiffany takes the rose bouquet across her body like a rifle. She's a natural. She makes her way down the runway, her sparkly gown growing larger and more white-blinding as she walks above the crowd. This makes the Treasurer seem miles from where we stand, a silver star receding into the background. Her shoulders sag a little. I squint, trying to decipher her expression, but she seems too far away. It's hard to imagine that everyone will show up on Monday as the regular versions of themselves: jeans and overdone eyeliner, talking too much or moodily silent, all of us counting down the days until spring break.

The applause for Tiffany has gone on for so long that it just sounds like static. Maya, despite having been upbeat about the whole pageant, now looks incredulous. I have seen her wear this confused expression before: the time, for example, that she didn't realize—because of her dyslexia, she claimed—that she had managed to play the first two lines of a guitar piece with her music score upside down. She turns toward me, as if to ask me a question.

I am supposed to stick around for the night's cleanup. But my body automatically follows her when she starts to leave, eager to beat the crowd out of the space. I turn away from the stage and the audience, through the double doors and the hallway filled with lockers and trophy cases, and then another set of doors—a very long runway into the outside world. Past the trailer condos. I step into the fog: for these early-spring weeks, it seems to have hidden everything except for what is right in front of us.

I lift up the bottom hem of my sweater, for air. In comparison to the school building, night somehow feels more like the real world, feels good against my skin. There are too many cars because of the pageant, so Maya has parked on the other side of the road: technically illegal, but who was going to stop her in rural Guilford County? "My car is parked in Egypt," she says jokingly, her tribute to the theme of the evening.

I ditch my shoes a few minutes into the walk, choosing the numbing, soggy ground over the feeling of high heels stabbing into my feet. When we get to the gravel edge of the lot, I stop.

"Do you want me to carry you?" Maya asks chivalrously, only half-kidding.

"Don't be ridiculous," I shoot back. I put my shoes half-on, teetering across the sinking gravel. The scene around us is eerie, like a giant X-ray. There isn't much light, but I can make out, in a few places, the gray edges of the rainclouds and the outlines of the trees, skeletonlike. The leaves are coming in, but we can't see them at all. It still looks like winter. We cross the ditch gurgling with rainwater and then the road.

In her car, sweat pools behind my knees. It's cold in the car, but I still fan myself with the pageant's paper program. I can see myself reflected in her windshield. The night's humidity has caused my curls to swell up to about three times their normal size. I could be a beauty queen from the 1980s with this much volume.

She sighs. "Well, that sucked. I really thought Jamie-Ann had this thing."

"What did you expect?" I ask.

"Things are changing around here," she says, hopeful. "A *goth* was in the pageant."

"Maybe she just wanted to put it on her college applications," I say cynically.

"I'm guessing you wouldn't put it on yours," she said. "Too rednecky for you, yeah?" She grins at me.

She is kidding, but she also has my number. I'm spending this year of high school trying to figure out how to build a road out of this county. Maybe out of the whole state. I am perplexed about why I came tonight. It certainly wasn't to support the contestants. Why was Maya here? Maya was here to help me.

I suddenly feel guilty. "I don't know," I say, finally.

Maya looks out the window. We've sat idly in the car like this many times, usually because we are waiting for a good song to finish playing. But this time, there is no music. We are totally alone, far away from the girls who will soon emerge from the school, hauling their makeup boxes and grocery-store bouquets into the parking lot. Across the road, I can barely make out the baseball diamond's scoreboard, a blur of white on leggy stilts.

I look at Maya, hard, in profile: the easy curve of her forehead, the sure, indelicate noise, the small flare of her upper lip. She doesn't turn the ignition or even reach for her key. Instead, she turns to me. As if sliding into some lateral world, I lean over the console, my mouth aiming for hers. My move is so sudden that I can hear her breath catch.

She turns her head forward again, at the last second.

"I'm sorry," I say.

"Oh." Maya laughs nervously. She pauses. "I mean, you just surprised me."

I surprised myself. I hesitate, searching for the right way to respond. I feel like Carly the freshman, asking, "Can you please repeat the question?" My brain has been emptied of its words. My whole body feels like it is composed of rhinestones, skittish sparks. I am filled with both terror and longing. I want to lean in again, but I've lost my nerve tonight.

After a long silence, she reaches over, her hand resting on top of my knee. We wait. I put my left hand on top of hers, tentatively. My fingers are not soft, I know, and I imagine she must be feeling, now, the places that the guitar has made calluses. And we sit like this for another minute, not moving. Then I reach for the back of her head, the place where the hair is shortest. It's thicker than I expected, bristling against my hand. This texture spreads through my limbs, another sort of strangeness. I'm surprised how good it feels. I've never found short hair attractive on any woman until just now.

I trace the back of her neck, then the hard line of her jawbone. My hand crosses over, intuitively, to the small patch just below her ear, where blemishes from some time ago have left a mark. It's strange, this skin: a bit uneven, weathered. I think of the runway in the now-empty auditorium, being stripped of its fabric and garlands. The Treasurer, wondering where I am, or maybe not caring at all, is zipping her beaded dress back into its vinyl bag. I imagine her turning off the auditorium lights. Maya tilts, letting the side of her face rest in my palm. Then she turns toward me just when I think she is going to pull away.

DYKE LITANY

You know them, the kids wearing jerseys sizes too big, shaggy hair in their eyes. Buying cigarettes and candy at the Kash n' Karry, the corner store in the middle of nowhere. Tucked in the back desks in Spanish class, tuned out but rarely making trouble. Eyebrow piercings and black sneakers. Chains clipped to their jeans. Their names feminine, like Angela and LaTisha and Kaitlin, soon to be Ange and Tish and Kait. Clips of the silver shears. *Scissor sister.* The girls laughing as they buzz each other's heads in some ugly bathroom. Hair piling on tile, a darker snow. *Rug muncher.* When one of them rakes her scalp with her palms, the cool touches back like a thousand rice grains in a barrel. She still might show up to church the next day, scalp showing and sore afraid. No corner to hide in.

The tall one in the ROTC uniform holding the flag. The fat one in the art room: black lipstick, clever noir silkscreens. The good one with the long ponytail, her As stacked in the gradebook. She's pouring sweet tea at Fran's, a secret spliff tucked under her bra strap. The one who is keeping kids alive in the artificial wave pool, its engineered tide tugging at her. Her feet turn green in chlorine. The one bagging groceries at Winn-Dixie, her name pinned to her chest. The capital letters look strange when you stare for so long.

The couple ducking behind the leggy scoreboard, up to no good. The ones who never get suspended: too good, too good at breaking rules on the sly. The debonair coach eyeing the student she thinks is hungriest, thin shirt and freckled shoulders. The one for whom she will write a dozen late notes. The one she tries to convince to cut history, buys biscuits for on her way back to town. It'll be an unexcused absence. Delay the presentation on Watergate.

And the girl in your older sister's class: Heather, who hung herself on a Wednesday. Why? Quiz bowl, Latin club, used to sleep during sad movies. *Butch.* You search for Heather's house years later, its rocking chairs and sagging carport. You don't know what you're looking for.

The one who still says *But I couldn't be, because. Bean licker.* The one looking up *lesbian* in the tome-sized reference dictionary, finding both "homosexual" and "inhabitant of Lesbos." Who discovered Sappho's poems but found mostly blanks: that ruined temple, columns open to sky. This was not what she was hoping for, her fear doubling and doubling. So that's why my aunt ran off to San Francisco, she thinks. *Muff diver. Taco licker.*

She with her silver ring, snake eating its own tail. Corona around the moon: she wants to press her whole body to this night. Who says *nerves* when what she really means is: inside, this moth keeps nudging me with its ugly powder. Who says *but I couldn't be* only because there isn't language yet for the joy, which is a shape not yet drawn, which is something almost infinite.

We lean into the sinuous rural road, headed fast toward the city's hem. An unnatural speed. A humming where we all touch down. *Bumper to bumper.* Her and her and them and me.

SHAME

My older sisters warned me about Ellen Owens, the high school substitute teacher with a big mouth. I can see her framed in the classroom's doorjamb, her eyes dark and sharp like a hawk's. Despite being a Quaker, Mrs. Owens wasn't big on the virtue of silence. She preferred to shout the latest news down the hallway during class changes, when the corridor got so crowded that students actually moshed. "Beth Rogers!" she'd yell, spotting me in the commotion. "Your granddaddy's cows got out this morning!"

When you're a teenager, there is nothing more embarrassing than broadcasts about your grandparents' livestock. I preferred not to think about the cows under any circumstances: the cows could have landed on Mars, and I still wouldn't have wanted to know. But the Owenses' property line was close to my grandparents', meaning that Mrs. Owens thought she was an expert on happenings at the farm. Convinced I hadn't heard her in the hallway, she once went so far as to follow me into the music room, where I was unpacking my guitar for class. "Did you hear me, girl?" she asked breathlessly. "Those cows were *all over* the road this morning."

In the back row, one kid snorted in response. Another looked up at me, perplexed, as if he'd summed me up incorrectly. Cows were nothing new in rural Guilford County. The Future Farmers of America club even sponsored a festival once a year, a sort of mini state fair at school, tractors taking over the school parking lot and livestock grazing on the grass. One of the big draws was a cow bingo fundraiser:

people bet on squares of grass and waited to see if they'd be lucky enough to have theirs shat on.

But I was not a member of the FFA, not tough enough to be one of the true farm girls. Instead I was a nerd growing up in one of the rural subdivisions off US 421, driving an old Volvo to school with moody tracks from the Counting Crows' *August and Everything After* blasting out the windows. I was going through my own personal age of enlightenment that year, one that included vegetarianism. After I renewed Upton Sinclair's *The Jungle* from the library for the second time, I told my classmates I had given up meat "for political reasons." To have grandparents who raised cows complicated the image I was trying to cultivate.

When Mrs. Owens shouted these livestock jailbreak announcements down the hallway, I felt my ears turn hot as branding irons. It wasn't just about the cows, though. The truth was that I'd been trying to steer clear of my grandparents for most of my life, always embarrassed by what their behaviors might say about me, what I might be made of.

∴ ∴ ∴

Carl and Rosa Lee Rogers's farm was on the other side of US 421, just twelve minutes away from our house, but their world seemed even stranger and more gothic than the rest of our rural corner. I still feel the shapes of the farm scrolling through me, like a cyclorama cranked to the tune of an Appalachian ballad. The sun beat down on their hillside pasture, the L-shaped farmhouse, barn, tractor shed. The roan-and-white cows drifted lazily toward the pond. A murder of crows shadowed the edge of the cornstalks. In the terrible dog pen, the black Lab clanged against the wires, forcefully nosing his big silver bowl full of kitchen scraps. My sisters and I pushed each other on the tire swing, its umbilical-looking rope always on the edge of rot.

My grandparents' farmhouse was full of broken telephones and shorted-out vacuum cleaners they refused to throw away, as if they might be useful when the Rapture occurred. Carl and Rosa Lee were God-fearing Baptists who took the Bible literally. They weren't poor so much as schooled in the mentality of the Great Depression, when their families *had* been poor. Both dressed like the cast of *The Grapes of Wrath.* My grandmother didn't own a single pair of pants, hadn't bought a new outfit in twenty years. The new blouses and skirt suits we gave her for Christmas sat in boxes, the tags on.

My grandparents' frugality seemed pathological at times. Their general attitude was that anything of public utility or convenience was a sin. Because I'd seen *The Bad Seed* one too many times, my grandparents' incinerator, a metal enclosure where they burned their trash, was an object of dark fascination. I once asked my parents why my grandparents didn't get their trash taken away by the garbage-men, like everyone else in Guilford County. Was the farm too deep in the country, I wondered? "No," my mother offered cynically, "it's just that they're too cheap to pay for it."

My father, parking the car across from the barn, nodded in agree-ment, but his eyes shifted downward. Although he'd struck out on his own decades ago, separating his life from his parents, some small part of him was ashamed. It was difficult for me to believe that these *American Gothic* figures were, in fact, my father's parents. My father was gentle, an analytical type who had gone to university in Raleigh to become an early-generation computer scientist. He'd retained his country accent, but he also began most of his sentences with *evidently*, a word no one else used. He had my grandmother's cornflower-blue eyes, but this was where their similarities seemed to end.

Our Sunday meals at the farm were compulsory and almost com-pletely identical. My grandmother cooked fried chicken, biscuits, and vegetables from her garden. My grandfather, the gruff, half-deaf patriarch, was always the one to say the blessing. Conversation topics included what Bill Clinton was doing wrong, church, and numer-ous great-aunts and great-uncles that my sisters and I couldn't keep straight, even with their litany of horrid health problems. Before dessert, my grandfather would announce one of his paranoid plans, which got even larger in scale as he got older. He wanted to have a secret road on his property in case he needed to escape; he wanted to build his own cemetery so that he didn't "have to be buried next to Mexicans and Jews and Catholics." Toward the end of the meal, he'd disappear from the table without explanation, falling asleep on the odd single bed wedged between the back porch and his desk. Jerry Falwell and a host of other right-wing Christians droned on the radio.

My mother, who had been raised in Raleigh before moving to Guilford County as a teenager, found fundamentalism especially distasteful. Our family had ended up at a more moderate Presbyterian church, a decision for which my grandparents had given my father considerable grief. "Do you want to know why your dad and I refused to take you and your sisters to the Southern Baptist church?" she asked me once when I was a teenager. "One reason is because women aren't allowed to serve as elders or preach. They're not allowed to do *anything.*" I never thought of either of my parents as feminists, because gender roles remained fairly traditional in our household, but clearly they had spared their daughters from some strictures of Southern Baptist life.

Years later, my parents would find letters my grandmother sent to her sisters in which she described the gendered frustrations she rarely voiced aloud. She had written candidly about her depression, her unhappiness on the farm, even my grandfather's occasional violence when something hadn't gone his way. She spoke of her faith in God to fix her, to fix the suffering within her own marriage. Even so, she seemed to subscribe to a God that was the same brand of controlling patriarch as my grandfather. She quoted Bible verses warning about his wrath, the possibility of her future damnation. She also quoted the old marriage mandate from Ephesians: "Wives, submit yourselves unto your own husbands."

In my lifetime, though, my grandmother was a hard person to know. She was a fastidious woman who rose at ungodly hours to tend to her vegetables. She wore a ratty pair of my grandfather's pajama pants in the garden to keep the bugs off, her enormous hat shadowing her face. The word *shame*, as I later learned in college, comes from the Old English word *hama*, a kind of veil women wore to signal penance. Although Rosa Lee's brim was meant to protect her from the strong North Carolina sun, I always got the sense that she was hiding, or else trying to protect herself from something bad I could feel but not fully grasp.

∴ ∴ ∴

During Sunday dinners, my father, desperate to make nonconfrontational conversation, would mention how well his kids were doing in school. When one of us made the honor roll or got an award, my grandmother's stoic face would twist into a half smile, a quiet sort of pride. "That's very good," she'd say. "You keep that up." Rosa Lee was in charge of her family's finances—she was always better with numbers than my grandfather—and even though we didn't have a close relationship, she made sure to set aside five thousand dollars for each of her five grandchildren, to be invested toward college. Reports about the college funds came in the mail, the blue arrow on the graph rising a little each year.

Rosa Lee had a silent ax to grind when it came to higher education. I learned that she had been the valedictorian of her high school class in 1937. She graduated at the age of sixteen, winning a scholarship competition worth a year's tuition at the local college. She went to study education, but her father refused to pay for the second year—either because he couldn't or because she was a girl. My grandmother dropped out and went to secretarial school instead. When she met my grandfather, she was working as a secretary.

Rosa Lee never returned to college, but she did later register as a local substitute teacher to earn extra money. By the time I was eight years old, she had made her way to my elementary school, which spelled trouble for me. A very old woman roaming around school with your last name was a sure way to get yourself teased. Whenever I saw the ancient-looking 1970s station wagon in the parking lot, I was on high alert.

In the fourth grade, changing rooms for math class one day, I walked through the door and froze at the sight of my grandmother, her knobby spine hunched over the desk where Mr. Plummer usually sat. She'd written *Mrs. Rogers* on the board, that same austere cursive I knew well from years of religiously themed birthday cards. When our eyes met, I immediately looked away.

"Whoa, wait . . . is *that* your grandma?" a boy asked me, slumping in the desk behind me. I nodded. "Man," he said, laughing, "like, how old *is* she?"

Given that my father was the youngest in his family—born some twelve years after his sister—Rosa Lee was already in her early eighties, older than most of my classmates' grandparents. She was a gray-haired woman who would wear a polyester orange dress to school, the kind that wouldn't be popular again until I was in college and students wore them to be ironic. *Why can't she be a normal grandma like everyone else's*, I wondered, *the type that lives in a brick*

ranch and dyes her hair? Who shows up at sports meets and dance shows
to cheer for her grandkids rather than showing up unannounced in math?

When Rosa Lee introduced herself to the class, her tiny voice
sounded like she was coming from thousands of years in the past. She
had us open our books to a chapter about how to convert one unit
of measurement to another, and she asked me to read the textbook
aloud. Snickers came from all over the classroom. This was taking the
whole teacher's pet thing to another level. "Stand up," she instructed
me, as if it were 1950.

I couldn't look at her. But I had been raised not to be rude. I wasn't
cool enough to be defiant or forceful enough to push back. She was
still my grandmother. I remembered the college fund, the hopes she
was placing in me. Cheeks burning, I obeyed. I rose to my feet and
started to read.

∴ ∴ ∴

My dad's much-older sister was the only person on either side of
my family to have a doctoral degree, which made my grandmother
quietly proud and my grandfather suspicious. Once a year my aunt
visited North Carolina from her cosmopolitan life in Los Angeles,
the time change making her sleep in. She'd want to talk late into
the night, entertaining us with stories about serial killers. She was a
forensic psychologist, not exactly the career her parents had imagined
for her, I suspect. The usual talk at the farm's Sunday dinners was
replaced with her client stories: some guy who'd strangled all his ex-
lovers by wrapping a telephone cord around their necks, for instance.
Later I'd wonder if the creepy gothic sensibilities of the Rogers farm
had gotten into her psyche, predisposing her to such a career.

My aunt could be tinged with the sort of darkness that didn't lend
itself to easy conversation with children. But I was drawn to her brand
of strangeness, fascinated by the bizarre life she'd made for herself in
California. She had a loud, raspy laugh and sometimes cursed like
a sailor when my grandparents weren't in earshot. On her visits, she
usually stayed at the farm for part of the week before getting fed up
and coming to our house, taking over our basement. "That goddamn
right-wing radio twenty-four hours a day," she'd complain. "I mean, I
held out for as long as I could. I just can't handle it any longer."

I suspect that she visited only because she felt a particular responsibility toward my grandmother, who used her once-a-year visit as a kind of therapy session. While my grandfather was out in the barn, according to my aunt, my grandmother would complain about what an ass he was. "She can't do this over the phone," my aunt reported. "Dad listens in on all of her phone calls. He's even got a phone installed out in the barn."

I began to notice Carl eavesdropping on my calls with Rosa Lee too, his labored breath in the background. *What was he was listening for?* I wondered. I was never sure whether he was paranoid or just socially unaware. I started to feel like something about my grandfather was to be feared, something more ambiguous than his blatant racism and conspiracy theories. Even when I finally heard the darker family stories in my late teens and twenties, I still wasn't fully prepared for them.

My mother shared a story my aunt had once told her. When my aunt was a teenager, she became exceptionally close to another girl, spending so much time with her that it began to make my grandparents uncomfortable. One summer night when she was sixteen, my aunt's second-floor bedroom at the farm sweltering in the heat, she'd come downstairs to sleep on the couch. My grandfather crept in and crawled on top of her. She'd pushed him away and gone back up to her room, having nowhere else to go. "No one believed her back then, of course," my mother said.

Stunned, I asked my father if Carl had ever hurt him when he was a child. "No," my father told me. "But he was never affectionate with me either." My dad paused, pensive. "I suspect things were worse for my sister because she was the oldest," he said, "and also because she was a girl." I started to understand why she had run off to the West Coast—and what my parents had potentially protected me from by never leaving me alone at Carl and Rosa Lee's.

I was horrified by this new knowledge. My aunt's story confirmed my lifelong psychic sense that the farm was a creepy place to visit. Perhaps my grandparents weren't to be trusted, weren't as virtuous as they claimed to be. By that time, I was a teenager wrapped up in my own life, my weekends full of social events, extracurriculars, homework. Occasionally I called my grandmother on the phone for an obligatory hello, but I was always conscious that my grandfather might be listening. When I did go to my grandparents', I often drove myself so that I could leave as soon as possible. Talking mostly to my grandmother—my grandfather had become so deaf that he could barely hear me anyway—I sat as far away as possible from him at the dinner table, eating just the vegetable dishes while he gnawed his pieces of chicken to their bones.

By then Rosa Lee's body was starting to wear down, her vertebrae protruding. She sometimes accepted my help cleaning up after the meal: I scraped the dinner plates, making a slop-scrap bowl for the dog out back before sliding the dishes into the sink of soapy water. I burned with resentment for the years she'd been doing these household labors without assistance.

Rumbling down the long gravel driveway toward NC 62 one evening, I brooded, feeling the heft of the farm at my back. *I hate this place*, I thought. There were no lights for miles; I edged down the driveway by muscle memory. *Why would anyone end up here by choice?* I wondered, as I pulled out onto the road, the night as dark as a crow's back.

∴ ∴ ∴

The general culture of southeastern Guilford County, even on my parents' side of the highway, suffocated me. I was itching to leave North Carolina, convinced that the rest of the world must be more enlightened than our cow-dotted pocket. I got good grades, so maybe there would be exit paths, options for me. A musician, dancer, and all-around dork, I wanted Oberlin to be my school: a small haven of intellectuals on the cold, blue lip of Lake Erie, a nine-hour drive from home.

My mother was suspicious. "But why do you want to go to school in such an extreme climate?" she kept asking me. "Do you know what the winter will be like?"

My father had other, practical objections. "This is one of those schools for wealthy people," he insisted. I felt myself prickle with shame, wanting a thing I might not be entitled to despite my hard work in school all those years.

We were past the economic boom of the 1990s. The small investment my grandmother had given each of her grandchildren had taken a huge hit in the years just before I went to college. The money there would barely make a dent in private-college tuition. After we filled out the forms and got the financial aid package, my family qualified for more relief from Oberlin than my parents had anticipated. But there was still a lot of money for which to account. I would take out loans, I told them; I would work all year and in the summers. I wore my parents down with my persistence.

At Oberlin I found the community I'd been seeking: weird intellectuals and queers and artists from all over the world, twenty-somethings who made their own tofu in basements and played in punk bands and rode overnight buses to protests. What I hadn't known is that I would feel an invisible partition of a different kind of privilege. Many of my peers had lawyers and doctors as parents, or even professors. Some had received private educations. They had traveled. And many had trusts set up by their grandparents, which meant college tuition wasn't something their parents had to sweat.

Compared to the other kids at Oberlin, I often felt like a hick. I'd never bought a train ticket or eaten food cooked in a wok. ("You're not supposed to *wash* it," an older student said to me scornfully, "because it rusts. *Obviously.*") I didn't understand the references people were making to *Monty Python* or *Rosencrantz and Guildenstern Are Dead*. There were fewer kids from the South at Oberlin than any other region in the United States, and from people's reaction to my accent, it sometimes felt like I was the only one. After I said something in my history class freshman year, two chic-looking students approached me at the end of class, gazing at me sentimentally. "We were just wondering where you're from," one asked. "Is it Texas?"

At worst, my Southernness became a mark of bumpkin shame; at best, it was a quirky novelty for which I was teased. My first college girlfriend, a hippie Jew from suburban Philadelphia—a woman who had never driven deep enough into the country to use the high-beam lights in a car—was even turned on by it. "When you guys first met," my friend Lydia told me, "she was so excited. She's all like, 'I just met this cute redhead. She wears a jean jacket, and when she talks, she sounds like this: *Hayy, gurl!*'"

With all of us eating bad vegetarian food and living in unrenovated dorms, it was sometimes possible to believe that we were all the same, that no one had an advantage. But my girlfriend's grandparents were paying full cost for her to go to Oberlin. She took unpaid internships in the summer, spent our January terms doing international-language programs not included in our tuition. When I visited Philadelphia for the first time—walking the shady sidewalks of her family's historic neighborhood, seeing her private high school behind its iron gate—it seemed to me that we had grown up in separate countries.

After what seemed like the millionth conversation with the financial aid office—I was always in danger of having to leave Oberlin as the tuition went up each year—my mother admitted what my father had been too polite to tell me. Neither of my grandparents had wanted me to go to Oberlin, and they had given my father a terrible time about it. Hearing that wasn't a surprise. After all, Oberlin was pricey, and its culture did contain several red flags for my grandparents: artists and weirdos, gay people and Jews.

But no: my grandparents didn't know anything about the college. Apparently, my grandfather had a vendetta against the whole Lake Erie region. In the years when he and his orphaned siblings had been shuffled between relatives, my grandfather had lived in Elyria, Ohio, the town next to Oberlin.

"Carl said that it's too cold up there and that there are too many Catholics who drink a lot," my mother reported. "You know. Back in 1939." I tried not to laugh.

"He also said that there were 'a lot of uppity Black people,'" my mother continued, "who tried to tell him what to do."

Having known my grandparents' bigotry all my life, I should have been prepared for this. But his words made me sting with shame, and I almost wished my mother hadn't told me. At Oberlin, many of my classmates were actively anti-racist and came from families with similar politics. They had grandparents who had been activists or public defenders, started social justice projects, fought segregation during the civil rights movement. By contrast, the Rogers family's legacy was typical American racism.

The longer my classmates and I were at college, the more our upbringings were subsumed by the microculture of Oberlin itself. After a few years, you couldn't tease me apart from any of the others: another queer college kid riding a secondhand bike to meet a bunch of activists, one pant leg cuffed at my knee to keep it from getting caught in the chain. Academically, I had no idea what half the people in my classes were talking about, but I could write well, so professors remembered me. When a paper came back with a B instead of my standard A-, with inked comments claiming "disorganization" or "muddled argument" or whatever other failure, I wondered whether there was something inherently wrong with my brain, some lesser quality that was finally being sniffed out. Perhaps those feelings of inferiority—the ones my grandmother and father held onto, however subtly, throughout their lives—were not as many miles from me as I'd hoped.

∴ ∴ ∴

I was often strapped for cash during college, despite working several campus jobs and also every summer. My senior year, I rented a small house on Hollywood Street with three friends, each of us forking over just two hundred dollars a month. It was a steal. Never mind that my housemate Rowan's room was the size of a walk-in closet, and my room didn't have a closet at all. The one-story house looked decidedly like a mobile home, especially when compared to our classmates' rentals, those worn-down Victorians and Queen Anne styles with rambling porches. Their parents, I suspected, were covering their rent.

As an act of self-mockery or self-consciousness, Rowan and I decided to throw ourselves a "trailer-warming party," inviting a huge swarm of friends and buying cheap beer. Rowan wore a man's undershirt; I wore tiny jean shorts and too much makeup, teasing up my hair into a 1980s bouffant. One guest arrived with a fake pregnant belly, another naked except for an apron with "Italia" written across the front. "I'm Eurotrash," she said. "Or at least the Italian side of my family is." There was a lot of enthusiasm for themed parties in general, but one of my activist friends picked up on this one's underlying prejudice. "Trailer-warming party?" she said. "I mean, it's pretty classist, right?"

I was used to discussing privilege with my college classmates, but mostly in terms of gender and race. But money seemed to be a more taboo subject at Oberlin, perhaps because so many people had grown up with lots of it. The woman calling us classist was wealthy, white, and from the Northeast. She'd gone to private school her whole life and probably didn't need a drop of financial aid. Still, she was right:

I was mocking a culture I couldn't call my own, making fun of people I'd grown up with.

Rowan—an androgynous queer Oklahoman who identified as coming from a "white-trash family"—spoke up. "OK, maybe. But I'm totally allowed to make fun of my own people. I'm pretty sure I'm, like, the only person at this whole school from Oklahoma." Rowan motioned at me. "And you, you totally get this too. Yeah?"

I paused before I responded. I *had* grown up in the South, sure. But I'd never lived in a trailer. My parents had never lived in trailers. My grandparents had one on the farm, but they rented it to people of lesser means. However, all four years at Oberlin, I had felt like a kind of Southern mascot and often wondered whether I was the only person there from a South that was not Chapel Hill or the wealthy outskirts of Atlanta. In fact, it seemed like my only classmates familiar with rural life had back-to-the-land hipster parents.

"Yes," I finally said, agreeing with Rowan's assessment, looking at our other friend. "My upbringing, you know, it was different than most people's here." Deep down, though, I had a clear sense that I couldn't have it both ways: on the one hand, implying that I was descended, at least in part, from so-called white trash, and on the other, having been afforded opportunities that my father hadn't had. All my life, each time I enter another space marked by privilege, I carry the shadow of my grandparents with me.

∴ ∴ ∴

"Call your grandmother sometime," my father would remind me, his voice crackling from the other side of the Appalachians. There was nothing about my life at Oberlin that I could share with Rosa Lee: not the liberal content of my courses, not my tofu making and occasional attendance at Shabbat dinners, not the women I dated. But the main reason I never dialed the farm is that I could not deal with my grandfather listening in.

On visits back to North Carolina, the Rogers farm somehow felt more mythic to me than it ever had. I got jittery as I headed down the gravel drive, promising myself I'd stay just long enough to be polite. My grandparents were in their late eighties and not doing particularly well. My grandfather's paranoid impulses—the decision to cut down all their trees to make money from timber, or a sudden obsession with Muslim terrorists coming to the farm—made him seem like a time bomb. My grandmother's mind was intact, but her bones were breaking down. She refused any help. The farm was becoming too big to keep. Life in an assisted-living facility was inching closer.

During my senior year, I accepted a two-year teaching fellowship in rural China and was slated to leave for Beijing just a couple of weeks after graduation. My grandparents approved for two ideological reasons, both of them unsurprising. First, they'd known missionaries who had gone to China. Second, my grandfather believed that communism was evil, and he behaved as if I were doing China a service by gracing them with my American presence.

"Terrific," I said to my parents. "I'm sure that's going to go over really well once I get there."

But I went to the farm with my father, to say goodbye. At the end of the visit, my grandfather tugged my hand back toward the barn where he kept the tractors.

"Come see my hideout," he mumbled. My father rolled his eyes.

His what? I drew my hand away, my grandfather's touch too aggressive.

"Don't take her back there, Carl," my grandmother warned disapprovingly.

My grandfather was insistent. Eventually my father and I followed him back into the tractor shed. A door inside led into a smaller room. My father and grandfather had to duck as they crossed the low threshold. The room was just big enough for the three of us to stand in. One wall held a shelf full of old paint and stains, with a small desk and chair beside it. The other three walls were plastered, floor to ceiling, with pictures of Ronald Reagan on his Santa Barbara ranch, cowboy hat and plaid shirt, horse beside him. An over-the-top shrine to Reagan, who'd been president more than twenty years earlier.

I looked at my grandfather and said nothing, wondered what the hell was going on in his brain. I wished I could blame his old age, but he had been like this for as long as I'd known him. "My hideout," he'd called this inner room. What did my grandfather think he needed to hide from? What was the likelihood that terrorists would target his crappy farm in Pleasant Garden, North Carolina? Carl was grinning at me in an unreadable sort of way. I began to feel like the ceiling was closing in on me. I kept thinking about my aunt's story, the one that no one had believed at the time. How could I share a name with this man? And who was he to be acting like the salt of the earth, claiming to be a man of God?

∴ ∴ ∴

I didn't start to write about my grandparents in earnest until graduate school at Cornell, after my years in China. "Wow. Who *are* these people?" my professor asked rhetorically, her attention drawn to a series of poems I'd written about the sick bean smell of my grandmother's kitchen; my grandfather's Reagan shrine and his diagrams of the Rapture; and their globe-domed Jesus, placed atop the piano, what my sisters once called "Jesus in the Jar." With more distance, I'd become even more interested in the gothic quality of both my grandparents and the farm. My classmates, unimpressed, leafed through copies of my work and said nothing. My face burned.

That series of poems ended up in the middle of my first book, published four years later. Knowing my grandparents would never pick up a book of poetry, I didn't worry too much about exposure. And the February morning I got the phone call about the book's acceptance, I had a gut feeling: a year from then, when the book was finally in my hands, my grandfather would no longer be living.

The following February, as I was checking into a Boston hotel for the conference where my book would debut, my phone rang. "Carl is in the hospital, and he's telling everyone he's dying," my mother told me. "It might be real this time." Well into his nineties and having lived with congestive heart failure for the previous twenty years, he had said it over and over again: "This might be the end."

"We'll see," I said, unsure.

In the morning I woke to the radiator hissing, snow moving horizontally across my window. Boston was in full whiteout, which was expected to continue for the next couple of days. Half the people flying into the conference wouldn't even make it. My mother called again. My grandfather had taken his last breath just a few hours earlier.

I sat alone on the bed, fazed. Then I got on the phone with a Delta Airlines agent, soon realizing that there was no way I was getting to North Carolina that weekend, the Boston airport officially in a ground stop until further notice. When I asked about a ticket for a few days later, I was put on hold. I waited an hour before hanging up.

"I'm stuck here," I told my mother. "There are no flights going out anytime soon."

My sisters sent me text-message updates: *Our aunt just got here from California. You're not missing much. Dad seems relieved, honestly, that he's finally gone.* I went through my conference events feeling distracted and displaced. Going back and forth to my hotel, I walked down Commonwealth Avenue past the snowy brownstones, stunned and numb, the wind blowing directly into my face.

When I finally reached my father on the phone, he sounded haggard. I listened for emotion in his voice, trying to parse out whether he felt grief or bewilderment or simply unburdened. I couldn't tell. He asked about my book. He was proud, I knew. But somewhere in me was a nagging feeling of failure, that the book was not as big a deal as we'd been making of it; that only a handful of people were going to read it anyway. At the conference, where writers were chatting at the book fair and sipping cocktails in chic hotel bars, I felt again like the clueless kid at Oberlin, hearing people talk incessantly about things I didn't know much about. Instead of posturing up here in Boston, pretending like a white-girl poet from the South was going to change the face of American literature, I should've been at home with my dad.

I had fantasized that when my grandfather passed, Rosa Lee might change. That she might throw off the burden of having lived with him, and I'd finally get to know her. "How are you feeling, Grandma?" I asked her on the phone. "Whatcha been up to?" She was almost as timid as when Carl had been listening in. Our conversations would struggle along for a few minutes before we hung up. It was too late, or so it felt.

When I went home to North Carolina once or twice a year, I rode with my father to visit her at Clapp's Assisted Living, just a couple miles from the farm, a brick ranch with a big sunroom on the back. Rosa Lee had outlived not only her husband but also all her siblings, and she spoke frequently of death. Although she'd push her walker down the hall to play bingo or make something out of beads, she spent a lot of the day lying fully clothed in her single bed, staring out of the window. At the front desk, nurses checked residents in and out for weekend activities off campus, but my grandmother refused to go anywhere except for the doctor's office. She didn't want to go to my parents' house; she didn't even want to see the farm again. The doctor put her on Zoloft, which might've been useful during the Carl years.

Rosa Lee no longer asked many questions about me—perhaps for the best. She didn't even notice the simple gold ring on my finger that signaled I had promised myself to someone.

"I'm not out to my grandparents," I had told my future in-laws. This came as a shock to them. How I could keep this crucial information from my blood kin was unthinkable to the Ohio family I was marrying into. In the Oberlin years, when my relationships with women were new and not that serious to begin with, it had been easy to keep my "deviant" sexual identity, as they'd have seen it, from my grandparents. Now it began to feel like a lie through omission.

What Rosa Lee *did* know is that I taught at a university, which satisfied her. School had always been my grandmother's domain; its order and purpose made sense to her. "That's good," she said of my work. "You are making sure they can write." She seemed confused by my moving around—China; Ohio again; New Orleans; Washington, DC; Arkansas—and I didn't have the heart to explain to her that I was taking fellowships and visiting-professor contracts, trying to make a more permanent life but mostly just waiting for the contract to expire, the academic bottom to eventually fall out. Every couple of years, it seemed, it became harder to find the next job. Even with my fancy education and publications, I wasn't quite living the life that either of us had imagined for me.

One Christmas, my sisters gone and busy with their small children, my parents and I joined my grandmother for lunch at Clapp's: chicken, mushy green beans, sweet potatoes, macaroni with tons of salt. The meal was similar to what my grandmother used to cook, but it had none of her garden's freshness and tasted mass produced. After an hour or so, I excused myself to use the restroom down the hall. When I returned, I found my parents standing awkwardly a few feet down from my grandmother's door. The custodian's rolling cart was beside them.

"She didn't make it to the bathroom this time," my father said, his eyes down. "We're giving her some privacy. The nurse is helping." I saw my father making a mental note to bring Depends the next time he came over.

So this is what late life is, I thought cynically to myself: shitting yourself on Christmas. I felt a pang of empathy, and then a sense that I'd shirked my responsibility. How many of my father's diapers had Rosa Lee changed? How many of his childhood accidents had she handled? One of us should be the one helping her. But I also knew how deep her shame was, how she likely trusted the nurses more than any of us. No wonder she was hesitant to leave the building.

When we later entered the room—my grandmother's soiled clothes wrapped in blue plastic, the linoleum smelling of Lysol—she was lying down again, refusing to look at us.

"I'm sorry," Rosa Lee kept saying, her apology directed at no one in particular.

It's really OK, we all said back. We sat there and watched the cardinals come and go from the feeder at her window, their flicker and bravado. All of us were embarrassed, and none of us had done enough.

When I arrived in the old sanctuary of the Baptist church, it felt airier than I remembered: white pews and opalescent stained glass, the aisles so long I could barely make out the faces at the back of the visitation crowd. My wife, Sarah, stood beside me in the receiving line. My father looked weary, the grief hitting him harder than I had expected. But he had his social graces turned on. "This is my youngest daughter, Beth," he told people he hadn't seen in at least thirty years, "and my daughter-in-law, Sarah." You could see the almost-comical confusion on some people's faces as they tried to do the calculus: vaguely remembering that Dad had three daughters, not being able to account for Sarah's presence. I had worried that Sarah, a secular Jew from Ohio, would be out of place. But the truth is that her qualities—practical, judicious, hardworking—were exactly the ones my grandmother valued. Now I was wracked with guilt, unable to decide whether I should have introduced her to ninety-six-year-old Rosa Lee.

The Baptist pastor said hello to Sarah and me with a cool smugness that I could read only as homophobia. When he took the pulpit, I tuned him out completely: his auctioneer preaching was typical of the Southern Baptist churches in North Carolina, all rhetoric and no substance. I never understood how people could listen to it and feel anything. It had been a long time since I'd been to any church, actually, and even longer since I'd been in a Baptist church. We'd never come here with my grandparents. The last time I was in this church, I was in middle school, unknowingly following a group of peers to a magic show that ended up including altar calls and a revival.

Mostly, though, I was amazed by how many people had come to the visitation and service. There were second and third cousins my parents' age, people whose names I'd heard but whose faces I didn't know, and people from this church and another small one that my grandparents had helped found in the early 1990s. Mrs. Owens, that cow-gossip high school substitute, was unusually quiet, looking more or less the same as she had when I was sixteen. It seemed like she didn't recognize me, and my grandparents' cows had been sold off to another farmer some years back anyway. There were people I couldn't easily connect to my grandmother at all. One sweet old man looked directly at me and said, "You favor Rosa Lee." The caregivers from Clapp's were there too. "She was the sweetest lady," they kept saying. "You're so lucky." I was stunned, having experienced almost nothing but emotional reserve from Rosa Lee my whole life. *I've missed something*, I thought to myself. But looking at my father—the gentlest man in the room—I remembered that his good qualities came from somewhere.

A month or so before her body shut down, my grandmother had begun expressing regrets. "She told me that she hadn't done anything important with her life," my aunt told me. "And when I listed all her accomplishments, including the children she'd raised, she didn't seem convinced." As she told me this, I remembered all the things Rosa Lee had given up, the years she'd spent under Carl's thumb. The privileges, the permissions I'd had that she never would. How smug I had been about these, as if I somehow deserved them more than she did. Still, I was not living the life I had imagined: working a visiting-professor job in Arkansas, a time zone away from my wife and the rest of my family for a career that would likely dead-end in a year or two. How had I used the freedoms I'd been given?

As frustrated as she'd been with my father's parents, my mother had sat beside Rosa Lee as she was dying, feeding her ice cream from a spoon until the day she wasn't hungry any longer. "She got a little wonky at the end," my mother said. "Lifting her arms like she was taking off to heaven. She just wanted to sing hymns. So we did."

My aunt and father had chosen the traditional "I'll Fly Away" as the final song for the funeral service. My sister got choked up as we moved from verse to verse. The grief that we felt was not uncomplicated. I couldn't claim to have been close to Rosa Lee, but something came over me, something different from when Carl had passed.

"She used to sing this song when your dad was a baby," my aunt whispered between verses, "and she'd hold him up in the air above her head, like he had just taken off." I couldn't picture my grandmother being that playful. Although I didn't believe in heaven, I could imagine, at least metaphorically, Rosa Lee's relief. I thought of her shame as a long shadow fixed to the soil. Above it, some new body winged its way up and up.

Months earlier, when I'd been passing through North Carolina, my father had taken me over to the farm to see the work he'd done preparing Carl and Rosa Lee's farmhouse for its first renters. I heard the familiar gravelly sound under the tires, felt myself leaning back at the expected angle as we headed up the drive. The ironic-seeming sign that my grandfather had once hammered into the ground— Rogers' Friendly Farm—still stood.

"Jesus, that thing is creepy," I said to my father. "You've gotta get rid of it." But there was also a new energy on the farm. Maybe it was the big oaks that had come down in front of my grandparents' house, the strong sun. Maybe it was the former cow pasture, an unblemished grass canvas.

I barely recognized the house when I swung the screen door open. The musty furniture and old beige carpet had been torn away, wood floors now exposed. My father had finished the floorboards, painted the cabinets in the kitchen, pulled down the heavy drapery so that the rural green landscape filled every window. The rooms were still modest and quiet, but there was a feeling of lightness that had never been in the house before. Some yoke thrown off. It hadn't been some fancy renovation but a kind of hollowing to make space for something new, an unveiling.

I paused over my grandmother's kitchen sink, my hands pressing its cool silver edge. I looked up and out the window. My eyes met the familiar slant of the barn. The darker pitch of the tractor shed leaned beside it, its old machinery sold off. In the window's opposite quadrant: the exposed rows of North Carolina clay, the eastern edge of her garden. The sun seared the scene into focus. All of this had been her view.

SOMEONE OLDER:
A CATALOG OF DANGERS

The Swimmer Person

When I was seven, my oldest sister was fourteen and utterly gorgeous. Dark waves cascaded over her shoulders. Lipstick stained her big mouth. She had several superpowers, one of them being that strangers thought she was much older than she was. Teenage mothers were not uncommon in our pocket of rural North Carolina, and twice—once at the Circle K and once at the Video Shack—someone mistook me for her daughter.

My sister and I had always had an unspoken understanding that I was free to enter her bedroom at will. On her bookcase's top shelf was the antique crockery where she stuffed babysitting money, fives and tens coiled into an enormous cash rosette. I had no interest in stealing the money; I just liked to unravel and count the bills. Touching them made me feel powerful. If she was home, we sat on the carpet together, listening to R.E.M.'s *Out of Time* or *Automatic for the People*.

Out in the world, my sister radiated confidence. I, on the other hand, was a "worrywart" who got stomachaches from math tests and competing in swim meets. My sister had somehow managed to extricate herself from the swim team a few years before, preferring to spend her summers in intensive ballet training, watching old movies with "mature themes," and working on her tan at the pool. I watched her stretched out on the lounge chair—her bikini-top straps pulled down, her skin preparing to turn olive—and wondered why it was that girls were allowed to go outside in their bikinis but not their underwear. Wearing my drab one-piece team suit and eating a firecracker popsicle, I sat directly on the pool deck, the concrete incubating my butt and legs. My sister wore aviator sunglasses and read a thick paperback book. The book was part of her overall look. She was always reading. She would finish the book in a few days.

No one else read at the pool, unless you count magazines.

She put down her book. "Do you see Ashley over there?" she asked me in her signature stage whisper. "She's a snob." Across the pool deck, a pinup-looking blond girl leaned on one of the boy's lifeguard stands, giggling and feigning a sort of demureness. This was the kind of gendered finesse I would spend my childhood and early adolescence envying, believing it was synonymous with power.

Ashley refused to even glance in our direction. But I felt the glances of both lifeguards—older guys, eighteen or nineteen years old—drifting toward us. My sister resumed her reading, sliding her aviators down her nose slightly, playing it cool. Already I was picking up on an early sense of her sex appeal. I could never tell whether she was fully aware of it or whether she wielded it purposefully. At any rate, she was too young for the guys who gazed at her.

When my sister entered high school, I watched a series of boys show up at our front door, reeking of cologne and wearing the standard North Carolinian "dude" uniform of belted khaki pants and polo shirt. She got sick of most of them pretty quickly: Mike the football player, Derek the lacrosse player, Paul the debutant from Greensboro. She'd see one of these guys for a few Friday or Saturday nights in a row, and then he'd disappear.

One morning after a date, she emerged in the kitchen later than usual, wearing her standard sleepwear of boxer shorts and a V-neck undershirt. I asked her, rather innocently, where she'd gone the night before.

"Went to the movies," she said, her tone glamorously listless. She swept her hair out of her face and changed the subject. "I had this crazy dream last night," she began, "about Jack Nicholson. You know, the actor." She halved a grapefruit and sprinkled it with artificial sweetener. My sister thought she was fat, so everything she ate was modified or missing something in a way that made it nasty. "So I'm sitting by the pool in the Biltmore House," she went on, referencing the Vanderbilt mansion in Asheville, "where Jack Nicholson is swimming. He gets out of the pool and comes over to me all the sudden. He's all wet and ugly looking, and his chest hair is dripping water everywhere."

"Gross," I said.

She ignored me, raising her spoon like a baton. "Then, oh my god. Jack Nicholson looks me straight in the eye and says . . ." her voice dropping a couple of octaves, " 'Well, hello there.' " She shoved grapefruit into her mouth and picked up the newspaper, pantomiming an adult life. That was the end of the dream, or at least the version she was willing to tell me.

The image of Jack Nicholson's soggy carpet of chest hair was enough to make me gag. But I already knew that dreams sometimes meant things we couldn't say out loud or fully understand yet. I sensed that this dream contained something elicit, maybe even dangerous. Maybe Jack Nicholson was supposed to be a kind of archetype, a warning about men's predatory capabilities. From her cavalier narration, though, I suspect that there was also an element of fantasy to this dream, a desire beginning to take on the shape of older men.

I was the one who answered the phone when Andy called our house for the first time, his voice so serious that it verged on comedic. Andy was our community swim coach, and he was rarely serious about anything, any awkwardness diffused with goofiness. But this guy on the phone was not the Andy I knew, the Andy who wore Umbros every day, sang fight songs about sharks, and let all the kids push him into the pool, fully clothed, when we won swim meets. This Andy said nervously, "Let me talk to your dad for a second." He was about to ask if he could take my sister out to dinner.

We lived in southeastern Guilford County, where chivalry was alive and well. If you were born female, you learned that men would open doors for you from the time you could walk until the day you died. Still, it was the late 1990s, not the antebellum period. There was a reason for Andy's formal asking permission. My sister was still only seventeen years old, and Andy was twenty-four. This was hardly Jack Nicholson territory but still pushing the envelope. On the one hand, Andy was like family to us. My parents had known him since he was a teenager himself. On the other hand, a seven-year age gap seemed pretty questionable when the younger person wasn't even eighteen yet.

My father's blue eyes cast out into space, then twitched a little. Perplexed on the other end of the phone line, he told Andy that he would have to think about it. What he really meant is that he needed to talk to my sister to find out what she was thinking, as well as my mother, who generally had final say about how we three daughters were raised. I'm not sure my parents' opinion would have mattered much, to be honest. It seemed that no one could stop my sister from doing anything she wanted to do. She was born like that, I guessed.

Because I'd never seen Andy anywhere but the pool deck, I hardly recognized him when he showed up at our house wearing a collared shirt and a belt. This was the guy I'd known my whole life, the guy whose skinny shoulders I'd once ridden on in a swim meet parade. Now he said nothing to me, as if trying to make a mental separation between my sister and the rest of the Rogers girls. (Our middle sister, fourteen years old, hid in the kitchen during this episode, mortified by the situation.) When my oldest sister appeared on the stairs and walked out with Andy—her hair soft rolled, pout full of lipstick, belt cinched around her waist—I was transfixed and bewildered. She had crossed into another realm. It had never occurred to me that she might be eligible to go out with the swim coach.

Mothers began to stop my mother in the Winn-Dixie, fishing for information. I pretended not to listen, feigning interest in yogurts with their various aspartame flavorings, a staple of my family's diet in the 1990s. My mother tried to demur when faced with questions. "They're just going out casually," she said. "It's not serious." My mother seemed embarrassed, apologetic of her own parenting choices, which I didn't quite get. Wasn't she in charge?

"Oh, Andy's such a nice *boy*," the other mothers would go on and on, wanting to approve. In reality, Andy was a full-grown man, a college graduate with his own apartment and a growing business. It wasn't as if my sister and Andy had first met in high school and he had moved on to college: that kind of thing was considered acceptable and normal dating behavior, even if one person was younger than eighteen. If you do the math, of course, you'll know this wasn't possible for my sister: when Andy was a senior in high school, she was in the fifth grade.

Perhaps my sister and Andy reminded those mothers of their own slippery longings. Andy was one of the community's hunky figure-heads. When moms came to pick up their kids from swim practice, I'd watched the way some of them behaved, how they smiled flir-tatiously and tousled their hair, nervous in the presence of Andy's lean, tanned limbs and jokey demeanor. They touched their faces or slouched toward one hip while they talked to him. Andy was tempt-ing. Even if no one pulled a Mrs. Robinson in earnest, watching these women then taught me something, early in my life, about how messy attraction can be.

At seventeen years old, my sister's precocious tastes included a fas-cination with scandal, as well as all things British, including Maggie Smith. *The Prime of Miss Jean Brodie* was one of her favorite movies, an odd choice for a high school girl in the 1990s. At the film's narra-tive crux, Sandy—a nerdy but insightful schoolgirl, the most trusted of Miss Brodie's mentees—admits to Miss Brodie that she's having an affair with Teddy, the forty-two-year-old art teacher. After she started dating Andy, my sister was half-joking when she walked around the house parroting Sandy's famous declaration: "You see," she would say in an exaggerated Edinburgh accent, "*I* am Teddy's lover."

"OK, *enough*," my mother snapped. The joke hit too close to home.

Seeing the film version again years later, as an adult, I found it curious that while Miss Brodie is fired for her "unconventional teach-ing methods" (which, to be fair, include narcissistic hero worship and promoting fascism), there's a lot less emphasis on Teddy's questionable morality. Sandy is only seventeen when she begins to model for forty-two-year-old Teddy. They start having an affair soon after. For Teddy, there are no real consequences. Maybe it's because Teddy feeds into a prevailing mythology about creative men, how they derive so-called inspiration from underage girls.

Perhaps, when she was a teenager, my sister thought of these girls as aspirational, or even cast herself as one of them. But her life was not like Sandy's. Andy was just another run-of-the-mill North

Carolina guy in his twenties, not some unbridled artist approaching middle age and looking for a young muse. At seventeen, I don't know how conscious my sister was of any of these dynamics or whether she thought to question why an older guy might be interested in her in the first place.

∴ ∴ ∴

The last time I saw Andy, he and my sister were still together. She and I were at the mall buying Christmas presents, and we ran into him unexpectedly as we were leaving. Andy was walking through Belk with another woman about his age, someone we had never met. He held a bag from Bath and Body Works—the store than sells the fruity lotions and sprays, the scents that choked my school's sixth-grade locker room.

"Hey," Andy said, gripping the bag handles. He shifted his weight awkwardly between his long legs. His summer tan had faded. He looked like Boo Radley, his hair too blond and spiky to be seen in December. "This is Amy," he said, motioning to the young woman next to him, trying to provide an answer for my sister's look. "She's also a swimmer. A swimmer person." Swimmer person? He had a deer-in-the-headlights look. My sister raised her eyebrows. "She was, like, helping me with some gift stuff." Andy acted like he had forgotten how to use words, seemed suddenly younger than my sister. He shifted his weight again, from one foot to another, like the boys in my sixth-grade classes as they waited in the lunch line.

She and I headed out of the mall without saying anything to each other and found her old Volvo in the parking lot. She turned the key forcefully in the ignition. The car let out a roar. "OK, who *was* that person?" she demanded. My sister always spoke to me like an adult, despite our age difference. "Oh, excuse me. *Swimmer* person," she said. "And I want to know about what's in that bag. Who is that for?"

"Maybe it's for you," I said, stating the obvious.

She sighed, turning the giant, ancient dial on the radio. "I hate that kind of stuff, and he knows that," she said. "If he's planning on giving that to me . . ." she started. "Well, let's hope it's for his sister or something. Whatever it was in that bag would likely make me break out in hives."

⋰ ⋰ ⋰

Andy and my sister broke up some time after the new year. "We just don't have enough in common," she said, sounding rational and mature.

She was finishing her senior year of high school, shocking no one when she got a full ride to a nearby university. By August, she had moved into the honors dorm there, made a bunch of new friends, and was back home only on the occasional Friday afternoon, waltzing in to do laundry for free and drink all the diet soda. But she never stayed long, usually getting angry about something my mother said to her within a couple of hours. Storming out of the front door, laundry basket in hand, she returned to Greensboro into her new life.

Within the year, she'd have her own apartment. She'd go over to her professors' houses for dinner and to parties with wine hosted by graduate students. She'd be cast in a bunch of college productions, including a production of *Hair*, which I was not allowed to see. Her personality remained unchanged, but things would not be the same again. My sister was finally an adult.

She seemed unfazed by Andy's engagement announcement in the newspaper about a year after they had broken up. His fiancée was someone involved with the City Swim Association, though not the person we'd seen at the mall. In the announcement, her age was listed as twenty-five, the same age as Andy. "Oh, I think he just wanted to be married," she said. "To anyone." He was in a different phase of his life, she reasoned, and he wanted different things.

⋰ ⋰ ⋰

Many years later, my sister revealed to me that she never slept with Andy. "Nope," she snorted. "He was one of those kooky Christians, so not before marriage," she said. Then, with a feminist sarcasm, "I was *pure*."

This reimagining of the relationship shifted my understanding, perhaps more than it should have. The someone-older taboo, especially when it relates to teenagers, is about power difference. If there's no sex involved, does it mitigate the danger? Level the playing field?

For my sister—the teen who devoured long novels and scored off the charts on every standardized test, a girl who easily passed for twenty-two when she was out in public—I wonder whether someone older, anyone older, might've meant a chance at an intellectual match, or at least an escape from banal culture of teenage romance. I couldn't picture her sticking with any of the boys from high school. Could she have really been an exception, one of those rare girls who transcends the usual expectations of age and experience?

Later in my life, however, I would begin to doubt whether that kind of girl exists. Maybe that line of thinking is the one that too often excuses the older person's bad behavior. Even Sandy, Teddy's young lover in *The Prime of Miss Jean Brodie*, eventually realizes that Teddy really wanted Sandy's mentor, Miss Brodie, all along. He used Sandy as a replacement, knowing she's young and susceptible to his wiles. "As this seems to be a time for truth," Sandy tells Teddy when she ends things, "You're quite a mediocre painter. You really should try some other line." She then delivers the washed-up artist a real zinger: "You are getting on, you know."

It's the kind of line that only a precocious seventeen-year-old can deliver.

A PhD Star Is Born

Over the next decade and a half—separated by our different life phases and then by geography, both of us eventually moving far away from home—my oldest sister and I loosely followed each other's romantic lives. There was her goofy actor boyfriend, Jared; my first college girlfriend, a trust-fund hippie from the East Coast; my second college girlfriend, a singer-songwriter from a Rust Belt town in Ohio. There were the flings not worth mentioning, and the ones too precarious to mention.

When I was twenty-four and she was thirty-one, we found the distance collapsed between us for the first time in our adult lives, both of us living in central New York by happenstance. I had moved to Ithaca to get my MFA at Cornell. She was in the second year of her PhD an hour away in Syracuse, where she was studying how to educate the next generation of psychotherapists. In Syracuse, she and her boyfriend had finally moved in together full-time, playing house in a snowy bungalow near the university. "Boyfriend" sounds hilariously infantile, since he had been a grown man for a very long time. In fact, he was fifty-two years old to her thirty-one.

By the time I arrived in New York, I'd known about him for a while: they'd already been involved, on and off and long-distance, for almost five years, since Jennifer's midtwenties. But the murkier truth is that they'd first met long before that, when they'd once performed in a ballet together. My sister had been only nineteen then, just beginning to edge into adulthood. He was forty and had been brought in from out of town, was a professional dancer in the last stages of his performing career. In photos I'd seen from his dancing heyday in the 1970s and 1980s, with all his stage makeup on, he resembled David Bowie. This association evoked pure cool, so long as I didn't think about Lori Maddox's fate in the process.

"Oh, *come on*, dude. It wasn't like that," my sister said. "We weren't involved back then." She gave me a dirty look.

But my parents were skeptical of the boyfriend, namely because he was born in 1957, making him just two years younger than they were. They couldn't seem to get their heads around it. This was also a man who had been married twice, someone who had a daughter about my age. At the mention of him, you could see my father's face go blank, my mother's eyes narrowing. I was familiar with these sorts of looks, as they were the ones I also got any time I mentioned a woman I was seeing.

I'm sure our parents would have preferred that she and I both find nice guys our own ages. Our middle sister had already fulfilled this role by marrying her college boyfriend when she was twenty-five. My oldest sister and I had become united in our pull toward the deviant romance: she because of the twenty-one-year age gap with her boyfriend and I because I was gay. When you come out of the closet, you learn pretty quickly that it's cruel to pass judgment on any sort of relationship. It was my own queerness, I suppose, that made me more open to her boyfriend from the beginning.

Although I'd met this boyfriend a number of times before, it was up in New York that I began to get to know him in earnest, not just as a shadow in my sister's life. By then he had retired from professional dancing and owned a small playground-construction business. If I wasn't getting dumb-drunk with my classmates and wandering down the slopes of Ithaca in the middle of the night, I'd sometimes go up to

Syracuse to see my sister and her boyfriend on the weekends. She and I ate cake from Wegman's and watched her HBO on Demand, avoiding coursework and our piles of student papers. Her boyfriend made soup, loaded the dishwasher, did silly dances in the kitchen, and sang show tunes to entertain us. He was more introverted than she was, but they shared the same irreverent sense of humor. Affectionately, he referred to her as "The Professor." Compared to a lot of people's clueless boyfriends, he appeared evolved. He was a grown-up.

My sister's boyfriend and I got each other, despite our huge age difference. We had easy conversation. He was the one who came down to Ithaca after my girlfriend and I broke up, helping me get a new mattress and move various pieces of furniture in and out of my third-floor apartment, where I was now living alone. "I'm slightly familiar with this process," he joked, and we both laughed, knowing he'd gotten divorced twice in his twenties. He had survived most everything you can think of by that point, he told me. He could offer me advice without seeming condescending. When I had trouble adjusting to living by myself, the late-night quiet of my apartment overwhelming me, he would text me with practical suggestions. "Put some music on," he'd say. "It'll take the edge off your loneliness."

I survived periods of my twenties in that way. And to this day, the trick helps when I feel that the bottom is about to fall out.

That first year in graduate school, I was an emotional disaster in the way that I suppose many people are at twenty-four years old. Having just returned from rural Shanxi Province in China, where I'd taught English for two years, Cornell felt impossibly regal and aloof to me, almost as foreign as Shanxi had been when I first arrived. Undergrads walked around in eight-hundred-dollar boots. My professors were moody and sometimes inaccessible; when we complained, they retaliated and held grudges. The MFA poets in the class year ahead of me, who dominated our workshop class, called me "the Southern Chinese lesbian," even though I was not Chinese. In class, they tore apart my writing. Everything and everyone hurt my feelings. Meanwhile, in the midst of my academic identity crisis, I screwed up things with my long-term girlfriend because I was falling for someone else: the star

PhD student in my department at Cornell, a glamorous butch with a big academic ego.

Star PhD asked me how old I was at a graduate party, our bodies wedged between a kitchen table and a bookshelf with dog-eared Arendt and Heidegger volumes. "You're twenty-*four*?" she said in disbelief. She laughed her most theatrical laugh. "Oh my fucking god." I smiled weakly and shrugged. There was nothing I could do about my age.

Although Star PhD was only seven years older than me—born in 1978, the same year as my sister—her habits exaggerated our nominal age difference. She hung out with faculty members who should have already retired and was the darling of the oldest and most famous member of the department. She constantly trafficked in allusion, casting me as the damsel, comparing me to every virgin, goddess, or daughter figure from the Western canon: Persephone. Beatrice. Petrarch's Laura. My new friends in Ithaca could see this as the condescension it was. "This is going to be drama," they said, even though almost everyone I knew had a slight crush on Star PhD. But I was too self-involved and self-loathing to have any sort of perspective. In true graduate school fashion, I was committed to learning everything the hard way.

For the next few months, Star PhD and I did the sort of thing that you're actually too old to do once you're out of college: meeting in secret, yelling at each other on the streets, having sex in the park in the middle of the night. Star PhD's feelings toward me swung from complete obsession to disdain and rage when I'd said the wrong thing. I was either the greatest person alive or a recent enemy, depending on the day.

"Are you listening to me?" my sister asked. "That woman is fucking diagnosable," she said. I was weeping into the phone. "Seriously. She's showing all the signs of untreated borderline personality disorder." This was a morning after I'd stumbled home from another fraught tryst. Star PhD had a bad habit of calling me up at 3 A.M. and asking me to come over. This time, it had been after her evening drinking absinthe with an infamous queer studies person on faculty, one who was rumored to have slept with students. This should have been a clue: *Run away. Run away.*

My sister was the first person to explain to me that the allure of the charismatic intellectual wasn't anything new; it was a well-worn trope in academia. Star PhD had been cast as the young luminary of our department before I'd even arrived, and I was just another person pulled into in her swirly magnetic field. I'd always prided myself on being assertive and independent, even as someone raised in the South, where paternalism feels like the dominant mode. But there was something about Star PhD's brand of paternalism (not quite the right word, but it certainly wasn't *maternalism*) that pulled me in. Say nothing of her physical attributes—her androgynous haircut, muscular shoulders, her perfect breasts, the way her skin smelled—that made me feel like I was on cocaine. I've always had a particular weakness for soft butches, especially ones who are a bit older.

Maybe what I was really looking for in my graduate school days was mentorship. At Cornell, most of my professors kept their office doors closed if they were even around, seemingly unmoved by my burning quest to be a better writer. But Star PhD (who already had an MFA and was quite an accomplished poet herself, having published in all the good journals) was transfixed by my poems, proclaiming me a *real poet*, in contrast to many of my classmates, who she referred to as *charlatans*. I would eventually discover that Star PhD had a romantic history with approximately one incoming student every year or so, the one she'd anointed as the most talented and/or most beautiful of the group. Her shtick was powerful enough that she'd even caused one straight woman in the PhD program to leave her boyfriend.

"Oh, that's classic narcissism," my sister went on. "She makes you think you're special just because you're associating with her." My sister was clearly putting her shrink training to excellent use. "What does your therapist say?"

My new therapist at Student Health, a solemn, no-nonsense butch in her fifties, was forced to listen to me describe my travails with Star PhD in obnoxious detail.

"Well," the therapist told me, with absolutely no sympathy: "I suppose you will stop this when you are ready."

∴ ∴ ∴

"You will stop this when you are ready" might have also been my parents' attitude toward my sister and her much-older boyfriend. It seemed to me that my parents were waiting to see whether things fell apart on their own, perhaps hoping that my sister would finally get the older man thing out of her system, meet someone from her own generation. So when she finally eloped with her boyfriend in Manhattan that year, my parents took it personally. They refused to speak to her for several months, the longest silence in my family's history.

I wasn't surprised at my parents' dismay. But hadn't they been the ones to raise and shape us, the ones who had never imposed strict rules? The ones who let her date someone older from pretty much the beginning of her romantic life? What did they think was going to happen? She had been with her now-husband for almost five years.

"But she did this behind my back," my mother complained when I called her trying to mediate the situation. "She doesn't understand what this will mean," she mused, "later on in her life."

Here, I got a different sense of why my parents were resistant to the twenty-one-year age difference. It wasn't so much about age as it was about aging. What my mother really wanted to say to my sister was this: Are you prepared for the burden of being the young one, and the inevitable grief in the years to come? Because you are going to outlive him.

I saw where my parents were coming from, but I still thought they had overreacted. My sister may have still been young, but she was thirty-one now: not a neophyte. If this relationship had been some fantasy she was playing out, that fantasy had likely passed and transformed into something else. Wasn't she old enough by now to know what she was doing? At what point could we finally consider ourselves reliable agents of our own romantic choices?

Soon after my sister married, my relationship with Star PhD fizzled out. She stopped calling, ignored my texts. I reconciled with my previous girlfriend, apologized for my bad choices. Star PhD began to work her spell on another person, an unsuspecting femme who'd just began the PhD program. When I think back, I can see Star PhD as just a variation on a theme, one that I hadn't quite gotten out of my system. My own young vision of an ideal romance had been needled by a strange, double-edged desire: wanting companionship with an equal I could trust but also fantasizing, as maybe my sister had, about the allure and attention of someone more experienced than I was.

I don't know whether my sister's innate interest in older men influenced me or whether my desire came from a stranger—queerer—place.

At any rate, my sister may have been one to really have a relationship, and eventually marry, someone older. But technically, she wasn't the first person in the family to consider a twenty-one-year age difference.

I, Too, Am Teddy's Lover

I was fifteen years old and ripe for impression when I walked into high school guitar class for the first time, thinking that the rebellious associations of the instrument might help me shake off my uptight childhood identity, transform into something breezier. And who was waiting for me at the door? The Guitar Teacher, your classic charismatic educator. Thirty-six years old, she was one of those iconoclast musicians who'd recently figured out how to turn herself into a professional. An androgynous Jean Brodie with a guitar strapped to her back.

"Give me a girl at an impressionable age," Miss Brodie brags to her class of young girls, "And she is mine for life."

When you're a teenager, it's supposed to be reasonably safe to have a crush on someone older. Who hasn't had that imaginary space where you can rehearse your desire, work through your desires without real consequences?

Of course I was obsessed with the Guitar Teacher, but so was almost everyone in my class. She came from high in the mountains, but she had the veneer of being a classical musician who was conservatory educated. She cursed. She could play almost any pop song you could think of from memory, but also Bach, Paganini, all the weird modern composers. A modern-day troubadour, she spent days commuting between several high schools and evenings teaching at a small college. She rode a motorcycle, she told us, on her days off. Of course. My affinity for soft butches began with her.

I started coming to class early, when the Guitar Teacher was teaching me how to shape my right-hand fingernails for tone production. "It's necessary," she said, "if you really want to commit to the instrument." With her metal file, orange stick, and the finest-grade sandpaper—its gradient so fine it felt more like walking on a rainy beach than it did a construction tool—she knew the exact angle and length that each nail needed to be in order to get the richest sound possible on the strings.

I'd never cared much about grooming my hands before. The Guitar Teacher held each of my fingers in her cool grip, disarming me a bit with this direct form of intimacy. I was beginning to learn the characteristics of each nail. "This one grows a little downward," she'd say, squinting at the tip of my middle finger, angling the file around its curve. "Best to keep it as short as you can." The Guitar Teacher's own nails were pristinely clean, her hands slender and unadorned, neither masculine nor feminine. I memorized them quickly.

In many ways, I was a mediocre guitar performer. I was nervous all the time, my hands shaking in front of audiences. Under my teacher's influence, however, I also progressed quickly on my new instrument, moving from two-line melodies to more advanced études within the year. Soon I moved on to real repertoire: baroque dance suites, moody modern compositions that switched time signatures. The Guitar Teacher took a special interest in me early on for reasons that I didn't understand. Her brow furrowed in concentration as she watched my hands cross the strings and fretboard. "How did you learn to make a rich tone like that?" she'd ask, ignoring any technical mistakes or the occasional buzz coming from my troublesome left hand. "Seriously. That's a rare gift," she'd tell me, her tone one of divination. "I've never had a student who could do that at this stage." She paused. "I believe you're inherently musical."

The verdict: I was talented enough, or at least had enough potential, to become one of the few teenagers the Guitar Teacher took on for private study outside of school. "In the old days, before my school job, I taught everyone to make a living. Now it's only a few students. So make it worth my while," she said, commanding and beckoning at the same time: "You'll have to work your butt off for me."

Thus began the idea that she had done me a favor, that I owed her something for what she had invested in me. In the end, I would end up believing I owed her my whole self. The longer I studied with her, the less sure I was of any self that had come before her.

In high school, the All-County Guitar Ensemble was an annual occurrence, a time of year when all the young guitarists in the nearby city and towns had their abilities sized up. In my sophomore year, I'd been ranked eleventh, a decent chair for someone who was just starting out, but nothing to brag about. After the audition junior year, when a group of guitarists listened in from the other side of a privacy screen, I was awarded first chair unexpectedly. The dark horse, I had out-seated everyone, including the cocky senior boys whose left hands zipped across the fretboard, including city kids in Greensboro who'd been studying guitar since they were little.

The Guitar Teacher, elated, called me with the news. "I *told* you," she said. "I'm not the only one who knows you're gifted." She paused. "And do you know you're the first girl to ever be awarded first chair?" The Guitar Teacher's professional history was one full of men and boys. All of her teachers, classmates, and most of her students. A girl guitarist was still a rare bird. "And you're not just some random girl who got this," she said. "You're my girl."

My *girl*, I repeated to myself. The possessive language startled me at first, then stoked me with its ambiguous sense of possibility. But for sure: I was the favorite. I floated through the hallways, suddenly feeling recognized. Visible. Already I could feel that this was the season in which everything would change.

One week after that phone call, the Guitar Teacher invited me to carpool with her and one of her college students to a concert in the next town over. It was February and unusually cold for North Carolina. I wore my fancy coat, cream-colored wool, usually reserved for church—and ducked into the student's Subaru, where the heat was blasting. The Guitar Teacher, dressed in black from head to toe, removed her leather gloves.

It was a long drive, and the sun went down early. Something baroque was playing: Bach? So many notes. The Guitar Teacher had taught this particular college student since he was a kid—she had a way, I'd soon learn, of making people lifelong apprentices—and they knew each other inside and out, joking and laughing. The three of us chatted, talking over and under Bach, our voices mimicking the frenzied arpeggios. "Baroque rock and roll," the Guitar Teacher proclaimed. I was alone in the middle of the back seat, leaning forward

so I could hear them more easily. The Guitar Teacher was in the passenger's seat. "Your hair smells good," she said, turning to me. Then,
in a dark stretch of highway between Greensboro and Burlington, she
reached her hand across the console and behind her, resting it on top
of my hand.

For guitarists, I would argue, nothing is as intimate as touching
hands. The hands are the world. She had touched mine before, many
times in lessons and while she was doing my nails for the instrument.
But this was different. For a few minutes, I sat still, unsure of what to
do. I felt a starry sensation under the surface of my skin, a fierce eroti-
cism. *Did this mean that she . . . ?*

No, I tried to reason. *She would never.*

Unless . . . ?

Later that night, on the ride back from the concert, the Guitar
Teacher got bolder. Her hand reached my knees now, down the outside of my calf and into my sock, her index finger teasing the high
arch of my foot. I grew warm under my clothes, unsettled but curious. I didn't know feet could be erotic. The college student drove on,
oblivious to what was happening just behind him.

At the end of the night, he dropped the two of us off back near
the Guitar Teacher's office at the college. She and I stood beside the
car I'd recently started to drive, my old white Volvo sedan, which
seemed to glow in the dark parking lot. The other student was gone
now. We were alone. Night felt like a new country, one without a
language. An enormous oak, a tree from another century, cast a lacy
black shadow at our feet. There was light coming from somewhere I
couldn't place.

The Guitar Teacher reached down—she was eight inches taller
than I was, regal and towering—and placed her hand on the collar of
my coat. Her finger brushed the side of my neck. I looked at her for
answers. "So," she said, as if we were already in the middle of a conversation. "You're OK?" The Guitar Teacher was both gentle looking
and androgynously handsome, a strand of hair falling into her face.

"Yes," I replied, looking up at her, although I wasn't entirely sure.

She came toward me then, her lips brushing my cheek. A small
move that somehow seemed habitual. But she'd never done this
before. It was enough to confirm that something had shifted. She
touched my shoulder again. I looked up. She looked at me tenderly.

"You look nice in this color," she said, a kind of non sequitur. It seemed that wanted to say more, but she was withholding something. "You should get home now. OK? I'm gonna go."

The Guitar Teacher turned away, her lanky, black-shouldered figure ducking under the oak and into the dark. She was heading toward the front of the music building, where the college's employees parked their cars. The light catching her hair was the last thing I saw before she disappeared. The cold air around me felt like something out of myth. It would take me until the next time we touched to realize that I hadn't made the whole thing up.

∴ ∴ ∴

When my rational brain fired—as rational as one can be at sixteen—I begin to see how this had been coming. I also did the math in my head. The year 1964 beneath the year 1985, the difference of her thirty-seven years to my sixteen. Twenty-one years. In the upcoming year, no matter how I acted or tried to change myself, no matter what excuses we made, I never really found a way to bridge the distance.

∴ ∴ ∴

Like the careful, artisanlike penciled notes she made on my sheet music, the Guitar Teacher's gestures toward me were small at first. A hand on my lower back during a concert. Her fingers teasing the curve of my knees as she talked to me at the end of my lesson. Calls to my cell—the little flip phone my parents had given me for emergencies— just after we'd seen each other in public. The calls got racier over time. *That shirt you're wearing today is distracting*, she'd joke. Or: *Do you think that maybe we knew each other in some other life? Do you believe in that? Because I kind of knew it the first time you walked into my classroom.* Between our phones, driving in separate directions—her toward the city, me deeper into the middle of nowhere—we created a small room of voice that no one else could enter.

Boundaries were crossed so slowly that often I couldn't put my finger on them: a hallmark, I realize, of what it means to be groomed. I spent my sixteenth year adjusting to this shifting reality, the mercurial weather of our relationship, my new status as someone who could attract a charismatic thirty-seven-year-old. Some days, she was just my teacher: giving arpeggio and slur studies, giving me grades, taking my mother's cash for private lessons. But it also seemed like anything could happen now.

Even more complicated was the fact that the Guitar Teacher had been partnered for twelve years: with a dancer who was forty-three years old, five years older than the Guitar Teacher herself. When I brought her up, the Guitar Teacher barely reacted. It was as if nothing between the two of us were significant enough to register in adult-relationship world. Flirting with a teenager, as it seemed some days, hardly counted as anything.

"I want to see you," the Guitar Teacher would say. "Alone." We'd strategize. What slivers of the day could we go unnoticed? We started meeting during her midmorning planning period, driving around town until I forced myself back to school, to wander into Spanish class. The Guitar Teacher wrote me late notes.

In her car, she introduced me to music I'd never heard before. "Listen to this," she'd say, turning up the volume, pointing out whatever it was that was capturing her. Often the artist was someone from the Guitar Teacher's generation, someone who had risen to fame before I was born. The music was part of my education. To this day, when I hear Queen or the Police or early Annie Lennox or Stevie Nicks, I associate it with my generation, even though I was born in 1985, decades too late for that to be true.

In her car, we pretended that the twenty-one year gap between us was water under the bridge. "The age difference," she once told me, "might mean something now, but it matters less and less as you get older." The Guitar Teacher told me about her lovers when she was my age: a local college student, the head majorette at her high school. Once, the drama teacher at her high school back in West Virginia, who was young and closeted. The Guitar Teacher and I held hands. She began to move her fingers through my hair, over the camber of each ear, down my spine, alongside my small breasts. On the first warm day of the spring, a few weeks before school let out for the year, she teased me by reaching into the low rise of my jeans, snapping my underwear's elastic.

The Guitar Teacher taught at a summer program for high school students out of state during July and early August, meaning I wouldn't see her for six weeks over the summer. After my last lesson before she left town, we went to lunch and then drove around. It was hot, and both of us wore shorts. Without warning, she reached over and down between my legs. Here, the Guitar Teacher was clumsier and rougher than I imagined she'd be, given how precise she usually was with her hands.

I didn't know what I was supposed to do. I braced myself, as if for a blow. I no longer felt like I had a say over anything. I couldn't move her hand to a place that felt better. Around us, the green leaves blurred in the windshield, the sun searing through the glass. Everything now moved at a speed I couldn't reckon with.

When it came to sexual stuff, the Guitar Teacher's rules never made sense. This was part of the mindfuck that would always keep me on edge. The one time I tried to kiss her—that very basic thing I wanted, so much more than anything else she'd done—she raised her chin above my head in avoidance. She refused to kiss me on the mouth, as if that most basic illicit act would finally mark us, undeniably, as lovers. "I'm waiting until you turn eighteen," she told me, unveiling the shakiness of her grown-up logic. She revised her statement, perhaps finally remembering she was essentially married to someone else. "Or," the Guitar Teacher clarified, as if suddenly principled: "I guess *would be* waiting until then. You know, if things were different."

But she had not waited. The fact that she didn't kiss me, or that she'd never actually get in a bed with me in earnest, didn't absolve her of anything. What was the difference? By the time I was seventeen, there was nowhere left on my body that she hadn't touched. What would really happen that next spring, I wondered, when I finally turned eighteen, that supposed threshold of adulthood? Would I really be such a different person then?

When I researched the laws a few years later, I learned the age of consent in North Carolina is actually sixteen, not eighteen. The Guitar Teacher had this wrong, too. If she and I had been in Virginia, just forty-five minutes up the road, my age alone would have made these interactions count as statutory rape. Maybe. But in North Carolina, a sixteen-year-old can "consent" to a sixty-five-year-old, and there are no penalties.

The thing that *was* against North Carolina law, of course, was the Guitar Teacher's status as my teacher and a teacher in the public schools: any relationship between an educator and a student is a crime. Fewer than four years of age difference, and it's a misdemeanor. More than four years of age difference? Felony, I remember reading, finally cognizant of the gravity of what had happened, the real reason it had all been a secret. The North Carolina law is less concerned with age than with the older person's position of power. The law is also geared toward men; it wasn't really written with women in mind, and certainly not with lesbians in mind, never quite specifying what counted as a sexual relationship.

It didn't take me long to realize that most people still fundamentally believe that women aren't capable of sexual abuse. To be a woman, even a woman in a position of power, means to have your agency eased, even the agency to harm. I suppose I shouldn't be surprised that no one—not my family, people at school, or even the Guitar Teacher's partner—ever suspected what was happening. The two of us remained unseen.

I did eventually get angry at the Guitar Teacher. I wandered my last year of high school in a sad erotic purgatory, feeling desire and hurt on a loop, but still not able to find a definition for what she and I were to each other or what had happened between us. Was I now old enough to have an affair, I wondered, the way that Sandy had when she was seventeen, with the art teacher, in *The Prime of Miss Jean Brodie*? Was the Guitar Teacher just fucking with me for fun? I sometimes asked myself if I'd made the whole thing up, kept having to reconvince myself that what had happened was real, conjuring our trysts over and over in my mind, the things she'd said, what she'd done with her hands.

I tried to bargain with myself: If I just waited until I was a bit older, perhaps the Guitar Teacher and I would have a better chance at a real romance. Perhaps she'd even leave her partner for me. "The age

difference matters less and less as you get older," she'd said the year
before.

Maybe she'd really meant what she'd said about me turning
eighteen.

But my eighteenth birthday passed uneventfully, the Guitar
Teacher busy with work at the end of the school year, making a five-
minute call to my cell phone as she drove home to her partner that
evening. It had been a few months since anything sexual had happened between us. She no longer made a point to be alone with me
outside of lessons.

I was beginning to see the writing on the wall. I would be leaving
for music school at Oberlin at the end of the summer: a place that the
Guitar Teacher had helped me access with her knowledge and teaching, a direction I suspect I'd never have gone without her grooming.
She'd helped me convince my doubtful parents to let me try for an
elite private higher education: *She is gifted. She is special.*

But the Guitar Teacher was also biding her time. She was doing
whatever it took to pretend she was not in the wrong, was hoping I'd
forget, too, about the previous few years. To the Guitar Teacher, I
began to realize, I might not have any lasting impact. While she felt
like my first love, to her, I was just another devoted student passing
through her orbit en route to adulthood. And now I was almost there.

"She did *what?*" my sister asked.

In Oberlin, where the snow was piling up and there was no sign
of my previous life, those events from my teenage years were slowly
coming into focus for me. Hidden under the ornate wooden staircase
in my nineteenth-century dorm, phone pressed to my ear, I immediately regretted that I'd lost my willpower and spilled everything to
my sister. For two years, I'd had to keep it a secret: the social ramifi-
cations, both for the Guitar Teacher and for me, would have thrown
everything into chaos.

I'd hoped my sister would take the news differently, given that I
was technically an adult now: she and I, for the first time, were practically peers. I had also assumed that she, with her own desires and

experiences with older men, might've kept an open mind about the situation. I was relying on her to see nuance, to think about how much pressure it can be when your desires are considered unconventional, when your relationship lacks a name. "It's not as bad as you think," I kept telling her, trying to backpedal my confession. "I mean, it's not like I didn't want her to . . ."

"No, no, no," she insisted. "You don't understand," she said condescendingly. "*She* is responsible. *She* was the adult." She was resolute. "So you're telling me this went on for almost two years?"

I started to panic. She didn't get it. *What is the difference between what happened to me and what happened over and over to you?* I wanted to ask her. Older men had always been interested in her. I couldn't see a clear distinction between me being half-heartedly pursued by my teacher at sixteen and my sister at seventeen dating the supposedly-virginal-but-still-twenty-four-and-a-college-graduate swim coach. And what about her boyfriend, the one she'd eventually marry, who she'd just begun to see romantically? He was forty-six years old to her twenty-five. The same gap as the Guitar Teacher and me. Why the double standard?

I had miscalculated. She didn't see my situation as analogous to hers. She didn't see how things with the Guitar Teacher had started out, the tenderness and the gray areas, how isolating it still felt to be gay in the South in the early 2000s, how I still wasn't sure how I felt about anything. My sister was focused on one thing: someone in charge had hurt her younger sister in a backhanded, careless way. With some distance from North Carolina, my mental state had gone awry, which meant I couldn't lie about this anymore. I was having panic attacks. My back and stomach hurt constantly. I couldn't sleep.

I couldn't decide whether I felt relief or annoyance at my sister's reaction. Maybe both, but she just seemed like another older person trying to tell me what to do.

"Now that I know this," she began, "I am also responsible for you." The seven years between us was starting to feel more like a generation.

Out of desperation or fear, she decided to call our parents with the bad news. It's an action for which I'd eventually forgive her, but not at first. "I'm really sorry," she told me. Then, something I'd never heard her say: "This situation, it's . . . beyond me. This is really beyond both of us."

My parents didn't take the news well. They were so stunned that they couldn't come up with the right thing to say.

I stared out into the lake effect clouds. Everything seem to erase me. I felt the beginnings of my adult self falling away.

It's possible that this self had never really formed to begin with.

Thanksgiving weekend, age eighteen: the out-of-body experience of my friends in the dorm walking me downstairs, zipping up my winter coat over my pajamas. The ambulance throwing pink light on the Ohio snowfall. Our college's small-town hospital followed by the nightmarish psych facility, an ugly cement box in Amherst, Ohio, where I waited for my father to arrive from North Carolina and collect me. "Yes, I know what day it is. Yes, I know why I am here." I told the story over and over again: I overdosed on muscle relaxants, a prescription for my back, which hurt all the time even though I was only eighteen. Not enough pills to die—I'd stopped before I'd gotten through the bottle—but enough to slur words, upend everything, scare the shit out of people.

For the rest of college, the word stayed in my medical file, haunting me: *suicidal.* Why not also *grief?* Or *situation that seemed to have no solution, especially when you're a teenager?* Why not *suffering because someone else was out of line?* Or *Adults in my life don't know how to conduct themselves?* Everyone feels sympathy for the young person who is in pain because of someone older, it seems, right up until that young person's suffering takes on the form of mental illness.

I remember having two clear thoughts in those blurry hours at the hospital. The first was *I'm fucking mortified.* I was old enough to be embarrassed, I guess, at failing to take care of my pain and of the depth of the pain itself. The second thought—what seems too obvious but was an epiphany at the time—was that there actually might be a reason my relationship with the teacher had been prohibited by law.

I'd always assumed that laws surrounding age difference were put in place for only the most extreme violations: to keep, say, pedophiliac men from having sex with kids. But I realized that the law was also there, maybe, to prevent things like, say, the state of mind that led to this hospital visit. Perhaps if the Guitar Teacher had followed the rules, I might have been protected from this kind of emotional aftermath. The brand of loneliness I felt back then was one without a name, despite its specificity. It is that mind-muck that results when you enter a forbidden relationship and then, almost inevitably, are abandoned by the older person who led you there.

Queer Age

Some days, when I am not thinking straight from the wound, part of me is tempted to reframe my narrative surrounding the Guitar Teacher. What passed between us, for better or worse, was a pivot point: in the years that followed, I emerged from the closet, intact and unashamed. One version of the truth, however incomplete, is that the Guitar Teacher helped nudge open the window to the rest of my life, a life in which I could embrace queerness, question assumptions, refuse to take things at face value. Am I allowed to write this story in a sort of archetypal fashion, the one where an older woman ushers a younger woman (OK, a girl) into an erotic life, helping her (even if only briefly) see a future of belonging after childhood years of feeling off, set apart, full of embarrassing longing, like the weirdest girl in Guilford County?

Even under the gauzy gaze of my reminiscence bump—what psychologists call that period from adolescence where we seem to remember everything, assign it more value than other parts of our life—what happened to me is not easily redemptive. But I'm curious whether someone else's story of someone older could be. I also wonder, perhaps irresponsibly, perhaps too theoretically, if things are different for gay people, whether queers have a sort of automatic peerdom that overrides age difference.

Some people seem to believe this, as least in principle. Queer theorists, for example, have been making this argument for decades. In the sex scholar Gayle Rubin's influential "sex hierarchy" concentric circle drawing, she puts cross-generational relationships in the same "bad outer limits" as other taboo categories: homosexuality, non-procreative, and solo and group sex, among others, and then makes the point that these categories are just deviations from the norm rather than universally bad. Because we are a smallish tribe, because we don't adhere to the heteronormative and reproduction-mandated motivations for relationships, because we have been throwing off binaries and embracing polyamory and camp and kink for centuries, could it mean that being queer shifts relationship paradigms entirely, which also means throwing out some taboos about generational differences? I have considered this theory on and off throughout the years.

In pop culture, generational crossing is a common plotline in gay films especially, one that even seems necessary to drive both characters' development. Consider Cate Blanchett (born in 1969) in *Carol*, playing the gorgeous, almost-divorced socialite and mother, falling for the barely legal burgeoning photographer, played by Mara Rooney, who was born in 1985, the same year as I was. In the book version, *The Price of Salt*, the age difference between characters is probably twelve years, but it appears more like twenty in *Carol*: Rooney seems very young. Or, for something more lowbrow: *Loving Annabelle* features thirtysomething Simone Bradley and precocious seventeen-year-old Annabelle Tillman in a rather cheesy girls-school drama—nothing like *The Prime of Miss Jean Brodie*. Simone gets arrested at the end of the film, but of course this feels like a tyrannical tragedy, their lesbian relationship squashed by the Catholic school's dogma. Simone is so closeted and traumatized, and Annabelle so sure of herself; the expected hierarchy sort of balances out.

In a film that made me breathless with its seductive beauty—the Academy Award–winning *Call Me by Your Name*—what do we make of seventeen-year-old Elio pining for twenty-four-year-old Oliver all summer, with the gorgeous, sculpture-strewn, northern Italian landscape around them? Never do I think to myself, *Oliver should really keep his hands off that underaged boy*. (I admit, seven years feels easier to stomach than twenty, but Elio is still in high school, and Oliver is supposed to be a graduate student. Why don't Elio's parents think this is weird? The real age difference between the actors is ten years.) But the characters' ages seem less relevant when you look at the homophobic beliefs and culture strictures they must overcome. We're all mostly rooting for these relationships. There is a larger sense of morality at stake, one that goes beyond age.

Even in real life, many queer folks seem to think that an age gap—even one that is traditionally considered abusive—is par for the course, not inherently unhealthy, when it comes to coming into a queer life. Once, when I mentioned my early experience with my teacher to a gay friend, he said he'd had a similar thing with an older man when he was a teen. "Happens all the time," he said. But he didn't use the words *abuse* or *statutory rape* when he told me about his experience. "It's totally different in gay world," he reasoned. "I mean, how else are you supposed to learn what to do?"

But I also wonder whether we queers are being honest with ourselves. Perhaps our casual acceptance of the someone-older phenomenon is because we've reinvented or queered what an age difference might mean. But it seems just as likely that we're not examining it closely enough. Maybe we're just buying into the same patriarchal crap as everyone in the heterosexual world, the traditions that say that the only agency youth has comes from wielding their sex appeal. Perhaps we're just making excuses for bad behavior, repeating a tired old song in a different key.

In the end, no one theory quite holds. I want to believe that it's self-knowledge that finally determines whether any relationship with an older person is instructive, judicious, not what we would assume, plain abusive, a mix of any of these, or none of the above. I want to believe it's not my place to draw hard lines. It does seem possible for the balance of things with someone older, whether it's a queer relationship or not, to evolve over time, even if the origins seem questionable. "The age difference becomes less noticeable over time," the Guitar Teacher said.

Not back then, but maybe between actual adults: When I see my sister, now in her forties, with her sixty-something-year-old husband, I can tell he's older than her, but they seem as seasoned and predictable as any long-term couple. She is the main breadwinner in the family; he is the oldest dad on the playground. Does he really still have more power than she does? Or she over him? He was never her teacher, never held a fixed position of power over her. I hardly remember who she was when they begin to see each other. Who cares how it all got started?

Still, for each relaxed ending like my sister's, there are a thousand others that go something like this: Older person meets young person.

Older person is careless with their power, or maybe denies having it even as they wield it. Young person almost loses everything in the process.

This is still the story I know best.

∴ ∴ ∴

The last spring I lived in Ithaca—twenty-six years old, recently graduated with an MFA, two years after my fling with Star PhD—I came home one night not quite sober after an evening at the bar with friends. In the quiet of my apartment, I was scrolling through Facebook when the Guitar Teacher's face suddenly appeared, an almost apparition on the edge of my screen.

In my "People You May Know" list, I thought, at first, that I had hallucinated her name. But no—there she was in all her pixelated glory, forty-seven years old but completely recognizable.

Oh, boy. There must be a word for the feeling you get when you first see someone older than they have stayed in your memory. She had glasses, which I'd never seen before. A few gray spots in her hair. The edges of her jawbone were softening. But it was still her.

I sat there, arrested. I closed my laptop, willing myself not to look. Then I opened it again, unable to stop.

She was too much a part of my history to just walk away.

For almost a decade, it had been easier for me to pretend that the Guitar Teacher was dead. At a certain point, I'd accepted I'd never resolve what happened between us, that it would always bother me, that I'd never get the justice or closure I wanted.

But this was predicated on her no longer being visible to me. Adrenaline flooded my circuits as I begin to click through her profile, finding photo after photo of her new life. (The Guitar Teacher, it seemed, hadn't yet discovered privacy settings on Facebook.) *Don't*, my rational brain said. But I was searching, even if in vain, for something that would shed insight into her, something I couldn't have perceived in my teenaged years.

Years ago, when I was still in college, I heard through the grapevine that the Guitar Teacher had quietly exited her public school job. Her resignation was mysterious, maybe had something to do with me or maybe not. What I *didn't* know is that the Guitar Teacher had since been promoted at the small college where she'd taught, the one where'd I'd gone for private lessons, where we'd fucked around in her office and back in the woods and on the surrounding roads.

In another Facebook photo, she held a plaque, a collegewide award for outstanding teaching. Clearly, the people at this college had no idea who I was.

What undid me most, however, was the realization that she and her long-term partner were no longer together. Her new wife was tagged in the Facebook photographs, a middle-aged brunette who smiled confidently as she settled in the crook of the Guitar Teacher's arm. They seemed to be from the same generation. When I googled this woman's name, I was surprised to discover that she was a prominent doctor back home. The Guitar Teacher had won, it seemed: she'd wooed someone who was powerful, smart, educated. A grown-up.

The complicated grief from discovering the Guitar Teacher's profile was twofold. The first sadness was the reopening of the abuse rabbit hole: my reckoning, for the thousandth time, with how irresponsible and careless she'd been. I didn't care that others thought she was a person of distinction. I burned with indignance toward these people who had let her career flourish. But underneath that pain was an older one, embarrassing and messy. Somewhere, in spite of everything I now knew, the adolescent part of me, the part of me that didn't *get* it, still longed for her. How could I feel both these extremes at once? Had I learned nothing in the past decade?

In some fantasy universe, I can imagine a different ending with the Guitar Teacher. She is, I remind myself, just a normal person I could have known under other circumstances. I have often wondered what might have happened if I had met her years later, maybe when I was in my twenties or thirties. Could we have had a passionate romance and then evolved into the usual, boring domestic partners who drink wine together? The ones who ask each other to pick up toilet paper on the way home from work? Or: if I'd been older, maybe I would've seen through her right from the start, her recklessness and flaws. Without the teacher-student power differential, it also seems possible that there would have been no erotic charge between us at all. Although she doesn't deserve the benefit of my doubt, I wonder what kind of person she's become in middle age, whether she is any better now than she was then.

It's hard not to remember the final thing she said to me, back when I was a teenager, the only time I'd tried—unsuccessfully—to confront her about what had passed between us. But when I told her, point-blank, that I didn't understand what had happened, she'd sighed.

"Oh, Beth," she'd said. "You know, I've never had a student who needed so much from me."

As ludicrous as it is, that was the story she told herself. Despite her age and her specific brand of power, she believed *she* was the tragic heroine. Or at least collateral damage in her own profession.

When I remember that day, I want to praise myself for being brave enough to speak up. I want to say that I did the best I could. But I wish I'd had the knowledge to throw her words back in her face. Why is it that the older person often feels that the younger one is the instigator, the one who has led them into a kind of passionate madness?

They really should know better by now.

On the Brain

Years ago, my sister was the first person to explain to me that the prefrontal cortex—the part of the brain thought to govern self-control, predictive decision-making, and managing emotions—doesn't finish developing in humans until around the time we're twenty-five years old. This might explain why, in our teens and early twenties, we seem impulsive and can't imagine what the consequences of our choices will be. It also explains why we feel so out of control.

Applying this logic to my sister's romantic life, I could reason that she had just become a fully formed human when she started seeing her now-husband at the age of twenty-five. (At seventeen, though, she wouldn't have the full capacity to decide about Andy the swim coach—yet, he wouldn't have either, since he was twenty-four himself.) Maybe that is sound enough reasoning for everyone to back off. For me, the prefrontal cortex is a polite way of excusing myself for those 3 A.M. booty calls with PhD Star: I was only twenty-four, after all, and technically still had a year of brain growth before the final fusing, when I'd supposedly come to my senses.

Perhaps this theory also explains why, as a teenager, I could feel desire for an older woman—and even understand why our relationship was happening in secret—but still couldn't have seen the emotional toll it would take, what the big picture contained. I want the prefrontal cortex, at least through metaphor, to provide the answers for the unanswerable questions about power and agency. But I know even it can't tell the whole story, can't account for the grayer areas. Since I work with college students, I think about the prefrontal cortex a lot: the way their brains don't work the same way mine supposedly now does, or how they often have no choice but to follow their reckless hearts.

Just a few months after my thirty-first birthday, I arrived at a small college as the visiting writing fellow. My new office was in the building housing the college's Department of Music. Everything about it felt like my own adolescent-and-early-adulthood territory: the layered harmonies wafting out of the choir room, the cluster of music stands in the hallway. And especially that music-building smell: old wood, sour metal, aging linoleum treated with wax. Sometimes, on a sleepy early morning, my brain still half-dreaming, I felt I had gone back in time as I walked down the hallways with my heavy school backpack. It's only when I reached for my office keys that I remembered I had been an adult for quite some time. I was not the student but the teacher.

A number of my students came to my office hours that first term, but one—I'll call her Liza—was especially consistent. She showed up at least once a week, sometimes twice, often following me back to my office after our class. She was a bubbly, bright, twenty-three-year-old lesbian who was discovering poetry late in college. Liza spent hours each week writing and rewriting her poems, trying to find a foothold in the genre. Two-thirds of the way through the semester, after our class discussion of the elegy, she wrote a poem whose energy and earnestness blew me out of the water. I read the poem over and over by lamplight in my living room, absorbing its incantatory quality.

"*This*," I told her, perhaps with too much of a sense of divination. "This is, like, light-years ahead of anything else you've written." When Liza left my office after that meeting, I saw her glide out the door, as if she had wings on her heels.

At a student event I went to later that week, Liza bragged about me by name to the crowd, announcing, "I have dreams about your class even when I'm not there." I tried to play dumb, but I was taken aback by her forthrightness. I blushed. My colleague, trying to maintain professionalism, looked at me sideways and tried not to laugh.

Later, as I was telling the story to my wife, she giggled. "Sounds like that girl has it bad for you."

I shrugged. Sexuality was not on my mind at work at this tiny Southern college, where I walked around campus in my slacks and senatorial blazers, the sensitive parts of my body hidden away.

"It's not like that," I told my wife. "She doesn't know the kind of mixed signals she might be sending out. You know?"

"Oh, come on," my wife said. "Remember that time she brought you a cupcake?"

The cupcake had been a little weird, I admitted, but totally harmless. Liza had recently made a bracelet for another professor I knew. But I had to admit this gesture felt different, especially given that the other professor was a straight woman.

"Prefrontal cortex," I insisted, parroting my sister. "Her brain. It's not fully online yet." I was probably just paranoid, I told myself, due to my own charged history.

The next time Liza was in my office, after we'd finished talking about one of her poems, I felt her stalling as she gathered her things. "Well, I'm going to get back to my grading," I said politely.

"Of course," she said. On the way out the door, though, she invited me to the open mic where she was playing a song set. *Of course she is a singer-songwriter*, I thought to myself.

I declined, politely, but wished her luck.

Liza accidentally left a shirt on the back of one of my office chairs. She must have been wearing it on top of whatever else she was wearing that afternoon. I sent her a quick email letting her know she'd left her shirt, that I would bring it to our next class session. But then I deleted that line, imagining how weird it would look to the other students when I handed this woman her shirt at the start of class.

I rewrote the email to say I was leaving my office for the day but she could pick it up in the file box outside my office. As I folded up the soft fabric, I saw that the tag read XS. I remembered being a size XS. Seeing this tag felt strangely intimate, like I was witnessing something I shouldn't. One long blond strand of her hair was wound around a button. Absently, I started to untangle it. In a flash,

I recalled the Guitar Teacher, in a lesson once when I was just fifteen years old, lifting one of my stray red curls that had fallen across my guitar's fretboard. An action that may have been innocent but takes on new meaning when I consider everything now.

I put Liza's shirt in the box quickly and closed the door behind me. I didn't want to tamper with anything that belonged to her.

Liza graduated that May and moved far away. But on a spring night the following year, I was driving home from work and listening to the local station when, inexplicably, I heard one of her songs come on the air. I knew her voice immediately: that bubbly timbre with bright major chords beneath it. I also recognized her lyrics, something about how a lover's freckled skin is like the sky and constellations, as one of her early poems from my class. It hadn't been a great poem, but as a song, it worked better—even if a bit saccharine and unapologetically winsome. *You do you, kid*, I thought. I felt a little embarrassed for her.

Was I ever that naive? I wonder. Or, alternatively: *When was the last time I laid myself so bare?*

I sat in the driveway, listening to the song all the way through before I cut the ignition. Her voice came at me from that great distance, another place in time.

ONE PERSON
MEANS ALONE

Before Taigu, people warned me: China was fiercely social country.
After I arrived, I rarely went anywhere unaccompanied. I was ush-
ered into crowded noodle stalls and corner stores stuffed with plum
juice, chicken feet, and hot-water thermoses. I often needed help at
the post office, with its hundreds of strict regulations and wisp-thin
envelopes you sealed with a depressor and paste. Students took me to
the White Pagoda and the courtyard of H. H. Kung, historical sites
in town that hadn't been destroyed during the Cultural Revolution.
Eventually, I'd be invited into my Chinese colleagues' small apartments, where several generations of the family often lived together.
I'd be generously served five kinds of dumplings, the bowl full again
before I had the chance to set down my chopsticks.

In the unheated, Soviet-feeling building where I taught university
English, I waited in line with other women to use toilets without
doors or stalls. At first, I tried to turn my face away from the others,
demurring. But there was no use trying to hide anything about our
bodies here: whose stomach was upset or who was crying or who was
on her period. We saw it all. We offered stacks of tissues when someone had run out of their own supply.

I lived in a tiny brick house, the tiles on my roof painted with evil
eyes to ward off badness. I'd often wake to the arguing of an unknown
college couple, shouting their insults right in front of my window, just
a few feet away from where I had been sleeping. I'd stumble into the

kitchen, startled to find a stranger outside the back door, shaking my (was it mine?) jujube tree and picking up the fruits from the ground.

Like most teachers at the agricultural university, I lived on campus and wasn't hard to find. My thoughtful students showed up on my front stoop, bearing jars of weird, floating grains and fermented vegetables sent by their grandmothers. "If you eat this for six days," they'd say, "you will be well."

The word was out: I was sick a lot. It was my first time living abroad, and the new microbes were hard on my body. In Taigu, there was delicious street food as well as contaminated cooking oil, air, and groundwater. Shanxi Province, even by Chinese standards, was an environmental disaster. The coal plants were next to the grain fields, pink and green smoke rising out of the stacks. On a good day, you could see the mountains that surrounded campus. Most of the time, they were hidden by pollution. Particulate matter caked the windowsills in my house.

People were curious about me. I was asked daily by strangers in the market square what country I was from and why I had come to Shanxi Province—sort of the West Virginia of China, except that it was on the edge of the desert—as opposed to the more glamorous Shanghai or Beijing. They also asked how old I was, how much money I made teaching at the university, if I'd eaten that day yet, and if so, what had I eaten? And why was I "a bit fat," they said, but not as fat as some Americans? How often did I need to color and perm my hair? (It was reddish and was curly on its own, I said.) Was that American living in the other half of my duplex my boyfriend? (He was not.) Well, did I at least have a boyfriend in the States? (Sarah, my girlfriend from college, was teaching on a similar fellowship in Indonesia. But I didn't explain her, for obvious reasons.) And, occasionally, from students and younger friends: What did I think of the movie *American Pie Presents: Beta House*? Was it an accurate portrayal of American university life?

Eventually, I borrowed my friend Zhao Xin's laptop so I could watch a pirated version with Chinese subtitles. I was horrified. One of the thankfully forgotten sequels of the original *American Pie*, it made me squeamish during scenes of a fraternity's hazing ritual, something about hanging a bucket of beer on some guy's genitalia. There was also one exaggerated fire-hose moment, a sorority sister experiencing female ejaculation for the first time. As for the question of whether this resembled university life in the United States, I told them, in all honesty, I wasn't sure. I had just graduated from a small, studious college in the Midwest. Despite its sex-positive atmosphere, things were, all in all, pretty quiet there, with some nerdily themed parties but no Greek life at all.

In truth, I'd had plenty of sex in college, but that had to be my own business. More specifically, I didn't reveal my lesbian identity to anyone in China, at least at first. I responded to boyfriend questions with a simple no. I didn't know what the consequences of coming out might be. I couldn't take the risk. Keeping my queerness a secret, I'd come to realize later, was part of what made me feel so isolated that first year in China, even though I was constantly surrounded by other people.

As a student in America, my life had been pretty communal. Still, like a number of Generation Y, middle-class, considerably selfish Americans, I thought I was fiercely independent and staged myself as the protagonist in my own life story. Very little prepared me for the level of social responsibility and interconnectedness that came with moving to Taigu. One of the first words I learned was *guanxi*, which can be roughly translated as "social connections," or maybe "relationships." If you had *guanxi* with others, you could count on them for most everything, and they could count on you; if you failed to foster a sense of *guanxi*, people would resent you or think of you as selfish, even though they might not say it out loud. *Guanxi* emphasized—or mandated— the whole you were a part of rather than the part you played alone.

I embraced this idea the best I knew how. My American co-fellow, Ben, and I mounted a disco ball in our living room and started hosting weekly dance parties for our Chinese friends: social activity for the greater good, something students reported as scarce on our small-town, farm-school campus. At these parties, at first we'd awkwardly stand in a circle. But then the sorghum-alcohol punch we provided began to take effect, and our loopy, arrhythmic movements took over the room. Over time, we perfected our playlist: a mix of American hits from the 1980s and 1990s and cheesy Chinese pop songs. By our second year in China, our living room floor was beginning to split from people's dancing enthusiasm.

This was one way we Americans got a wild reputation on campus. Our parties were on Thursday nights, but then we got a noise complaint from the university's vice president, who happened to live in a house just thirty feet from our front door. When we showed up on his porch the morning after, with a giant fruit bowl and profuse apologies, he smiled and invited us in, as if nothing bad had happened. Our *guanxi*, the neighborhood harmony, seemed to be restored.

Overall, however, I was not the best at fostering *guanxi*. I often found myself hungry for space between others and myself: a necessary measure to quiet the buzz in my dislocated brain. I'd draw the curtains and hole up in my side of my foreign-teacher duplex, the door to my side closed. This action was usually perceived as hostile or a symptom of possible depression.

"Why is she not coming out here?" I heard someone ask Ben on the other side of my door. "Is she sad about something? Why is she alone?"

The word *alone* in Mandarin can be translated in various ways. The expression I heard on the other side of my door, traveling by myself on a train, or walking down the street solo was *yi ge ren. Yi* is "one"; *ge* is a kind of counting word, placed between a number and an object. And *ren* means "person" or "people." The expression "Are you *yi ge ren?*" when translated literally is "Are you one person?" In context, though, I began to understand this as a way of asking, "Are you on your own? Are you alone?"

Of course, I was rarely 100 percent alone, unless you counted when I was asleep or in the single-person bathroom in my apartment. I had come to Taigu paired with Ben, another recent college graduate, and there were more Americans living in the house next door to us, doing their second year of the same teaching fellowship we'd all received. Most of our life outside of class involved a mixed group of American fellows and Chinese graduate students, with a few older Chinese undergraduates mixed in. We ate dinner together most nights at the hot-pot place, just outside the campus gate, or at one of the noodle stalls at school.

Every once in a while, though, I'd find myself walking alone in public. I was not afraid: not near my house, not on the other side of campus, not even in the bleak brick-and-mud village alleys scattered with trash and piles of used coal pellets. There were terrible stories, real or imagined, of people getting snatched up around here and having their organs harvested. There was a line of massage parlors, a sort of red-light district, the neon signs flickering on and off.

When I passed another person, I'd see what I came to know as the Look: not threatening but a look more of curiosity or even shock, mostly due to my obvious non-Han appearance. Some would ask me where I was from. Some would say nothing. Some would ask me if I was OK, if I had eaten, and where I was going.

I don't know whether it was the fact that we lived in the ultra-militarized People's Republic or just that Taigu men are not the type to catcall, but I always maintain that China felt like the safest place I'd ever lived. Perhaps my outsider status as a Westerner protected me. Years later, when I returned to the United States, finding myself living in a host of smaller towns, as well as cities like Chicago, Washington, and New Orleans, I was shocked at how often some stranger on the street would whoop at me or stare for too long or walk too close. It was in my own homeland where I felt the most unsafe being by myself.

In a country of a billion people, personal space isn't just something that's frowned upon; it's often impossible to find. Even a small town like Taigu—just forty thousand people—was no exception. If you wanted to be alone in the daytime, you could ride your bicycle past the grain fields and the coal- and bauxite-processing plants to the even smaller village at the edge of the mountains, where there were several temples in the outcroppings.

In China, university dorms are not named after famous educators or benefactors but are referred to by serial numbers: 26 Building, 27 Building, and so on. I soon discovered that the undergraduates were living eight to a room: four sets of bunk beds pressed against the walls, one shared table in the barely existent center of the room. The graduate students, thought to be deserving of a bit more space, were also in dorms but housed in groups of four. The first time I entered a dorm room at the agricultural university, it was as if I were entering a unit in a warehouse. I saw schoolbooks, clothes, shoes, packages of dry noodles, and clothes-washing bowls crammed beneath the lowest bunks and around the perimeter. The room's one narrow window was strung with several drying lines for shirts and underwear. It was the middle of the day, so the students were elsewhere.

My friend Wang Yue, a twenty-year-old English major, pointed disapprovingly to one of lower bunks and told me that a pair of her roommates—two nineteen-year-olds who preferred to be called by their self-selected English names, Sky King and Toni—always slept side by side in this single bed. They were obviously in the early stages of a romance. "It's like they wish the rest of us weren't here," Wang Yue told me, rolling her eyes.

It was unclear to me where her disdain came from. Was it homophobia? Was she annoyed because these women had upset the *guanxi* and balance of the group, prioritizing their personal interests over the harmony of whole? Or was it because they were two women, finding a loophole in the single-gender dorm, the thing that was supposed to keep students focused on school, not sex?

Everyone on campus, it seemed, was struggling for intimate space. The foreign teachers' houses were adjacent to a small, circular garden where the willow and birch trees created a shadowy canopy over a few park benches. This was hardly a hidden place, but it was more secluded than the rest of campus. If I passed by at nightfall, I could see the flash of someone's limbs wrapped around another body, and then another couple on the next bench, just a few feet away. This was the official campus hookup area, a kind of twenty-first-century drive-in theater. The students called it Qingren Shulin, or Lovers' Forest.

Even the privacy in my half of a duplex was not a thing I could always count on. My girlfriend Sarah managed to visit China the first fall I was there, during her Ramadan break. We'd spent a large part of our senior year of college in bed together, but coming to teach in Asia, and our resulting physical separation, left us almost celibate. Desperate, we tried to cram as much sex as possible into the two weeks of her visit.

One late Friday afternoon, we got interrupted by Ben's frantic knocking on the door to my bedroom. He warned us that Xiao Zhang, a staff member for the Foreign Affairs Office, had just come over, and she was about to walk in any minute. She needed to see something on my side of the house, and *right now*, apparently.

A wave of indignation passed through me that was immediately replaced by panic. I didn't have any closets to hide inside. There were no locks in our house, except on the front door. And it was no use to pretend to be out: Xiao Zhang and the office staff members, for all sorts of reasons, regularly came into our apartments when we weren't home and would have no trouble coming into the bedroom. The units belonged to the university, after all; we were just living in them.

Flushed, I pulled on my tossed-off clothes and rushed out into the foyer area, apologizing for my delay. I tried to close the bedroom door behind me, but like most doors in the house, it didn't fully latch. Xiao Zhang advised me, in the slowest Mandarin she could manage, about getting some sticky paper to try and trap the mice that had invited themselves in just after the weather had turned. "Right," I kept saying, nodding, hoping to make the conversation as short as possible. I stopped understanding her instructions after a while. My language skills were not up to snuff, especially when I was panicked.

But it was clear from her hand motions that she was describing what happens when the mouse actually dies its horrible death inside the adhesive. She even went so far as to mimic a rodent scream, just so I would be prepared. I stood fidgeting. On the other side of the partially cracked door, Sarah was hidden under the duvet, still undressed and trying not to move.

Besides teaching, eating, and the lessons with my Chinese tutor, I spent a few late afternoons a week at the campus's indoor swimming pool. The idea of swimming, especially in a poor, dry province like Shanxi, sounded luxurious in theory. In practice, the pool felt like an environmental apocalypse, so gritty and chemicalized that you could barely make out the *Ts* on its tiled bottom. The water smelled like a mix of spoiled vegetables and bleach. The chlorine powder was dispensed in satchels that looked like giant artificial jellyfish floating just above the underwater jets.

We swam there anyway.

One week, I ran into my student and his friends on their way back from the pool building. He told me they had closed the pool down for a couple of days. "They must change the water this week," he told me assuredly, in English. "It is the first time in seven years they will change the water."

I hoped something had been lost in translation.

The pool scene was, despite all this, pleasant enough. Of course, if you headed there with the sole intention of swimming a bunch of laps, you'd be frustrated. Like everywhere else, the pool was full of bodies, especially in the shallow end. For every fifteen meters I swam, I'd usually stop to talk to someone: a student, or a friend, or sometimes a complete stranger. If I didn't stop, I'd likely collide with them in the water anyway.

Right away, I noticed that most of the women stayed in the shallow end, trying to develop the basic skills to pass the university's swimming test. The lifeguards or pool keepers, all middle-aged men with beer guts and sagging swim trunks, were impressed with my sessions in the deep end and with my swimming skills. "You have a good *shui jue*," one of them told me, which translates to "feeling of the water."

But my sense of the water wasn't intuitive so much as it was another marker of my Western, middle-class upbringing. I thought of the series of photos in my mother's albums back in North Carolina: me at six months, fat and smiling, at baby swim class at the YWCA; me at four, splashing in the waves at the beach; my first swim-team picture at the age of six, posed next to the diving board. In China, however, swimming pools were scarce, and most natural bodies of water seemed apocalyptically contaminated. For most of the Chinese students, the university was the first place they'd had access to any place where they could swim.

The women at the pool intimidated me. It was not because of their swimming. It was the locker-room shower scene that I found daunting: an enormous, packed-to-the-gills mob of bodies and steam.

Unless you are wealthy, in Shanxi, most homes do not have a shower. Instead, towns have public bathhouses. At university, similarly, there were no showers in the dorms themselves; showering was something most people did a couple of times a week in one of the university's provided facilities. Or, if you bought a swim pass, you could take your showers at the pool.

At any given time, the showers at the pool had four or five people gathered around each showerhead, taking turns to rinse. To pass through this shower room, even just on your way to or from the pool, was to push through a crowd of women and soap and hair. Much to my Puritan dismay, it was almost impossible to find unscented anything in rural China, including laundry detergent or pads, and the shower room was no exception. The air was overwhelming with its shampoo and soap perfumes, freesia and juniper and lavender. In the fog, it was a humid, scented forest, with limbs reaching in every direction.

I had never seen so many naked bodies together, been close to so many people at once. Most of the women, being students, were in their twenties: their skins completely smooth, their breasts small, their bodies angular and narrow by my own Western standards. Many of them had tied a red string around their hips, with a jade pendant for luck. There were some older women, too, who were teachers or lived in the community. Their bodies were considerably rounder, more weathered by time. Some had Cesarean scars that had never faded, their bellies divided by the pink line.

The level of intimacy here terrified me. In this shower space, my own shame came from what I couldn't hide: the obvious strangeness of my Caucasian body and its larger proportions of fat, muscle, and hair. It was one thing to walk through Taigu, wearing jeans and a jacket I'd bought in town, and be stared at immediately because of my red curls and pale skin. It was another to enter the shower room, for it to be obvious that the hair in my crotch was as red as that on top of my head.

"Wow," my friend Wang Hui Fang said the first time she got a look at me, not long after we had met. We weren't even showering then; she and I and our other friend were just changing into our bathing suits, stuffing our clothes into a shoebox-sized locker with no lock. "Name hong!" she exclaimed, meaning "really, really red."

When she saw my embarrassment, she switched to English and tried to reassure me.

"It is very interesting," she said with enthusiasm. She grabbed, then, at the nonexistent flesh on her own waistline. "I am really getting fat," she said, as if this was meant to comfort me.

So I usually rushed through the shower room at the pool, being there only long enough to rinse off, my businesslike attitude probably causing even more attention than I would have otherwise. Sometimes I avoided the shower room altogether, opting to walk home shivering, the chlorine eating away at my hair. I was choosing, then, to use my

own showerhead in my apartment, which was simply attached the
wall and got everything else in the tiny bathroom wet: sink, toilet,
trash can, floor. Even in the privacy of my own bathroom, showering
was a messy, unbounded experience.

Once I went with Wang Yue to visit her hometown of Datong in
the north of Shanxi Province, another cold, dusty, coal-mining city
that borders Inner Mongolia. On Saturday afternoon, we went to
a public bathhouse near her family's apartment. The showers were
strangely empty that day, much less crowded than the pool building's
at school. Several middle-aged women turned to look at me incredu-
lously and then went on with their scrubbing. With all that empty
space in the tiled room, I actually felt cold despite the hot water beating down on me.

I admitted to Wang Yue then that I felt embarrassed showering at
the pool at school. To make things even weirder, I pointed out, I was
a teacher. The shower room called to mind one of those teaching-
anxiety dreams, I explained to her, when you suddenly find yourself
naked in front of one of your classes. Wang Yue looked me at, confused. It hadn't occurred to me that the "teaching naked" dream
might be specific to my cultural background.

"Like, what if I see my students in the showers?" I asked her,
reframing my point. "That would be totally embarrassing."

"Why?" she asked. "I mean, like . . ." she said, her English collo-
quialisms flawless, "they are also there taking a shower, right? They
don't care. They are doing the same thing as you." She offered me her
bottle of soap. She had a point.

In this new phase of my life, where I felt exposed all the time, there
was still so much in the culture that seemed guarded, so much
information I'd never be privy to. At the start of the day's classes, I
frequently got notes from missing students who gave vague excuses
for their absences. "Dear Teacher," the notes usually read, in English.
"I am sorry I will not attend class today. I have something to do."

In Mandarin, the expression *you shi* means you have some kind
of business to deal with, the specifics of which might be private and
need not be explained in detail. There is no good translation for this

phrase, at least in my experience, although my students tried. What these *somethings* were, I never found out.

Despite the communal culture, there was a limit to how much of myself could be seen. I had my own secret. My first year in Shanxi, I felt I couldn't explain to any Chinese person—mostly because of the conservative social mores of where I was living—how much I longed for Sarah and how impossible communication had become, given unreliable internet access and my crackling phone, as well as the unpredictable restrictions from the government in Beijing. We found our Skype calls going silent for reasons we couldn't place.

As exhilarating as it was to be living abroad, there was also, for me, a day-to-day panic I didn't know how to explain to others. It came from an accumulation of small things: not being able to read all the characters on the bus schedules or figure out how to send a package. Not knowing what to do when you eat something that gives you diarrhea all night and the water source to your toilet is cut off, in a province with severe shortages, between 10 P.M. and 7 A.M. When I think back on China, even my good days had an undercurrent of deeper, untranslatable anxiety. It was a dislocation that comes only when you find yourself living, all of a sudden, on the other side of the world and not understanding how anything works. On bad days, I felt that I shouldn't have come to China. As an outsider, maybe I had no business being in Shanxi at all.

At night, I lay awake in my cold little bedroom, listening to the mouse inside the radiator vent toenailing his way out onto the dark floor. China is a pretty loud place, but at night in Taigu, there was only the mouse plus one other noise: a train, about a mile away, from Xi'an on its way to Beijing, sounding its horn into the crisp, landlocked night. I could hear its pitch shift as it grew closer, then farther away. A sort of reverse alarm clock: I heard it every night at the same hour. Years later, when I think of the word *alone*, I still hear that sound.

That first spring, when I'd been in China nine months, Sarah finally broke up with me over the phone, the result of a multicall argument we couldn't seem to resolve while in two countries. Neither of us would back down. "This is impossible," she admitted and then hung up, as if some unknown force in the universe was responsible for what was happening to us. Despite that we were already physically separated, and knowing the unlikely odds for relationship survival—several countries between us, two new cultures to adapt to, no plans to see each other until later in the summer, and being generally immature, in our early twenties—the breakup blindsided me.

I wasn't out to any of my Chinese friends yet. I spent the night after the phone call wallowing in the company of the Americans next door, eating, in alternation, seaweed-flavored potato chips and beef-flavored potato chips. We would eventually start calling them "breakup chips," since hardly any American's long-distance relationship survived while one member of the couple was living in China. We drank large bottles of Xue Hua, a mediocre Chinese beer. The next morning, I woke at dawn, hungover and disoriented, to the loudspeaker narration of a campuswide exercise routine. I couldn't decipher any of the voice's directions except for the counting parts. "Three . . . four . . . five . . . six!" the voice kept saying, the reason for the emphasis unclear to me.

My grief that spring was enormous, maybe even out of proportion. Before China, I had never been particularly weepy. Now I cried any time I was not in front of a group of students: during dinner, during my Chinese lessons, after I bought vegetables in the square, while sweeping my floor or wiping the black coal dust from the windowsill. In Shanxi, all my usual emotions became augmented in ways I didn't understand, and the boundaries for who should and shouldn't know my feelings became more and more unclear.

Everything I ate made me sick. I started to resent hosting the usual dance parties, giving a thin-lipped smile as twentysomethings flooded my house. It wasn't long before my new Chinese friends put two and two together, even though I had never directly explained to them that Sarah, who had visited in the fall, was my girlfriend. I didn't have to spell it out. "Oh! You have *xin shi*," they would tell me, letting my lesbianism be implied rather than stated outright.

When it comes to emotional matters in China, there is a variation of the vague expression *you shi*, the usual "I have business" or "I have something to do." If you say "you xin shi," it means, more specifically, you have a matter of the heart to deal with, or something is weighing on you, or that you're worried in an all-consuming way. The word *xin*, written 心, is an actual pictograph meaning "heart." *Xin shi* was how my friends referred to struggles with their boyfriends or girlfriends, or, occasionally, even more sensitive matters. (One close Chinese friend, I eventually discovered, had three abortions in the previous four years, all of which she'd kept a secret from her family and most of her friends at school.) The phrase is useful and can serve as a euphemism if you want it to, allowing you to both guard the details of your situation and offer the gesture of an explanation.

The first time I uttered the phrase, it was because it was a bad day for me, my eyes still red and swollen when I entered the grain seller's store to buy a half kilogram of flour. After I asked for the flour, the woman nodded, looked hard at me like an all-knowing mother. "You xin shi," I said, and she seemed to accept that.

"This poor foreigner," I heard her say to her husband, shaking her head, as I was heading out of the door. But that was the last time she'd refer to me as "foreigner." I'd always be one, but the next time I came in to buy something, she called me Luo Yi Lin, the name I'd been given by a Mandarin tutor just after I'd arrived in China.

Not surprisingly, being with other people could sometimes distract me from my breakup. But I preferred to hang out with my friends one-on-one rather than be in the crowd. My favorite thing to do that spring was to sit on my stoop late into the evening with my Chinese tutor at the time, Zhao Xin (or "Maggie," she sometimes called herself), drinking cheap beer and talking. Maggie had slowly become my closest friend in Shanxi. She was less demure than most of the Chinese women I knew—she cursed and was undefeated at badminton, and she also got angry at her boyfriend a lot. With the formal hour of the Chinese lesson long past, our conversations tended to get crasser and crasser as the night went on. The "real talk" quality of those sessions, I maintain, is how I finally got conversational in Mandarin. It's a lot easier to learn a language when you're using it to talk to someone you really like.

Maggie showed up at my house one spring night, appearing like a ghost on the dirt path leading up to my porch. She was coming from her graduate program's class party. "I had DRY WHITE WINE,"

she kept saying, over and over, in English. Something was off about
the translation: there was no dry white wine, at least the kind made
from grapes, anywhere in town. What she had really been drinking
was some kind of grain alcohol. Maggie spoke full-on English only
when she was drunk; it was her secret code to let you know what
she'd been up to.

She had missed her dorm's curfew, so she stayed with me. We
shared my double bed, talking loudly and rudely for a while, scaring
off the mice. She kept asking me, in English, with a strange British
accent I'd never heard, if I had any beer in the kitchen. I didn't.

Far away, we heard the train pass, its timbre more muddled than
what I remembered in the colder months. Why was that so? We lay
on our backs next to each other, our shoulders just barely touching.
The ends of her black hair crossed onto my pillow. I could smell her
shampoo. The room felt still, big around us. What was this? It was a
closeness I hadn't felt in a long time.

I was thinking about what could happen, what would not happen,
between us. We got quiet. I wanted to know what she was thinking.
Finally, she rolled toward me and reached across my arm. I held my
breath and froze.

In a teasing, nonsexual way, she grabbed the hem of my shirt and
tried to tickle me on my stomach, the way my sisters would do when
we were kids. She stopped suddenly, with the heel of her hand just
below my ribs.

"It's strong here!" she said, jubilant and surprised, pointing to my
upper abdomen. "I like it."

When I exhaled, it came out as a laugh. She rolled back onto her
back. A thin sliver of moonlight was wedging its way through the
bedroom curtains. Our chattering thinned out, and the room went
still again.

I heard her breathing shift toward sleep. Our shoulders were still
touching.

Language-wise, I finally gained the confidence to spend a good chunk
of that first summer traveling alone. On a warm night in June, I stood
beside the railroad tracks outside Taigu's railway station, balancing

my backpack across my feet. Alongside me was a small group of students with tiny suitcases, farmers with burlap bundles across their backs, and a handful of men and women who carried nothing except poker cards and the sunflower seeds and pears they would snack on. When the train to Beijing approached, a red light and a low honking in the dark, it slowed only long enough for the twenty or so of us to climb on: not from a platform but directly from the dusty ground. A train attendant reached her hand out to grab mine.

From Taigu to Beijing, a trip I'd made many times, it took nearly eleven hours in 2008, meaning we'd wake up just before the train pulled into the Beijing station. And then it was another twenty-four hours to Inner Mongolia, the first new place on my journey, where I'd end up, for several nights, sleeping in a yurt, under quilts and on the floor. A hole at the top of the tent showed the pollution-free, star-spangled sky.

On that train to Inner Mongolia, we passed through a dry mountain range that eventually leveled out against the grasslands: a kind of lush prairie filled with long shadows, the sky enormous and flat and blue. The herds wandered in the distance, a scatter of white coordinates. I sat on a foldout seat by window, talking to strangers for hours. "Are you *yi ge ren?*" they would ask me, surprised, wanting to know whether I was really traveling by myself.

I was, I said. And I wasn't, in another sense. At night, in my train compartment, I slept on the high bunk with my backpack nestled under my head. There were two strangers on the bunks below me, and three more against the opposite wall. We were together, if only for the night. A man across the way snored rhythmically, precise. I could still feel my grief from the past year close to the surface, but it felt good not to be alone as I drifted into an on-off sleep. The six of us jostled across the terrain, passing towns and villages in the dark. Occasionally, I woke to the train's deceleration and the *thunk* of a new rider being hoisted aboard.

Back in Taigu, I had finally gotten over the showers at the swimming pool. Because my American co-fellows were men, they couldn't help me with the challenge. Instead, I faced my fear by always entering the shower surrounded by my women friends. This is what all the women did. I don't know why it took so long for me to figure out that it was my aloneness, not my foreign body, that made people stare.

After a long afternoon in the pool, with our hands turned as wrinkly as Shanxi's jujubes, we climbed out of the water and slipped into our plastic slippers, careful not to fall as we headed into the tiled corridor. We passed the open toilet stalls, the stench pricking my nose, just before the perfumed smell of the shower room took over. We peeled ourselves out of our suits and wrung them out with our hands. I could feel my breasts swaying a little as I stepped over the ledge, the cold air grabbing my bare skin.

As I crossed into the foggy threshold, I heard, in English: "Teacher!"

I had finally run into a group of my students. They were undergraduate freshmen, English majors. I had seen most of them only when they were wearing their glasses, so I hardly recognized them at first. Luo An, who introduced herself as "Annie" in my class, looked at me in a dreamy, blurry sort of way. She was one of her class's leaders and the most forthright in English, talkative and clear. "Do you come here often to have a shower?" she wanted to know immediately. "And are you by yourself?"

"I usually shower at my house," I told her. I motioned to my friends in front of me. "We are together today."

The smallest student, who called herself Stella, nodded at me demurely, her wet bangs and bob still hanging in a perfect square around her face. She was less than five feet tall. Undressed, her body seemed to be solely composed of bones and skin, barely pubescent. Her chest was almost flat. At this point, I remembered my own shame, that I was also naked. They must all be looking at the weirdness that is my body, I thought to myself: my red bush, sturdy thighs, sizable butt. I could feel my face growing hot despite the cold air.

But I resisted the urge to turn away. *There is nothing weird here*, I told myself. I was twenty-three years old. The students were nineteen: barely even women yet, but still women, nonetheless. Toward the end of my conversation with my students, it hit me that they were treating me in much the same way they had at the times we'd run into each other in the marketplace, fully clothed. Seeing their teacher out in public was seeing their teacher out in public, regardless of the circumstances.

I slipped further into the steam, the showers' whooshing noise, the clamoring of female voices, their exact words getting lost in the larger din. I placed my plastic caddy at the edge of the room, with the dozens of others, what seemed like hundreds of bottles of shampoo and body wash crammed inside, washcloths draped over the handles. By now I had run out of all of my preferred Western toiletries—my last holdout from my day-to-day life in the United States—so it was next to impossible to tell my basket from the others.

On the one wall where there were no showerheads, I saw a dozen undressed women lean against the tile, as if poised for a series of painful tattoos. Instead, their friends vigorously scrubbed their backs. The scrubbers wore hand-shaped loofahs, what looked like textured oven mitts, and rubbed—or more like scoured—so hard—that the top layers of skin began visibly pilling in some places. Of course, I had no loofah mitt of my own, but Wang Hui Fang insisted that she use hers on me. "You first," she said. "Then me."

Eventually I turned, putting my hands on the tile wall. I glanced over my shoulder. There had been a handful of women staring at me since I entered the shower room, but once they realized that I was with friends, they went back to their showering, seemingly losing interest.

The scrub hurt almost as much as I imagined it would. Wang Hui Fang worked in long, shoulder-to-butt strokes, the friction so fierce that it felt like my skin was lit. At first I thought the force was unnecessary, but then I remembered the swimming pool's chemicals and what the bottoms of my feet looked like: almost black in the dry, dead parts at the edges of my heel, and the ball of my foot its own dingy plateau. I had made the mistake of trying to go barefoot in my apartment a few times, earlier in the year, and I had paid the price. I couldn't seem to get all the Shanxi dust off my body, no matter how hard I tried under my tiny home showerhead, no matter how many times I mopped my apartment.

Pronouncing me done, Wang Hui Fang handed me the fluorescent pink mitt, and I looked for an open showerhead to wash it out and rinse myself. There were none. "Just push your way through," she suggested. I edged slowly into the crowd, waiting and waiting, my backside getting cold, until finally a woman stepped out from under the spray, and I got my clearance.

I rinsed the mitt off first and then myself. The water was hot, and the pressure was good, much better than the lukewarm trickle of the sad shower in my apartment. I was not alone. I was so close to the stranger next to me that when I bent forward, my shoulder brushed hers. The woman and I turned to look at one another at the same time, both of us sort of smiling in acknowledgment. The collision was inevitable; the room was very full. Neither one of us felt the need to apologize.

THE YEAR ON DESIRE

Weddings had never been for me. I'd always gagged a little at the traditional pageantry: the father giving the daughter away; the poufy dresses and hairdos; thousands of dollars spent on rings, mediocre buffets, and drunk people doing the YMCA. Weddings were exclusively tethered to the domain of heterosexuals. As a card-carrying lesbian, I wasn't interested. I was allergic.

But when my queer friends began getting married, I softened. Every few months, same-sex marriage became legal in another state, a victory when you're a person who has spent your life thinking that your country will never take your relationships seriously, let alone recognize them under the law. When Ezra and Drew stood under the chuppah, I teared up when the rabbi touched their shoulders, imbuing them with same sanctity as he would a man and a woman. When Rowan and Caitlin got married, I flew out to Portland to stand beside Rowan as their groomsperson. Wearing a tuxedo was a lot more fun than the strapless pink bridesmaid's dress I'd worn when my middle sister got married. It was a lot easier to dance in a tuxedo.

Still, when Sarah and I got engaged, I told her that the courthouse thing would be fine with me. I couldn't imagine myself doing the pomp and circumstance of anything beyond. But Sarah was more sentimental about the idea of a wedding, especially about having family witness this new phase in our relationship. "We only get one chance to do this," she pointed out. "Let's think of a compromise."

In the end, we drove up to Ithaca and had a flash-mob ceremony in the corner park in front of Cascadilla Falls, with our parents, siblings, six friends, a city councilman, and a handful of random sunbathers lying around in the grass. Sarah and I exchanged the plain metal rings we'd paid for with debit cards. I wore a short lace dress I'd bought for sixty dollars; Sarah wore a black peplum and a 1960s pillbox hat with a veil. We'd found the hat in a dead relative's attic. Before we said our vows, one of our friends read Wallace Stevens's "Final Soliloquy of the Interior Paramour," the most intellectual, unmushiest love poem I could think of. My mother read a selection from the *Goodrich v. Department of Public Health* opinion, the first of the same-sex marriage cases.

Even our choice of readings was suspect, I feared. Wallace Stevens had a terrible marriage, and every lesbian in America knows that the Goodriches eventually got divorced. "Don't you think that's a really bad sign?" I asked Sarah. "Doesn't this doom the marriage automatically?"

She rolled her eyes at me, signaling the end of discussion.

Neither of us cried at the actual ceremony, but Sarah—a new attorney, still unabashedly sentimental about the law—got choked up at the Ithaca City Clerk's office as we were filling out the forms for our marriage license. "It's *real*," she'd whispered tearfully, looking down at the pile of red tape. We'd chosen New York because it was important to us that the marriage be a legal one. If we were going to do this death-do-us-part business, we didn't want to screw around with a category that was only symbolic.

Despite my skepticism around tradition, our own tiny wedding made more of an impact on me than I'd expected. Saying our vows seemed transformative, which, I guess, is the whole point of ritual. Maybe it's more that I was hyperventilating slightly during the ceremony, simulating a bizarre, liminal experience. As I held both Sarah's hands, I studied her face—her strong nose, blue-green eyes, and dark, serious eyebrows—and it was almost as if I were encountering it for the first time. In real life, we'd been together eight years, most of our adult lives. Just shy of twenty-two when we met, I'd fallen for her almost immediately, her ambition and maturity a whole new category of person for me. Up until this point, my girlfriends had mostly been whimsical, pot-smoking, iconoclast types, the kind who worked on organic farms and eventually trained to be Reiki practitioners. Part of me craved someone who lived a bit more in the mind, someone with an edge, someone with a long-term plan for life.

When our families left town, Sarah and I holed up in a cabin on one of the nearby Finger Lakes: our modest but blissful form of a honeymoon. We kayaked and dared each other to swim in the lake, still numbingly cold in mid-June. Afternoons were for sex: the earthy, unrushed sort, the skylight above us filled with the trees of New York. In the evenings we cooked, drank on the porch, played gin rummy, read books.

Finally, we drove eleven hours back to Chicago, where Sarah was finishing up her district court clerkship and where I'd lived with her on and off during breaks in the academic year. Sarah and I had done the long-distance relationship thing a number of times throughout our twenties, prioritizing education and careers over everything else. Most recently, I'd held a writing fellowship at a small college in Ohio: a necessary step, I told myself, that would one day help realize my dream of being a professor.

We would be moving to New Orleans in August because Sarah had been awarded a second judicial clerkship, this one on the Fifth Circuit Court of Appeals. In law school, Sarah been one of the best of her class—high grades, an editor of the law review. An appellate clerkship was a big deal in her world, an honor afforded to rising superstars. With no set plans after my fellowship, it made sense that I follow her stardom down to Louisiana, where we would finally live together full-time for the first time in many years.

The day she'd gotten the offer from the appellate judge and asked me to move to New Orleans, I'd been away at a writers' conference in Boston, in a particularly good mood as I coasted in my own professional success: my first book of poetry had just been published. As Sarah and I discussed her clerkship offer over the phone, a blizzard was pummeling the East Coast. From my hotel window, I watched the suffering of New England, the miserable, puffy-coated pedestrians fighting their way down Commonwealth Avenue. New Orleans was appealing. I imagined the warm air touching my skin, eating beignets and riding a streetcar with Desire printed across the front. I imagined a Juliet-style balcony with a cocktail in hand, a brass band parading below while I looked up from writing some literary masterpiece. Yes,

I told Sarah. Louisiana could be good. After all, I was a Southerner at heart. And for our first year of marriage—I thought, gauzy with a tourist's sense of sentimentality—what better backdrop than the streets of New Orleans?

Seven weeks after our little flash-mob wedding, we loaded the Penske truck in the Chicago summer heat. We'd moved apartments so many times in our twenties that we could have performed this task in our sleep. Sarah drove and I followed her in the Honda, our two big orange cats crated in the back seat. The industrial clutch of Chicago gave way to the green and gold heartland, cornfields seemingly choreographed into a graceful undulation. I found myself strangely calm as I looked at the landscape; I didn't even need the radio to distract me.

The next day, an hour or so over the Louisiana border, the trees thinned, the colors faded, and the land appeared to empty. We found ourselves on a raised highway with water on both sides, the swamp trees white in the distance, like the masts of ghost ships. As I turned the radio knob slowly down to nothing, it was as if all sound, too, had fallen away from the world. We had arrived at the swampy edge of the country, where the land goes under the water and then surfaces and then goes under again. I'd lived in the South before, but I was from the Piedmont, not a place like this. Overwhelmed by the landscape, I tried to keep my eyes on the back of the yellow moving truck. My face began to tingle the way it had on our wedding day: excitement or panic, it was hard to say. I felt the gravity of the commitment I had made: inserting myself into this strange landscape, promising Sarah that I'd follow her down here.

New Orleans was a city of smells—garbage, fried food, gasoline. Mildew covered anything that stood still. Our street had so many potholes that every passing car sounded like it was breaking in half. More than once over the course of the year, I looked out the front window and cringed, finding a passerby casually peeing on the gate next to my house. "New Orleans is a lover," a Louisianan friend had once explained to me, "but it's a gritty one, for sure."

Before I moved, I'm embarrassed to admit that most of my impressions of New Orleans came from two sources. The first was from news reports after Hurricane Katrina, ten years before, when I'd been a college student in Ohio and helping with relief efforts: horrific images, thousands of people stranded in the Superdome, whole neighborhoods underwater. The second version, the overly romanticized one, was from watching Marlon Brando and Kim Hunter in the film version of Tennessee Williams's *A Streetcar Named Desire*. In a lot of ways, the actors in this film really do seem like they're living in urban Louisiana. The interior rooms are smoky and narrow and overflowing with people and objects. People's faces are shiny with perspiration; someone's shirt is drenched all the way through.

In *Streetcar*, when Blanche Dubois arrives at the train station in New Orleans, she's told she needs to "ride a streetcar named Desire, then transfer to a streetcar named Cemeteries, take it six blocks, and get off at a street named Elysian Fields" to get to her sister Stella's apartment where she lives with her new husband, Stanley. When we moved to New Orleans, I figured out that the newlywed Kowalskis would have been living in the Marigny, a funky neighborhood that borders the French Quarter and the river. Sarah and I stayed in the Marigny while we were looking for a place to live, charmed by its outrageously colored shotgun homes and narrow streets. But *Streetcar* takes place in 1947. By 2014, when we moved, the neighborhood was almost fully gentrified, with most rents out of our price range.

Instead, we'd crossed the edge of the Marigny—Press Street, where the train tracks meet the Mississippi—and ended up renting half of a shotgun house in Bywater, the next neighborhood over. The Bywater, I discovered, is where Blanche would have ended up if she'd stayed on that first streetcar and taken it all the way to the end. In fact, our new address was 1025 Desire Street, a literary coincidence that delighted me.

On the five small blocks of Desire Street between our house and the river, houses ranged from run-down shotguns to restored cottages with lush tropical gardens. Mimosas, crepe myrtles, and magnolias lined the street in whimsical, uncalculated ways. Claw-foot bathtubs full of herbs and hibiscus flowers also had statues of Mary, her neck strung with Mardi Gras beads. In the vein of the absurdly comical, a 1970s El Camino was parked on the street with a large purple canoe strapped to its top, soon deemed the Purple Canoe Named Desire.

Then crossing out of the Bywater and over St. Claude Avenue, Desire Street begin to give way to houses even more run-down than the roughest ones on our block. Other houses had the clean starkness of new construction. There were boarded-up businesses and lots with nothing on them but grass and tangles of weeds: an ambiguous, fecund emptiness in the middle of the city. This is what things looked like ten years after Hurricane Katrina. By contrast, our next-door neighbors explained to us that, on our block, the water had risen to only about the level of our front steps. The roof of our shotgun had been damaged by wind, but no water ever entered the house. The blocks south of us were untouched; the ones north, submerged. This particular strip of Desire Street had been right on the cusp of fortune and misfortune. It was a tenuous place to have landed.

Across from our house, there was an empty lot that functioned as a public garden, the chromatic focal point of our block. I put my writing desk in the front room so that I could see it while I was working: the sunflowers, crazy vines, and the gorgeous tree whose huge, antebellum-dress-shaped blossoms bloomed white but then turned pink late in the day. "Confederate rose" is what the tree was called, our neighbor Edmond told us, though it was technically a kind of hibiscus.

"The city hasn't gotten ahold of this lot just yet," Edmond explained, motioning toward the garden. "So I try to help keep it looking good." Edmond, a gay landscape painter, told us that Desire Street's residents had collectively nicknamed the vacant lot the "Garden of Desire."

"It's our own sort of Eden," he joked. "This is a great block, by the way. I've lived here a long time. And the good news is," he said, looking at us knowingly, "the Bywater is still full of queers, at least for now." He winked at us. "Welcome to the neighborhood, newlyweds."

Despite the grit, it was easy to throw ourselves into the ramshackle romance of New Orleans. We took walks down to the river bend, watching the enormous boats stacked with boxcars, and then tried to outrun the cloud walls before they drenched us in rain. Once, we took the ferry to Algiers for no reason other than to cross the river by boat. We took the comically slow streetcar—the real one, on St.

Charles—to a couple of cemeteries, wandering through two hundred years of mausoleums, examining the flowery Victorian names of
the long dead. We decorated our house, spending pocket change on
drawings and maps from the junk shops on Dauphine Street.

Mostly, though, we ate. We were addicted to the fried oyster po'
boys at Frady's. The bakery around the corner made cinnamon rolls
the size of our faces. We discovered our favorite watering hole, a tiny
restaurant on the corner of Louisa Street that made cheap Sazeracs
and Old-Fashioneds.

Sarah and I found that drinks were stronger here than we remembered them being in the Midwest. We flirted as we walked back on
Desire Street, teasing each other as we tripped over the uneven sidewalks. At home, we undressed each other in a performative way, our
bodies pressed up against one of the nineteenth-century pocket doors
of our new bedroom. Having been together most of our adult lives,
we were already a couple who knew each other backward and forward. But New Orleans—the hot night air and the drinks and flowers
blooming in all seasons—was heady, bewitching. I felt like the clumsy,
sex-crazed college students we'd been when we'd first met—or maybe
like Stanley and Stella, the Big Easy's most dramatic newlyweds.

∴ ∴ ∴

Unglamorously, most of what we did in New Orleans was go to
work. Sarah shined at her new job, no surprise to anyone, given her
general overachiever status. She spent her days researching and writing opinions on which the judge eventually signed his name. "I can
rely on her to get things right," the judge told me once when I popped
into the courthouse to pick her up. "Sarah's truly the best," he assured
me, as if I didn't already know it. "Terrific work ethic."

I glanced over at Sarah's desk, the most immaculate looking of the
four clerks'. In the left-hand corner was a picture taken at our wedding. The two of us posed by the cascade in the gorge, hugging each
other by the waist and shoulder—Sarah is about five inches taller than
I am—as we looked at each other and tried not to laugh. Above this
photo, Sarah's court case binders neatly lined the shelves. Her writing
utensils, legal pad, and coffee mug were poised carefully around the
twin computer monitors, as if painted into an office still life.

I thought about my sad little office desk at Tulane University, which wasn't even really mine: I had to share with a bunch of other people. After some hustling, I'd gotten two adjunct teaching contracts for the academic year. At Tulane, I taught two sections of creative writing to undergraduate students. Across town, I was also a teacher at an early college program, where I was replicating a college writing course for gifted teenagers, students pulled from the remains of the New Orleans public school system. I got schooled pretty quickly in that first semester. The early college kids rolled their eyes at the very first assignment. A group of boys—who hadn't actually signed up for this writing elective—spent the period goofing off or else slumped over in silence, their sweatshirts pulled up and obscuring their faces. They were not my fans.

Some of those early college kids turned out to be terrific, with far more spark than the partygoing Tulane students across town, who seemed to take everything at face value. My early college students laughed out loud when Flannery O'Connor's Bible salesman ran away with Hulga's wooden leg; they liked writing sestinas on the board, seeing the same words looping over and over again. A lot of the time, though, I didn't feel in control of my own classroom: some days, students flat-out refused to do anything I asked. Once, after a boy plagiarized an assignment, he came back from his meeting with the program head and yelled at me, slamming down into his chair and hurling his notebook across the classroom. The unpredictable nature of the class, and of teenagers, was exhausting.

When my meager paychecks arrived, it was hard not to feel deflated. I joked about this to a few of my colleagues, and they looked at me with contempt. "Realize that you're teaching at the two places that have the highest adjunct pay in the city," one teacher said to me. "And do you know how many writers would kill for your classes at Tulane?" she asked. "I've been fucking trying to get work there for years." I swallowed my pride, remembering I'd been lucky to get teaching work in the city at all, especially as a newcomer.

Sarah, impeccably organized, opened the spreadsheet as we paid bills every month, nervously examining whether we'd overspent. The conversations made us tense. We were eating at restaurants more often because food was a part of the culture here. But groceries and utilities were also surprisingly expensive. One month, the water bill was ninety dollars: surprising, since we had been under boil alert for the previous two weeks. I was earning about what I'd made as a graduate student, which didn't help with expenses.

"It doesn't matter," Sarah said practically. "We just have to be more disciplined." But I felt guilty that we were not saving anything. I felt guilty that I was working all the time but not making more money, especially since I was almost thirty years old and had two degrees.

Each day, after my classes, I made my way back to Desire Street, where I removed the sweat-drenched work clothes and considered whether I should take a nap, try to write something, or tackle the enormous stack of student writing assignments in my charge. In the hour before Sarah got home, I usually made dinner in our small kitchen at the back of the shotgun, so far away from the front door that she startled me when she appeared in the doorframe of the kitchen, her face hot from biking home along the river.

It was rare that Sarah had a bad day at work. Most of her reports were of the office group lunches that pushed well past the one-hour mark (normal in New Orleans, I came to realize), where the judge and his clerks discussed nerdy legal issues over sandwiches and cake. I imagined them in a kind of seminar, taking pride in the fact that they were all contributing to something important: the judge as an already important person and the clerks on their way to great things.

At the stove, I would listen to her recount the day, sometimes with interest or patience, and sometimes with envy, depending on how my own day had gone. I would long for her before she got home, feeling so relieved to see her tall frame darkening the kitchen doorway. But as the year went on, if I'd had a bad day at school, I'd begin to get paranoid and resentful. It was easy to worry that we were falling into traditional marital roles, the ones I'd actively planned my life against.

I was worried I was destined to become a lawyer's wife.

"I want to be more ambitious," I announced to Sarah one night after dinner. "You know, in terms of career." What I meant is that I should have gone on the national academic job market the year before, which is what people are supposed do when they're really trying to become a professor with any sort of stability. You're supposed to go where the job is, or so I had been told. Instead, I had prioritized our marriage and committed to moving to New Orleans.

Although we had only just arrived in the city, we'd come knowing that Sarah's contract, as with all federal clerkships, was only for a year. If we wanted to stay in New Orleans longer than that, she'd need to study for the Louisiana bar to get another law job. There were bigger questions, too: Did we want to set up shop here, a two-day drive from Ohio and North Carolina, where our parents and siblings lived? What about the fact that our marriage wasn't legal in the state of Louisiana? Bigger than that: What about climate change, the natural disasters, the broken-down infrastructure?

"I mean, of course you should stay in New Orleans *forever*," one of our friends, a New Orleans filmmaker, joked to me once as we were walking in the Bywater. He pointed to the Mississippi River. "But just a warning: don't ever buy a house here. This whole fucking city is going to fall into the water eventually."

Academic jobs on the national market were already being announced for the following year. It made sense for me to begin applying. "Preferably in a city where I could also get a job," Sarah said. We came up with a tentative plan: I would send out applications all over the country and see what happened. If I had followed Sarah to New Orleans, I reasoned, the next move could be because of me.

At night on Desire Street, we watched all kinds of people pass by: workers getting off the bus on St. Claude; teenagers with their mini-bikes; Edmond coming home on his cruiser; Pat, who lived in the house next door, leaving town for Bay St. Louis, where his wife had lived since Katrina. After dinner, our neighbors Rob and Emily—well-known civil rights attorneys, according to Sarah—pushed their new baby down Desire in the stroller, trying to get her to sleep while their toddler wheeled alongside them on her scooter. When they passed by us, Sarah's expression was longing when she looked at their little kids.

Kids. I'd always been on the fence. "Maybe," I'd said, "if the time is right." But Sarah had felt called to parent for as long as I could remember. I wondered how long it would be before I felt like I was secure enough to be in charge of another human. It was not an unreasonable age to start thinking about children. But approaching thirty, I had not pictured myself working two ill-paying jobs, as a writer with a book I think only a handful of people had actually read. For most of my twenties, I had believed, or at least hoped, I was on the path to something bigger when it came to career. I was beginning to be nagged by the sense that things might not turn out the way I'd envisioned.

⁘ ⁘ ⁘

Many of the teenagers I taught, most of whom had been born and raised in New Orleans, were growing up in neighborhoods struggling with violence and crime. That fall, two local tragedies shook up my classroom at the early college. First, my student Farrah's cousin was shot and killed at a nearby apartment complex. "She was just at the wrong place at the wrong time," Farrah told me glumly. I never learned the specific circumstances. Her cousin had been a college student, just twenty-one years old. The few poems Farrah turned in that semester were lyrics about her grief, filled with images of tears and screaming and bullet holes. Her life had been changed forever. She was absent for weeks at a time, and no one seemed to know when she was coming back.

A few weeks after Farrah's cousin died, George Carter, a fifteen-year-old boy who had been the childhood classmate of some of my students, was murdered on the street in New Orleans. I didn't know him, but I read the articles about him in the paper. The shooting was a mystery: some guessed a random act of violence or that he'd been mistaken for someone else. A convenience store clerk claimed that George and his friend had robbed him in the hours before the shooting, but the rumor was never confirmed.

The day after the news about George, there were more absences in class than usual. A few students were staring off into space; others were quietly discussing George's fate. "He was up in Desire when it happened," Bryra reported. She was referring not to Desire Street but to the Desire neighborhood, dozens of blocks north of where I lived, where Desire Street dead-ended into the Florida Street Canal. I had driven through the area a couple of times, noticing how the streets were all named for benevolent concepts: Abundance, Treasure, Benefit, Pleasure. George Carter had been gunned down on Piety Street—which also ran through my neighborhood, which was many blocks south of where he'd been killed.

The irony of those names was not lost on any of us. That morning, after we'd spent ten minutes or so writing in our notebooks, Bryra read aloud from the quick elegy she'd composed. "He was out walking in Desire," Bryra recited, "a place they should rename for all the lost lives." Her classmates snapped in appreciation. As I listened, I pictured the Desire Street north of my house, where some people had warned me never to walk after dark. And I thought, too, of where I'd lived when I was my students' age: rural North Carolina, where, even in the midst of homophobia and racism, small and large instances of bigotry, I'd still been protected by the woods around our house, by privilege, by my white skin. There was not much in my life that prepared me for the worries my students at the early college were facing.

No wonder some of them didn't trust me.

After the class, I made my way to Uptown for my seminar at Tulane, passing the auto shops and the strip malls on Claiborne Avenue, the potholes shaking my rickety old car as I drove over them. I begin to circle Tulane's pristine campus, its grandiose live oaks and manicured lawns, those emblems of prestige and white supremacy. I was circling because I was trying to find a parking place allowed with my employee permit, which had cost something like a month of my adjunct salary to purchase in the first place. Everything about this situation, including how annoyed I was, struck me as petty and ludicrous. But I had to find somewhere to park to go to work. There were many days like this one, times when I felt that I had no place being in New Orleans at all. Despite how friendly all our neighbors had been, how quickly I'd found work, and the fact that we'd made friends: *This city doesn't belong to transplants*, I told myself.

In the weeks after submitting my many national job applications, I heard nothing. It became clear that I had not been competitive for even the first-round interviews. My years of good luck and privileged access—getting into graduate school, getting my book published, having a writing fellowship, finding teaching work—were promises of nothing. I'd had a false sense of confidence going into the application process.

When I came to this realization, seemingly sudden, I closed my laptop and stared up at the small cracks in our shotgun's unreachable fourteen-foot ceiling. I walked from room to room, starting in the front parlor and ending in our busted-looking bathroom in the back, whose floor sloped dramatically toward the backyard and where roaches routinely died underneath the clawfoot tub. *The city is sinking, the city is sinking* played on a loop in my head.

Instead of being realistic about all the possible reasons I wasn't being considered for jobs, I began to wonder about direct cause and effect. If I hadn't moved to New Orleans and taken the adjunct jobs, would I be in a different position? If I hadn't gotten married, would I still have felt the pressure to move to Louisiana?

Sarah wasn't a stranger to my strong emotions. "This is what happens when you marry a poet," she often joked when I had strong reactions to things. But as I grew more and more despondent that November, her patience started to wear thin.

"What's the point of dwelling on this?" she kept asking me. "You're working right now. I'm working. I'll be employed somewhere next year. Maybe you'll try again. What can you do? Move on." My wallowing, as she saw it, wasn't doing any good.

In more lighthearted times, I would have teased her about her midwestern stoicism, joked about how she was secretly jealous that I was expressing my negative feelings. "Southerners deal with our feelings out loud," I always told her. But it felt like she was trying to sweep my desires under the rug. For weeks, I didn't want to go out or hear about anything in Sarah's life. When she made suggestions for me, I'd snap at her, telling her she didn't get it.

One night I found myself suddenly sobbing on the couch, unable to explain myself.

"You have *got* to pull yourself together," she said. "Your depression is messing with our marriage," she said point-blank.

That stung. Not only was I failing at my career, I was a terrible spouse. In contempt, I found myself imagining Sarah's perfect academic transcripts spread out on the coffee table, her tidy résumé and its list of ever-impressive entries.

"You've never failed at anything in your life," I proclaimed. "How can you possibly know what I feel like?" I looked around the room, unable to make eye contact. "I should have never come to New Orleans in the first place," I said coldly. I knew, even without looking at her, that I was hurting her, but it didn't stop me from pulling out the big guns. "I'd probably have a better job right now," I said, "if I hadn't sacrificed my career for yours."

I said it even though I knew my logic was shaky at best. As a writer, I knew how much doom was built into everything I tried to do—projects that stalled, prizes I didn't win, publication dead-ends, job rejections.

Failure was an occupational hazard. But this time, I couldn't put anything into perspective. Sarah pointed out that I'd picked a career path on which the jobs were next to impossible to get. (Every job rejection I'd received had listed the number of applicants as in the hundreds.)

"You made a choice," Sarah said. "This is why I went to law school," Sarah pointed out. "I wouldn't want to do what you do. I want something *reliable* for my fucking career." (What she wasn't saying: "I am paying most of our rent. I am carrying most of the load.") Her voice started to waver. "And you know I never made you move down here. It was your decision to come to New Orleans," she reminded me. "I just wish that the marriage—that *I*—was worth it to you." She stormed out of the room, a combat technique that had been declared off-limits since arguments of our midtwenties.

We were regressing. For hours we kept walking out on each other midconversation and following each other into the next room of the shotgun, our voices raised in accusation. We said things meaner than we had ever said before. It was the kind of argument that feels like maybe it will do permanent damage, our first awful argument since we'd gotten married. Years earlier, a fight like this would be the beginning of us breaking up. It had happened twice in our early twenties: once when we were living in different countries, and once my first year in graduate school. Things were more precarious back then, or so I'd believed.

Now I was haunted by the sense that we had no idea what we had gotten into, getting married. Maybe we weren't mature enough to handle all the compromises and sacrifices that marriage seemed to require. Or maybe I was not the marrying type. I'd never been sure. Regardless, the year seemed to be taking a bad turn.

The next morning was a cruel one, neither of us having slept much. I looked outside and found that a cold snap had gotten the hibiscus tree across the street. The blooms, which had stayed a deep pink throughout the early fall, were turning brown. Sarah got up and went to take a shower, saying nothing to me. She was about to go out of town for something work related. We wouldn't resolve anything before she left. Our argument had been poorly timed.

I watched her disappear through the automatic doors at the terminal, and my sleep-deprived brain went into panic mode. What if, finally away from me for the first time since we'd moved, she decided we had made a huge mistake, getting married? Maybe I was the one who felt we'd been foolish, trying to tie our lives to each other before we were settled in our careers. I knew, anecdotally, that career imbalances caused couples to fight, laid groundwork for resentment and failed marriages. What if we couldn't work it out? How had I not seen this conflict coming, having known Sarah for so many years? Why couldn't I be happy for her success? And how terrible was it that I was jealous of the person I loved?

After work, I came home to find Mae and Henry, our neighbors on the other side of the shotgun, sitting on our shared front porch, drinking cocktails out of vintage glasses. I stood there making small talk on the porch and watching them interact. Mae, a part-time manager at a vintage clothing store, was also a professional swing dancer who taught workshops all across the United States and Europe. Henry was a professional trombone player. They'd recently gotten engaged. It was hard, somehow, to picture them living anywhere but Desire Street. Their relationship seemed complementary, easy: he the musician and she the dancer, both of them artists in fields that overlapped but were separate. Sound and movement. Yin and yang. Masculine and feminine.

Despite cultural pressures from the moment I was born, despite growing up in North Carolina, where I sometimes felt queer people were rare or invisible, I'd never envied a straight couple, not for any reason. I'd known who I was for a long time. I'd never struggled much with accepting my queerness or the relationships that emerged from it. It had made me not take anything in life at face value. It had helped me escape oppressive forms of femininity and understand that there was more than one way to walk through the world. It was one thing that had made me attuned to the struggles of others. I was grateful to be queer.

At the same time, I wondered whether Henry and Mae found themselves wrestling power questions as much as Sarah and I had in the previous months. Even before our careers were involved, my relationship with Sarah had required an almost constant negotiation of agency. We'd never tied ourselves to roles or the expectations of gender. Our relationship was not butch-femme in the traditional sense. Even when we'd gotten engaged, no one got down one knee to ask the other one. Rather, deciding to get married had been the outcome of many conversations in which we weighed various aspects. That wasn't the traditional way of things, but it was the only way that made sense for us.

Now, having moved to New Orleans after getting married, there was something almost ironic—maybe even fatalistic—about the fact that Louisiana wouldn't recognize our marriage. Of course, I knew that our marriage was every bit as real as Mae and Henry's would be. But when it came to *how* to be married, it sometimes seemed like there were no models for Sarah and me to look to, or at least no model that seemed like the right one.

Depressed and alone in the house that late November weekend, I found myself sucked into *A Streetcar Named Desire*'s version of New Orleans. I watched the film on my laptop, blanket over my head, as if in mourning. The cats draped themselves lazily on my lap, finally favoring me in Sarah's absence.

But really, if one is looking for an example of how to be married, they should do the opposite of everything they see in *Streetcar*. For all my whimsical musings about the film, I had forgotten how violent the relationships are. All the great love scenes are preceded by yelling, or Stanley beating on Stella, or Stella pushing Stanley, grabbing him, or ripping his shirt. In a dramatic moment—what eventually leads up to Brando's famous bellowing, "STEL-LA!"—he throws a radio out the window in anger. The next morning, Stella appears to be naked under the sheets, presumably after their makeup sex. She giggles as she tells Blanche that Stanley's gone off to get the radio fixed. "He only broke one tube!" Stella announces gleefully, delighted by the limited casualties of the night before.

I watched an angry Brando let his own insecurities, masquerading as machismo and bravado, get the better of him. As Stella and Stanley flirted and fucked and then punched and screamed at each other, I began wondering how the hell anyone manages to stay with one person for the rest of their life.

For advice, I called my oldest sister. "Well," my sister said, "almost nothing good comes out of saying everything you feel. Save a little bit of your breath next time." I frowned on the other end of the phone. This seemed like terrible advice. "But marriage," my sister argued, with great older-sister authority, "is where you discover just how fucked up each of you really is, separately and especially together." As if this were a consolation to me.

I thought back to my early twenties, remembering how most of my friends said they'd never get married. They regarded marriage as patriarchal and unforgivingly capitalistic in nature: something that people did without thinking, and not necessarily a "right" that any queer person should be fighting for. Who wants to tie themselves down and get the state involved? people would ask each other, and then we'd all smirk in superiority.

"Well, the good news is that you don't have to deal with a man in your marriage," my sister joked just before she hung up. "They're way more fucked up than women. Trust me."

Although I laughed, I wasn't convinced.

As I hung up the phone, I finally realized that a small part of me had been afraid to get married in the first place. But my fear, I suspect, was less about what marriage stood for and more about the possibility that I might fail at being married. I guess I had known all along that vowing to intertwine your life with another's—both people's desires and hang-ups tangled up, along with whatever new mess the future might hold—was likely to be hard at times, maybe even impossible.

Sarah, a midwesterner at heart, attempted to repair our domestic wounds with an onslaught of traditional holiday food. When my parents came at Thanksgiving, she insisted on cooking a twelve-pound turkey for four people. During Hannukah—Sarah is Jewish on her father's side—we hosted a latke-making party for the law clerks in New Orleans, potato starch and frying oil somehow making it into every room. (The party's mess gave one of our cats a bladder infection.) We bought a Christmas tree and decorated it with 1970s ornaments I'd found in my grandmother's attic the year before. This is what married people did, right?

By Christmas morning, we were back in our power struggle. This time, though, it was not about careers; it was about the construction of the yule log cake. I was overseeing the bake, but Sarah tried to hijack the project.

"You're bossing me around," I insisted, brandishing the spatula at her. "And you don't know what you're doing, either." The yule log was in danger of becoming a metaphor for our marriage. When my in-laws arrived on Christmas Day, hours before they were expected—like true midwesterners, they'd gotten up at 4 A.M. to start driving south—Sarah had just slammed the bathroom door in my face.

Despite its reputation, there is a winter in Louisiana: gray, damp-winded days where you can't seem to get your house to heat all the way through. But in New Orleans, the glumness in January is counteracted by Carnival season, when it's pretty impossible to take any responsibilities seriously. The parade schedule is too full. At my early college job, about two-thirds of my students were missing or very late to class because of closed roads or the bus getting caught behind parade-float traffic.

I loosened up my lesson plans. I stopped working so hard, since no one else appeared to be. "Parade, parade, work a little, skip work, parade," is how my friend Brad described the season's agenda.

Slowly, Sarah and I begin to embrace the weird pageantry of parade culture, making glow-stick crowns and joining the crowds in the street. One parade consisted of miniature shoebox floats; another, dogs in tutus. Things improved at home. For a while, I was able to stop obsessing about marriage and career and focus on, well, costumes.

For Mardi Gras, Sarah and I planned to joined St. Anne's walking parade, which started in our neighborhood and ended in the French Quarter. Rummaging through our closet for costume possibilities, I made it all the way back to the garment bag that contained my wedding dress, which I'd never intended to use again. Sarah looked at me, and we both got an idea.

What better day to do a mock wedding than Mardi Gras, the day of pleasure and pageantry. This time, though, I would wear a fabulous veil (gold tulle, purchased by the yard at Walmart) and we'd both carry fake flowers. We raided the CVS for all the glittery makeup we could find. We made ourselves, as we'd seen other people do, look garish: turquoise eyeshadow, pink eyeliner, black under the eyes.

On a bitterly cold Mardi Gras morning, preparing to step into my white dress for the second time, I remembered my hopeful anticipation that June afternoon of our wedding in New York. But now, as Sarah zipped me up in the back—an intimate gesture she'd performed many times over the years—she paused.

"Um," she said, trying not to laugh. "I think this is going to be a little more challenging than it was last year."

The New Orleans Fifteen—maybe more. When she finally got the zipper up, I couldn't breathe. (I gave up. I left the back zipper half-open and wore my coat on top.) When Sarah tried to put on *her* black peplum dress, it was even worse: she found that she couldn't even get the skirt part over her hips.

"Well," she said good-naturedly, "they don't call it Fat Tuesday for nothing." She found another dress in the closet that would work as a substitute.

Just before we headed out the door, we pinned signs to the backs of our coats. They read, Just Married?—our own sad, private joke, since we'd spent our first married year in a state where our marriage wasn't legal. Mardi Gras costumes have a history of taking on Louisiana political issues.

Not everyone got the joke. Most people took the signs literally. "Congratulations!" strangers called out. A number of people applauded and cheered, as if we had just said our vows and were in the process of doing the recessional exit. The brass bands made for an exuberant wedding march.

We followed our feather-covered parade marshal on Rollerblades out of the Bywater, crossing through the Marigny and entering the French Quarter. People around us were dressed in tinfoil and papier-mâché, glitter and sequins; some were topless or had phalluses pinned to their costumes. Sarah held my hand tightly, grinning at me through her flamboyant makeup. There was something both profane and holy about processing under these festooned balconies. It was probably the whiskey talking, but it occurred to me that maybe we had both been too earnest in our first wedding ceremony. Maybe pageantry was best. Maybe we could take ourselves a little less seriously this time around.

With Lent season, the weight of real life returned. Decisions about the next year were looming. Sarah's contract would be done in August. As things stood, I could likely get my New Orleans teaching gigs for another year, but there would be no contracts until the last minute, as is the case with most adjunct teaching work. One of us needed to get a long-term job.

Sarah sent out some applications, had her judge make a few calls: something that actually has weight in the world of law. "Again," she said, "this is *why* I went to law school."

She ended up with a couple of offers, including one at a small firm in Washington, DC: something neither one of us had ever pictured. It was a good job. She'd have a salary that would allow us to rent in the District and begin to save some money. We'd be in driving distance from almost everyone in our families. One of my sisters was across the river in Virginia. But if we moved, we'd also be giving up the nascent thing we'd started in New Orleans, having not been there long enough to know what could have become of it.

"I don't know what to do," I confessed to her. "I mean, it doesn't make sense to stay here, does it?" I asked.

As these decisions were looming, we both turned thirty: Sarah in March, me in May. A Saturn return, as the astrologers would say, is the thirty-year event that makes you feel heavy with responsibilities and limits. I dreaded my thirtieth birthday, not because I was precious about my twenties, but because I'd imagined thirty as an age by which I'd have more of my life figured out.

The Sunday before my birthday—as if feeling the weight of the year and the hot, sweaty city all at once—we decided to get out of town for the day. I advocated for wide-open water, something bigger than the river. We headed west on the rumbling, sun-bleached stretch of I-10, and then south until we reached the winding swamp roads of South Louisiana. The idea of New Orleans faded as the land grew emptier and emptier, occasionally interrupted by a strip mall, a stretch of run-down Creole shacks, or the aluminum glint of a trailer park. We passed sugarcane acres, their unruly tendrils tittering in the breeze. On the shoulder, people parked their trucks and leaned over the shallow ditch water, fishing and raking the mud for crawdads.

Finally, the road turned sharply eastward, and we found ourselves on a barrier island: the edge of the country, a spit of sand out in the Gulf of Mexico. This was Grand Isle, Louisiana. Driving through its rows of weathered, midcentury beach houses was like watching an old photograph coming into color.

We were surprised to discover almost no one at the beach, despite the fact that we were accessing the Gulf through a state park entrance. I crossed the sand and walked straight into the surf. The waves were high and breathless that day.

Once I got out to about waist height, the first big wave hit me, and I let myself go with it, my feet lifting from the bottom.

Sarah hung back for a moment, watching me from the foamy hem of the water. I watched her short, dark hair rising gracefully in the wind, the sun hitting her shoulders and impossibly long arms and legs. I'd always been attracted to tall women, always drawn to what was the opposite of me. Even her physical features were like the inverse of my own—long lines where I was short and curved, her hair dark and smoother where mine was light and unruly. On our wedding day, when I'd worn the traditional white, she had opted for black.

Sarah came forward in the water, but I could see her hesitating. Because of how long I'd known her, I could already guess why. In opaque ocean like this, I knew she was obsessing over sharks. This was not a totally irrational fear, since they're everywhere in the Gulf.

I called out to her in encouragement, and she made a face. Finally, she began to move deeper into the surf. "I'm terrified," she said, out of breath when she reached the place where I swam. "I don't want to get eaten alive out here."

"You won't." But the truth was that I couldn't promise.

In the water, I pulled her close to me, startling her into a nervous laugh. Although Sarah claimed to be terrified, she stayed out there with me. Like kids with no one telling us not to, we were in the water for a long time that day, playing in the waves: sometimes letting them knock us down in a melodramatic way, sometimes diving under them. There was no point to any of it. Occasionally, a breaking wave surprised us, smacking both of us in the face. As if helpless to defend ourselves, both of us started laughing.

Sarah eventually accepted the job offer in DC, what seemed like the responsible thing to do, despite our ambivalence. The end of the school year came; I finished grading and turned in my office keys, and—for the first time in my adult life—became officially unemployed. We were leaving town in a matter of weeks, and despite all my hustling and emailing and searching for work, I hadn't landed anything in Washington.

Our first wedding anniversary snuck up on us. Like my birthday, its approach made me anxious, the random date pressuring me with supposed deep significance. Sarah and I had always celebrated our dating anniversary, which was in February. But something about this first wedding anniversary felt terrifying. When we woke up the Sunday morning of June 14, we realized we hadn't made any clear plans.

We agreed that we wouldn't do a fancy meal, given that we were on a tight budget for the summer. We bought cheap breakfast sandwiches down the block and picked at them nervously, as if we were people who didn't know each other well.

The truth is that the year had been a mixed bag for us: plenty of pleasures but also arguments, conflicts we didn't know how to solve, conflicts that might not have solutions. When, after a long silence, I finally admitted this out loud, Sarah nodded. "Truth," she said. "Maybe it's better not to be perfectionists about it," Sarah, the perfectionist, said. "We'll try and do better this year."

Back home, we got the courage to pull our wedding photos off the bookshelf: a made-it-ourselves album that we'd bought for ten dollars, printing off photos at the CVS. In the pictures, we look like the absolute best versions of ourselves: poised but not overly posed, dressed to the nines, holding hands, confident, promising each other everything. At the back of the album, there were two blue squares of paper, the vows we cowrote for our wedding day.

We read them with amusement, remembering almost nothing of what we'd written the year before. The vows we'd chosen were a blend of the mushy abstract ("I promise to always seek adventure with you, to prioritize our love, to be better and better for you") and the practical ("I promise to respect your independence and persevere through challenging times"). Still, after a year of marriage, we agreed that some of the promises we'd made were pretty vague, didn't fully match the life we were leading.

"Let's add something specific about resentment," I suggested, "and about not bringing up divorce when we're having a fight." Sarah, who lives to write lists, took this down along with her own notes. When I looked over her shoulder, Sarah had written, *I promise not to be a dick when you are feeling sad about your career.*

We drove up to New Orleans City Park for the rest of the afternoon, where there are dozens of mythical-looking live oaks. We made our way to the Singing Oak, a locally famous tree hung with dozens of wind chimes. I handed Sarah the new slip of paper. In our revowing session (we whispered, too embarrassed to perform in front of the random passersby) we pledged not to be immature assholes to each other in the second year of marriage, both of us of knowing that we might fail, perhaps even miserably. Above us, the crazy chimes rung out at random intervals, their effect both Zen-like and bizarrely postmodern.

"The end," I declared dramatically when we'd finished. We agreed to revisit our promises in a year.

The next year, as it turned out, would be easier in some ways. DC would turn out to be a pleasant place to live, the cool air of the fall a welcome relief after the past year. We would be upset with each other far less often, even though our careers would remain imbalanced. But the year would also present us with new questions. The glow of Sarah's clerkship years would fade as she became a sleep-deprived associate, positioned at the bottom of the food chain and saddled with long hours. I'd get my final adjunct teaching job, one far worse than in New Orleans: bad enough to quit after six months. For a while, I'd take another fellowship at a college in Arkansas, both of us spending our weekends traveling back and forth between Little Rock and DC. This, too, was a compromise, a major decision that we agonized over for a long time.

But as we loaded up our moving truck that last morning on Desire Street, not quite a year after we'd first arrived, I could feel some local changes already in full swing. Mae and Henry, after they got married, bought their own place across the water in Algiers. Our next-door neighbor, Pat, sold his run-down house—for four times what he'd paid for it—to a developer from Texas and moved to Bay St. Louis to be with his wife. In true gentrification fashion, a construction crew was adding a "camelback," a second story, making it a noisy site that I was happy to no longer be living next to. There were rumors of a luxury hotel going up in the neighborhood. And the City of New Orleans, just before we left, was preparing to take the Garden of Desire lot back. Edmond broke the news to us. They'd be clearing it for development.

Maybe we made our exit from the neighborhood at the right time.

Even now, we can't say for sure. On our last morning, as we walked through the empty rooms of that shotgun house, I could already see us far in the future, still wondering about Desire Street, its romance and rough edges. Still thinking about that first, imperfect year of our marriage.

"Maybe we'll move back one day," Sarah said, her hand on my shoulder. I closed the door behind us, pushing our old keys through the mail slot. "I mean, you never know. Right?" Sarah grinned at me for no obvious reason. She is an optimist. It is one of the reasons I'm drawn to her. The fierce Louisiana sun was catching on the very first flecks of gray in her hair: my wife.

PUBLIC SWIM

In New Orleans summertime, air conditioners rattle out of house windows, dripping yellow slime onto the concrete below. Shade is rare in most of the city. Dogs wander down the hot sidewalk and turn around after a block or so, ready to go home. A flat, bleached-out sky hangs low over everything: the crisscrossed metal of the Industrial Canal's drawbridge; the long blocks of shotgun houses; the bends of the Mississippi River, where cargo boats stacked with boxcars seem like the only swift-moving things in the world. When a storm is finally conjured—usually around three o'clock in the afternoon— you can see the entire cloud formation as it moves in over the river, purple and gray in three dimensions. The rain is brief and hard, cooling the air for half an hour or so. And then the city, bathtub shaped and full of steam, often feels twice as hot as before.

All week I crisscrossed invisible borders of New Orleans, from downriver to Uptown and back again, for my two jobs. Back home, I peeled off my work clothes and my sweat-soaked underwear, putting on the most lightweight clothes I could find. I dreaded turning on the stove or the oven to make dinner. I lay on the cool, beat-up floorboards of our rented shotgun on Desire Street and dreamed about going swimming.

Wherever I am living, so long as there is water nearby, I usually find a way to swim. And in a city like New Orleans—warm and party-happy, surrounded by water—this seems like it should be easy enough. Of course, the river itself is dangerous and illegal for swimmers, not to mention full of industrial traffic. The actual Gulf of

Mexico is far away. Lake Pontchartrain, the large estuary north of the city, has public beaches, but the largest one had closed some years earlier. And the water is considered risky: a higher salt content (read: global warming) means shark attacks, especially in the summer. A friend recalls getting salmonella in a cut on her foot there when she was a kid in the 1990s. A pristine beach just over the Louisiana border—in Bay St. Louis, Mississippi—can be reached in under two hours. But in New Orleans itself, there isn't anywhere that's naturally safe to swim. Before I figured out the locations and erratic schedules of the city's municipal pools, the only place I knew to go was the Country Club on Louisa Street: an ironically named, formerly secret swimming spot close to where we lived.

Housed in a nineteenth-century raised-hall cottage, with six white columns framing the front entrance, the Country Club looked like the quintessential small Southern restaurant as you entered the double parlor. The establishment was fronted by a respectable-looking café, although I rarely saw anyone eating there. Most folks tended to go straight to the bar at the back of the house and then out the rear door, where a sign proclaimed that no one under the age of twenty-one was allowed. Buying just one drink got you access to the pool deck, an area completely secluded by its lush tropical garden—palm and banana trees, flowering jasmine and hibiscus, unruly ferns. The swimming pool itself was just a small rectangle with ladders. But the distinction of this pool was its clothing-optional policy, something that had become local legend.

In the 1970s, the Country Club's pool deck first opened as a kind of gay men's cabana. Too far from the French Quarter to be easily accessed by most tourists, this swimming spot was a hub for queer New Orleanians, although it was frequented by allies as well. (Rumor has it that women strippers who worked in the French Quarter would come to sunbathe alongside the gay men: a kind of refuge, perhaps, from the carnivorous eyes of straight men on Bourbon Street.) But the Country Club, I learned, was badly damaged during Hurricane Katrina. When it was renovated afterward, the facility was upgraded: chlorination replaced with saltwater, a new bar installed. At the same time, the millennial population exploded in New Orleans, with many do-gooders and hurricane relief workers contributing to a gentrification wave. There was no way that these nonnative, queer and queer-friendly twentysomethings were going to let the swimming spot remain a secret. For the past decade, people said, the clientele had been shifting and included more folks in my own demographic: younger, college educated, born outside of Louisiana.

I didn't pay much attention to the Country Club in my first couple of months in New Orleans, even though it was just a few blocks away from our place on Desire Street. But in October, our best friends from up in Memphis—a couple, a lesbian and trans man, Portland transplants to the South—came to visit us over a long weekend. The heat was still relentless. We wanted to cool off but also to show them our new neighborhood's culture. The four of us strolled onto the porch at the Country Club, where a large rainbow flag was displayed. We bought ourselves Bloody Marys garnished with hipster-inspired pickled okra pods and green beans. As I slipped into the pool, the water felt cool against my skin for approximately sixty seconds—a welcome relief—and then felt warm enough to be a bath.

I glanced around the pool deck, observing the population, diverse in terms of race, gender, age. Even though the Country Club was most famous for nudity, only about half the patrons were stripped down. A number of women in bikinis, some topless. Some ambiguously gendered folks, clothed and unclothed. A few naked men, mostly straight looking, their genitalia swinging as they jumped into the water. A cluster of older gay men in tiny Speedos lounged on one corner of the pool deck, stoic behind their sunglasses, ignoring the rest of us. Near the bar, just to make it clear, a sign read No Public Sex.

In spite of the heat, the four of us ended the day in the hot tub, tucked in the most secret-feeling spot on the pool deck, under flowering bushes and the shade of giant ferns. Beside me, two gorgeous, full-figured lesbians in shorts and sports bras made out for about twenty minutes, ignoring everyone else completely. The heady effects of the alcohol and heat were working their way through our bodies. My wife slipped her arms around me, relaxing into the scene. The two women kept kissing, touching each other's backs and shoulders, pausing occasionally to smile at one another. Despite the fact that the Country Club had supposedly lost its primarily gay identity, I still felt, for a moment, that I had stepped into some queer utopia, a kind of lotus-eaters' island made up of orange hibiscuses and warm water and beautiful people kissing.

How I perceived the Country Club at first, however, was not the whole story. The space was now frequented by more adventurous tourists, along with the occasional celebrity. Beyoncé, Jay-Z, and Solange had made a stealth visit to the Country Club just a few months earlier, rumors said. With increased exposure, some friends of mine, mostly gay men who had lived in the city for a long time, worried about how the Country Club's social dynamic had changed. Depending on the time and day, the Country Club didn't always feel like a gay haven, they said. "Straight men," they complained. "Everywhere."

The growing presence of heterosexual folks, especially heterosexual men, was slowly shifting the feeling—and the power balance—at the pool. Nothing made this more glaringly apparent than hearing the story of Maria Treme, a local woman who visited the Country Club one afternoon the year I was living in the Bywater.

Maria Treme arrived at the Country Club that day for a few margaritas and a swim in the buff. Someone, she guessed, slipped something into her drink. That afternoon, she was raped by two different men: once in the locker-room sauna and once in the pool itself. She woke up the next day in her bed, not remembering exactly how she'd gotten there. How this violence came to light, and why no one tried to intervene, is unclear to me and unthinkable.

A local Louisiana paper first reported her story. Then it made national news. In a strange and reactionary response to Treme and the press, the Alcohol and Beverage Control Board threatened to revoke the Country Club's liquor license unless its clothing-optional policy was ended immediately. Conservative politicians believed that nudity was responsible for the atmosphere that lead to Treme's assault. The underlying logic—that rape culture might go away if everyone wore swimsuits—seemed pretty shaky. But political pressure and the press around Treme's incident was so bad that the management of the Country Club felt they had no choice but to rescind the clothing-optional policy.

The pool stayed open to the public but lost some of its flavor after the policy change.

"Why do straight people literally ruin everything," another friend said in response, referring to the men who assaulted Treme and, more generally, to all the conservative Louisianans who had gotten involved in the politics surrounding the Country Club.

His comment made me think back to my graduate school days, faraway in central New York, to a time I'd been hit on by two men at Felicia's, the lesbian-owned bar where I was a regular. I'd had to clue the men in on where they were, explain to them that it was not a space where men went to find women. "You guys obviously don't come here much," I joked, embarrassed. "This is not your space" was what I meant. Felicia's was not explicitly a lesbian establishment. But unofficially, and not unlike the Country Club, the bar had long functioned as a queer safe space.

After a number of months living in New Orleans, I began to wonder whether it was people like me—newcomers to the city, mostly young—that had essentially colonized the pool at the Country Club, slowly taking it from the gay community that it served. Or if, as part of the neighborhood LGBTQ community, I belonged there more than the recent influx of straight patrons. Certainly I belonged more than the tourists taking cues from their guidebooks, where the Country Club was listed as a do-not-miss spot. I was a registered voter and local to the neighborhood, not just someone visiting for the weekend.

Either way, the story of Treme's rape disturbed me and raised questions. I was wary of the power dynamics and violence that could play out when strangers plunged into this shared water in the name of recreation, especially when alcohol was involved. I questioned the function of the Country Club, given its history. I wondered who defined the terms of belonging there and what sort of public, if any, the space was meant to belong to. The complications were thorny enough to keep me away. I passed by the pool almost every day, but I never went back. I would find somewhere else to swim.

Even when alcohol and nudity are not involved, swimming pools are a place where bodies are on display. Growing up in the 1990s and early 2000s, I remember the pool as a gathering ground but also a public arena for gossiping and, well, voyeurism: who had a new bikini, which shirtless lifeguard was on duty, who was flirting with whom. It's not news to anyone, I suppose, that recreational swimming pool culture in this country has long been intertwined with the white male gaze and sexuality. In his book *Contested Waters: A Social History of Swimming Pools in America*, the historian Jeff Wiltse claims that pools in the United States have been tangled up with erotic culture ever since the 1920s, when Americans were loosening their sexual mores and developing an interest in leisure culture, building new swimming pools at an exponential rate.

Before the twentieth century, inspired by Puritanical ideals, swimming in America was mostly for men and boys and was considered a homosocial activity. Wiltse writes that the first public pools were in large Northern cities, meant to stand in as bathing facilities for the urban poor across cultural and racial lines: Black and white, American born and immigrant. These poor urban folks were considered "unwashed" by those in wealthier classes, who believed dirtiness lead to questionable morals. But the men and boys who patronized the pools were not interested in being "reformed," instead bringing a roughhousing and play subculture into them, a kind of rule bending and antiauthoritarian attitude.

When pools became mixed-gender spaces in the 1920s through the 1940s, bathing suits—which had once been loose, heavy, and covering most of the body—began to shrink. Men began swimming in short trunks and bare chested; women's suits evolved into tight one-pieces that showed off curves. The modern bikini was invented around 1946. Teenagers and twentysomethings flocked to the pools, and they became socially acceptable places to convene, to meet people, even to find a romantic partner. On the one hand, these changes signaled a kind a throwing off the yoke of Victorian ideals, the swimming pool as an emblem of sexual liberation.

But with that "freedom" was a clear shift toward seeing swimmers, especially women swimmers, as sexual objects. In 1925, at the Price Run pool in Wilmington, Delaware, for example, city officials began charging a five-cent "spectator fee" to the patrons who came to "see the bathers enjoying themselves." Newspapers reported on pool activities, photos of teenage girls in revealing suits filling leisure pages in the summer months. Public pools even became the site of some beauty pageants, people coming to watch the "bathing beauties" compete. This is one likely origin of the swimsuit competition included in the Miss America pageant, a tradition that persisted until as late as 2018. As a young child, I remember watching the pageant on television, never questioning why the women were wearing swimsuits when there was no water nearby. (I also remember my first bikini around twelve or thirteen years old, an adolescent rite of passage. The *swim* in swimsuit was not the point anymore; revealing my body to the public was.)

Girls' and women's appearance and behavior at swimming pools, it seems, have always been governed by the presence and desires of men. Sometimes the results have been violent: In the 1990s, as I learned from a *New York Times* article by Michel Marriott, the most infamous sexual assaults took place in New York City municipal pools, boys and men in their twenties raping multiple teenaged girls. "Whirlpool incidents" is how these assaults were described in the media, since the groups of boys often circled around their victims, making sure they couldn't escape. Some girls were assaulted in pools filled with hundreds of swimmers, in broad daylight, with lifeguards on duty: events that raise some of the same questions as Treme's assault at the Country Club.

These assaults are part of a longer history of American pools as erotically charged playgrounds, especially for the heterosexual boys and men who have claimed them for the past century. Stories like these make female-bodied folks wary of entering pools in the first place. At the very least, it gives many of us the sense that belonging in these spaces is transactional, that we are not the ones in charge. But when it comes to swimming, gender and sexuality are just one set of cultural considerations. Historically and currently, they prove not to be the primary policing force.

∴ ∴ ∴

My second summer in New Orleans, my colleague Elizabeth, a native New Orleanian, introduced me to the outdoor public pool in Gentilly. "It's a pool for everyone," she said. "My favorite spot in town. I swim almost every day." The pool was a few miles from my house. A couple of times a week, I'd bike up Esplanade Avenue, my favorite street in New Orleans, lined with live oaks and run-down, brightly colored Creole mansions. Eventually, I'd work my way up through the Treme and hit Broad Street: traffic, strip malls, auto shops, and a

strangely placed Whole Foods, a symbol of New Orleans's gentrification. I turned off into the neighborhood that surrounded the pool, a
mix of shotgun houses and bungalows, locking my bike outside the
Stallings Gentilly Pool's chicken-wire fence. The adjacent basketball
court had a few straggling palm trees at its perimeter, but the pool
itself was totally exposed, no trees for shade or privacy. In this sense,
it was the opposite of the Country Club.

Anyone could enter the gates here, no one asking for ID or money.
Like many municipal pools, the Gentilly pool was as humble and
utilitarian as they come: a large twenty-five-yard rectangle with no
lane dividers, no diving boards, no slides. The facility was worn down
but clean. The concrete deck was too hot to walk across. People's
shoes lined the perimeter of the pool. There was no lounge furniture,
so poolgoers simply piled their towels, clothes, and phones along the
inside edge of the fence, directly on the concrete. I was shocked to
see this at first, because no one in New Orleans left their belongings
exposed. My own wallet and phone had been stolen out of my bag
earlier in the year in the school where I worked; my wife's bike had
been cut from its lock; our car had been broken into. But at the Gentilly pool, there was an implied community trust.

On late afternoons when it didn't storm, Elizabeth and I sometimes met up to paddle slow laps back and forth across the deep end
of the pool. We often kept our heads above water so we could gos-
sip, mostly complaining about our work lives as writing teachers: the
instability, the last-minute contracts, the low pay. For the most part,
the deep end stayed pretty empty, only a few people swimming across
it at once. The water's aqua expanse was uninterrupted and quiet. As
the weeks passed, however, I begin to notice something. While this
deep end was frequented mostly by a few white people around my
age, the shallow end of the pool was filled with Black women and
men, along with kids splashing and chatting.

The reason for the age divide seemed obvious to me at first: in any
pool, kids and their caretakers tend to stay in the shallow water. But
there were also adults in this shallow end who weren't there with children, and a number of older teenagers. As I watched these poolgoers,
who stood and chatted in the shallow end but never let the water go
past chest level, I begin to think consciously about the pool and its
racial dynamics.

In my lifetime, New Orleans has been considered a largely Black city. Hurricane Katrina displaced more Black people than people of any other demographic. Ten years later, many of those people had rebuilt and returned, although the city's white population had also grown considerably. Desire Street, just below St. Claude, where I lived, had been racially integrated for many decades and was home to a mix of Black, white, and brown folks, at least in the years I lived there. A number of couples and families were interracial, the city's fastest-growing demographic category. Most of the spaces I frequented in my neighborhood and nearby neighborhoods—the corner stores, libraries, the riverfront, bars, jazz spots on Frenchman Street— were racially mixed, with folks of different races in community and in regular interaction with one another. In some ways, the Gentilly pool felt similar.

But when you looked at how the actual square footage of the Gentilly pool was being used, there was something more nuanced— hostile, even—going on. This public pool that gave the semblance of being an integrated space was actually segregated, an invisible border somewhere around five feet deep. I begin to ask myself what was least aggressive: for me to keep swimming in the deep end, where the people mostly looked like me, or to insert myself, very consciously, into the shallow end, where I would be the only white person swimming. In the end, neither choice seemed right. Although I often entered the pool at the shallow end, I also drifted toward the deep end during the course of the hour, as feeling a pole-pull of history.

It could have been a coincidence, for sure. But I suspect the divide I observed at the Stallings Gentilly Pool was not just in my imagination. It was evidence of something that spanned the whole history of the South and of the country in general. "Social segregation," the pool historian Wiltse concludes, "is the most persistent theme in the history of swimming pools." At the root, the story of American pools is a story about privilege and, more directly, a story about race.

When swimming pools were desegregated along gender and class lines in the early twentieth century, swimming in America became synonymous with racial segregation. The reason: most white people didn't want Black men swimming with white women. James Weldon Johnson, the writer and civil rights activist, put it this way: "In the core of the heart of the American race problem, the sex factor is rooted." He means that stereotypes about Black men's sexual urges drove segregation pretty much everywhere white women were allowed, which included swimming pools.

In the early twentieth century, pools' segregation policies depended on location and local laws, but the results were similar almost everywhere. Up north, pools were usually built in neighborhoods that were exclusively Black or exclusively white, discouraging mixed-race social interactions. Black people who tried to enter "white" pools were often turned away, or otherwise they were met with bullying and vigilante violence. In the South, Jim Crow laws codified Black exclusion from pools where white people swam. In New Orleans, for example, the largest public pools—City Park, Audubon Park, and elsewhere— were segregated for the first half of the twentieth century.

New Orleans's local government, recognizing that most Black people didn't know how to swim or have a place to learn, opened four pools for Black residents. But white residents in New Orleans had nineteen pools. "The number nor quality never equaled that of those related to the white population," an introduction to an exhibit by the city archives on New Orleans parks pointed out. "Separate, but of course *not* equal," it said, echoing the famous language in *Plessy v. Ferguson*, the Louisiana case that became the basis for many Jim Crow era restrictions. Outside of New Orleans, most Southern towns and cities had no swimming pools for Black residents. One result: generations of urban Black Americans never touched water, never learned to swim at all.

When public pools were federally desegregated in the 1960s, many cities chose to close pools altogether rather than deal with the changes, and the white-perpetuated violence, that resulted from Black people and white people swimming together. In New Orleans, most public pools were closed in 1964 by the segregationist mayor Victor Schiro. As in most of America, only the wealthiest residents—people who had access to the new, private, white-only "swimming clubs" that proliferated after desegregation—had consistent access to swimming. This is a trend that shaped American swimming as a whole, with swimming knowledge, or lack thereof, passed down from generation to generation. There are exceptions, of course, but the historian Jeff Wiltse puts it bluntly: "Swimming is a predominantly white activity." The Stallings Gentilly Pool appears to have been a "whites only" pool in the years of segregation, even though Gentilly has been a racially mixed neighborhood for quite some time. A 1947 photo from the city archives shows dozens of children participating in the Every Child a Swimmer water safety program, but all of the children I can see are white. Under the mayor's orders, the pool probably would have closed in 1964, with the other public pools in the city. I'm not certain what year Gentilly's pool reopened, or when Black residents began to slowly grow the community of swimmers here.

Swimming in Gentilly, it was impossible not to feel the ghost of segregation haunting the twenty-first century: Black folks in the shallow end, and white folks in the deep. I began to ask myself questions. Was one group consciously avoiding the other, despite coexisting in the pool? Perhaps Black folks hung at the shallow end because they could socialize more easily there, using the pool as a community gathering space. Perhaps they were the ones most likely to bring their children, whereas white patrons were more likely to be childless people in their twenties and early thirties, associated with the beginnings of gentrification. Or did some Black folks avoid the deep end because they were less comfortable swimming, in general, than their white neighbors? Did white folks have a different relationship to the water, or were they avoiding Black folks?

The summer dragged on in New Orleans, and the pool water grew warmer and warmer, beyond the point of being refreshing in the afternoon. Only in the early morning did being outside feel bearable. A few times, I entered the Gentilly pool when it first opened for the day, finding the clientele more homogeneous than it was in the afternoon. The lap swimmers, the ones who wore caps and goggles and racing suits, filled the pool, swimming back and forth from the shallow to the deep. The early sun rose and lit the pool's bottom, where there were no painted lines, only a blank, sloped surface, and long fissures in the concrete. With no lane rope dividers, we did our best to swim in a straight line, trying not to run into one another, our bodies stitching regular patterns across the water.

A predictable rhythm: *four strokes, a breath, four strokes, a breath.* To learn to swim in that rhythm had taken me years of practice, starting almost from the time I was born, although I obviously don't remember it. My mother took me to a baby swim class and then a swim club in the summer. (My father, who'd grown up as a rural kid, could swim enough to survive, but not as well as my mother, who'd mostly lived in the suburbs.) There were the swimming lessons in the winter my parents paid for at the Y and then, later, team practice at the swim club for the better part of my childhood, where I became a skilled swimmer, if never a terrific athlete.

These histories became more palpable to me as I moved through the water that summer. And during early morning lap hours, the water felt charged in a way that was hard to put into words. All the swimmers had come for the purpose of getting their heart rates up. Although we shared the space with one another, no one stopped to talk. People kept their heads under the water. And—so unlike the heterogeneous neighborhood where we found ourselves, and unlike New Orleans as a whole—almost every person swimming in the pool was white.

My time in New Orleans emphasized to me how knowing how to swim—and especially being able to think of swimming as exercise or sport—is a pedigree. In America, to be a swimmer is often the result of having had a privileged life. It often means that whoever raised you could probably swim themselves, and thus taught you how, or they may have even paid someone else to do it. It means that you likely had regular access to water that was safe to swim in, that you had access to a public pool or money to pay for a private pool, or both.

It means that you were born into a body that the dominant culture deems acceptable for swimming alongside others. It also means you were born in a time in history when your presence in a pool is legal, so you can swim without being a victim of violence.

This violence has not been limited, as people might assume, to the South.

In 1932, after the Highland Park Pool in Pittsburgh announced the end of gender segregation at the pool, two Black men, Clyde Crawford and August Ross, entered the facility. They were beaten with clubs by a group of one hundred white swimmers.

In 1938, at the Dowd Pool in Elizabeth, New Jersey, Black swimmers were punched and held underwater by white swimmers.

In 1949, when the mayor of St. Louis announced that all pools
would finally be available to all races, a group of Black men at the
Fairgrounds Park pool were attacked, the mob composed of hundreds
of white men. Ten Black citizens went to the hospital for their injuries, which included stab wounds, skull fractures, and broken jaws.
Police arrested eight people, and only three of them were white. Black
arrestees were charged with riot and assault and disturbing the peace.
White arrestees had their charges dropped, except for one, who paid
a five-dollar fine. The mayor responded to the violence by officially
segregating the city's public pools once more.

In the 1950s, in Cincinnati, white people threw nails and broken
glass into public swimming pools once they became desegregated
along racial lines.

Meanwhile, at the dawning of the civil rights era, the National
Association for the Advancement of Colored People, today the
NAACP, filed lawsuits against public pools all over the United States
that denied access to Black Americans. Like lunch counters and buses
and other public entities, pools in the South were often locales of
resistance. In one demonstration, a series of "swim-ins" spearheaded
by Martin Luther King Jr., other Christian clergy, a group of rab-
bis, and Black and white protestors stormed the segregated pool at
the Monson Motor Lodge in St. Augustine, Florida. When protestors
refused to come out of the water, the owner poured acid directly into
the pool. Protestors were dragged off to jail in bathing suits. Congress
passed the Civil Rights Act soon after. This legislation effectively
desegregated public spaces, including pools, for good.

But after segregation ended, as with so many public spaces in this
country, most public pools frequented by Black Americans either
fell into disrepair or closed in the decades to come. With "white
flight" and many middle-class Americans fleeing to the suburbs,
some white Americans built their own swimming pools behind their
homes. Many others started private "swim clubs" in their suburban communities. Some of these clubs were officially "whites only,"
while others unofficially kept people of color away through location
choices, antagonism, fees, selection processes, and other intimidation
tactics. Although official "whites only" pools no longer exist in our

country—at least to my knowledge—excluding Black Americans from "members only" pools remains a common form of exclusion.

The second summer I was living in New Orleans, a news story related to swimming—just one state over, in McKinney, Texas— grabbed my attention. Tatyana Rhodes, a Black teenager living in a racially diverse suburban area, brought a crowd of her graduation party guests to her housing subdivision's neighborhood pool. Kids who already had pool "member" access passed back their guest cards so that all their friends could swipe and enter the gates. Some kids scaled the fence.

But it got loud with a huge group of teenagers on deck, and then things got ugly. White neighbors showed up, some yelling racial slurs at the party guests. When police arrived, they claimed the kids in question had "bad attitudes." Officers handcuffed and arrested a number of teenagers, most of whom were Black. Eric Casebolt, one of the officers, warned a number of kids to "get their asses on the ground."

Dajerria Becton, a fifteen-year-old Black girl, was also thrown to the ground and then dragged by Casebolt, who is white. When I saw the iPhone video of the altercation—taken by Dajerria's class-mate before being uploaded to YouTube and shared by major news outlets—I watched, horrified, while Dajerria struggles and cries, Casebolt pinning her on a strip of grass. When two of her classmates try to intervene—two Black boys—Casebolt appears to get even more angry. He responds by brandishing his gun, sending these boys running, literally, for their lives.

Just before Casebolt forces Dajerria to lie face down on the grass, you can hear her begging, "Call my momma at home!" Instead, he puts both his knees on her back while she tries to lift her head. Her bare legs are sprawled out on the ground as he twists one of her arms behind her. Twice in the video, he is seen grabbing Dajerria's long braids, an image that haunts me for its embodiment of racialized vio-lence. She's wearing a neon bikini, most of her body exposed—all the more vulnerable when a burly white officer uses his knees to hold her down.

When I first watched the video, the word *rape* crossed my mind, a word that won't leave me. Seeing her makes me think about the "whirlpooled" teenagers from the pools in the 1990s. Becton's assault occurred less than a year after Maria Treme was raped by the group of men at the Country Club.

Dajerria Becton's abuse struck a national nerve, partially because of how it aligns with other stories of police violence, the injustices that fuel the Black Lives Matter movement. But Becton's experience is also a reminder of how swimming pools, specifically, continue to be emblems of white supremacy and spaces of segregation in America. In his reflective piece responding to the event, Hari Ziyad writes: "Black people still can't swim. Pools unplagued by our bodies and the haunting flashbacks they bring have always occupied a special place in the white imagination." Reading this makes me think back to the deep end of the Gentilly pool, the preferred zone of white people.

To say that a container of water is for certain people only—by dividing it in two, or putting a fence around it, or using a lock that requires a special card or code—makes zero sense, even goes so far as to defy the amorphous, mutable nature of water itself. But it's that very amorphous nature that makes white people so nervous and angry. "Swimming pools are more sensitive than schools," Judge Roszel Thomsen once said, attempting to defend racial segregation in one of his decisions, "because of the visual and physical intimacy that accompanies their use." In water, with our street clothes, jobs, houses, and credit cards left elsewhere, it becomes harder to maintain divisions and hierarchy. A shared body of water also forces people to encounter others who aren't like them and recognize them as part of their community, and as human.

Thinking back on my own childhood, I see how my experiences swimming in North Carolina were racially coded, maintaining strictures of white supremacy. In the winter, my mother sometimes took us to a YWCA in the city, where the swimming clientele was diverse but trended predominantly Black. In the summers, though, I learned to swim at a swim club—one of just two pools in the semirural portion of the county where we lived—with pristine, aquamarine water and annual membership fees. This was a space largely, if not exclusively, populated by middle-class and upper-middle-class white families. I remember only one nonwhite family, the Chins, an Asian

American family with three daughters. How many nonwhite families had applied to be members? Who had been turned away, and what justification was used? Who could not apply?

Safe in my white privilege, I was never forced to think about the implications in that water, about who was missing. Only later did I consider the silent aggression inside the gate around the pool deck, and what it would have meant to be a person of color trying to enter the water.

❖ ❖ ❖

I worked as a lifeguard at the downtown YMCA in Greensboro, North Carolina, after my first year of college. Nineteen years old, I came back home that summer grumpy and reluctant, feeling that I had a life elsewhere. I worked my lifeguarding job while many classmates from my fancy liberal arts college did fancy, unpaid summer internships for nonprofits or magazines in New York or Philadelphia or San Francisco, their living and eating costs subsidized by parents or relatives. Some went to prestigious music festivals to study and perform while others spent the months traveling in Europe or hanging out in South America to work on their Spanish. And then there were a few of us in the same crappy minimum-wage jobs we had as high school students, trying to squirrel money away. What I made lifeguarding that summer I would spend the following year on textbooks, toiletries, and printing out papers for class.

The lifeguarding job was largely mindless and didn't pay well, but it was not something I'd do forever. Some moments of the job were sensory enough to be interesting. At the beginning of each shift, as if attempting alchemy, I took the chemistry set to the side of the pool, filling the beaker with water and adding the magic potion that turned it a deep shade of magenta, assuming the pH levels were what they should be. I tested the chlorine in a separate tube, shaking it up and holding the amber color up to the light. If anything looked out of sorts, I called my supervisor. Otherwise, I climbed into one of the faux-wood lifeguard stands and people-watched. Working five days a week, I began to know some of the swimmers.

Unlike the swim club of my childhood summers, the YMCA pool truly felt like a space for everyone of all ages and races and abilities.

Despite my boring shifts, I liked the way the pool seemed like a microcosm of the real world. People conversed here when they were not underwater, the regular patrons seeming to know one another. One middle-aged man, Daryl, made a point of always saying hello to all the guards on duty, often engaging us in conversation if we were not busy. He did slow laps in the lane closest to my stand, drifting back and forth with a red kickboard, his head above water, making chatting easier.

"How old are you?" he asked me one day. I was nineteen, I told him. "You go to college?" Yes, I replied. "Up in Ohio. But I grew up here," I told him.

Daryl looked at me for a long time, and then asked me something I wasn't expecting. "Your parents both all the way white?" he asked me.

I paused, confused. No one had ever asked me this before. My skin was about as pale as it gets, even in the middle of the summer. My eyes were green, my hair reddish brown. Daryl was a Black man.

"Yes," I said after a pause, perplexed.

He nodded, passing the red kickboard between his hands. "You look like you maybe got some soul in you," he said. "Are you sure that, say, maybe your great-great granddaddy wasn't a little bit Black?"

"I don't think so," I said. I paused again, considering. "Well, I guess I don't know for sure," I admitted.

He smiled. "I don't know what it is," he said. "Something in your face. Or the hair, maybe?"

I touched my head. I'd been cutting my hair shorter and shorter over the past year. My cut the previous week had shorn my curls to a about an inch, so short that what was left of the curls coiled tightly. If I ran my hand across the top of my head, I felt a bristling sort of undulation, almost as if I'd placed my hand in the path of turbulent water. After I'd returned from that hair appointment, my mother took one look at me and became despondent, then angry. "You look like a boy," she said out loud. I think she saw my haircut as a rejection of my former identity, or at least the one she had assigned to me. Something about the haircut, I discovered, made my assumed identity categories less readable to some people.

The evening after my hair appointment, I met up with Courtney, a high school friend. She was out at a restaurant with her college-aged Bible school class from St. James Baptist, a well-known Black church.

"Come out with us," she'd said over the phone. When I arrived at her table and met her friends, she studied my haircut quizzically. I waited to see if she would comment, the way my mother had, on how the haircut was unfeminine. But she said something else.

"Oh, it's totally fine," she said with her signature, sometimes brutal, honesty. "But it's funny. You have the haircut of every middle-aged Black woman I know."

A guy on the opposite end of the table motioned at Courtney, and she went over to talk to him. When Courtney returned, she was laughing again. "Marcus just asked if you're Puerto Rican," she reported.

Maybe "Puerto Rican" was a question about whether I might be a white Latina, or something else. Or it was a joke, or maybe a real question about my white presence among Courtney's church friends.

Thinking on Marcus's question and on Daryl's question at the YMCA pool, I began to understand that my whiteness was partially contextual, that it was not just about my appearance but about the other white people who often surrounded me, along with the privileges and places I accessed because of my whiteness. The summer swim club of my childhood, for example.

Daryl's line of questioning about my family history suggested something less binary. He really seemed to see me—or maybe just wanted to see me—as something other than "just white." I don't know why for sure. Maybe it was my haircut, which emphasized the thick texture of my hair, maybe even appropriating a style not associated with white womanhood. Maybe Daryl wanted to give me the benefit of the doubt, eager to see something other than my whiteness. Whiteness is not friendly. It often means an unwillingness to engage with people of color, unless the relationship is one that clearly reinforces white supremacy. Whiteness also often means unwillingness to enter spaces where people of color are the majority: Courtney's church group, for example. White culture, when boiled down to the bones, is exclusivity and gatekeeping.

Before the lifeguarding job, shaped by my own privilege and general naivete, the teenage me seemed to think that on some basic level, everyone knew how to swim. I knew that babies, in the first six months of their lives, automatically held their breath when underwater, a reflex carried over from the womb. I knew something seemed to get lost after that. I thought kids took swimming lessons to sharpen this thing that's basically intuitive. Because I didn't remember not being able to swim, some part of me believed lessons were for teaching people to swim *better*: to go under without holding your nose, to swim with your head down, to use your arms and legs at the same time.

It never fully registered for me that swimming lessons were about survival.

Drowning is one of the top three causes of injury-related death in both children and adults younger than age twenty-nine. In their article "Drowning in Equalities: Swimming and Social Justice," Donald W. Hastings, Sammy Zahran, and Sherry Cable state that the risks of drowning are not shared equally across populations, including race and socioeconomic status. But even when age, sex, *and* income are accounted for, "being Black," they state bluntly, "reduces the odds of swimming participation by sixty percent" (*Journal of Black Studies* 36, no. 6 [2006]). It's the inaccessibility of swimming spaces that is to blame. It wasn't until I became a lifeguard that I really understood how dangerous the water can be, and how many kids never learn to swim and why.

When I was working at the YMCA, school-age day campers often took over the shallower of the two pools for an hour in the afternoon. The camps served kids from all over the Greensboro area and a number of backgrounds, but tuition was partially subsidized for children from low-income families. Most days I worked, a new group would come in, noisy with excitement, and clamor into the small recreational pool, where the water ranged from three feet to almost six at its deepest point. The pool had a small water slide that emptied into the deepest water. When the pool opened for the day, we flipped the switch that turned the slide on: water flowed down the tube, creating a small rapid where it tumbled into the pool below.

We always had an extra guard on duty during the day camps. I wasn't on especially high alert as I watched the campers all rush into the water at the same time. The kids stayed on the outer edges of the pool, where they could stand; an occasional confident swimmer would cross into the deeper part, showing off to their peers. There were counselors on the deck, two frazzled-seeming women in their late twenties. They always appeared busy with their clipboards, looking up on occasion to scold the kids for being rowdy.

I saw the boy only out of the corner of my eye at first: just another kid in the sea of other kids. He must have run over to the slide and scaled up the ladder, sliding down before I registered what was happening. I don't know whether the counselors had given the campers permission to use the slide. But I do remember seeing the boy hit the pool. At the bottom of the slide, his head bobbed up and down in the frothy whitewater. He raised his hand once, then slipped completely under the water's scrambled skin. Because of the aeration—the bubbles, water's white noise—I couldn't see him anymore.

People were yelling. I stood up on the lifeguard stand and leaped forward, startled and graceless. I felt my body hit the water at a strange, non-aerodynamic angle. My red lifeguard T-shirt ballooned around me; my sandals slipped off my feet and floated to the surface. I dragged the torpedo-shaped rescue buoy behind me, which I'd learned how to use in my training: you're supposed to grab the person with your left arm and yank the buoy down with your right, submerging it and forcefully threading it under your left arm. If you do this correctly, you and the person in trouble should rise effortlessly, their mouth instantly breaking the surface so they can get air.

Because the rescue buoy is meant to float, pulling it under the water—and then putting it where you want it—requires force on the lifeguard's part. It's a maneuver I had practiced. What I hadn't practiced was trying to go through this process when the water was churning, making the boy's body almost impossible to see. I panicked, the edges of him lost in that blurry pocket of whitewater. I tried to rely on my sense of touch rather than sight. Underwater, I felt my skin slipping against his. I felt the small bulge of his arm muscle, the bones in his back. I managed to grab the boy in the "rescue" position, but he continued to thrash when I embraced him.

I couldn't get the buoy underneath him with the movement. This had not been covered in lifeguard training: what do to when the person in trouble is reacting for fear of their life. Perhaps he intuitively didn't trust that I would be able to pull it off. I didn't fully trust myself. It was too deep here for me, at just five feet tall, to touch the bottom. My own legs thrashed furiously beneath us. My instinct was to move the boy away from the deepest point. I thrust my body backward, pulling him with me on my back, and kicking as hard as I could to move our bodies together.

His head bumped my chin as I yanked him. In a few seconds, we were in a place shallow enough for both of us stand. The kid rose, coughing violently.

"Are you OK?" I asked him after his coughing had slowed, my own voice shaky. The boy nodded but didn't speak or look at me. Several other poolgoers surrounded us. The boy didn't say anything. He was muscular but still small, about the same height as me. He had on long red swimming shorts and wore his hair in cornrows. I helped him out of the pool and onto the deck, where the counselors were now standing.

The boy was OK, it seemed. He had started to breathe normally again. Still shaken, I turned off the water source to the slide. I stepped away to call my supervisor on the wall phone, a protocol if we'd done a "rescue" on our shift. My supervisor told me where to find the forms: paperwork for all the adults to fill out, for legal reasons. This felt strangely banal in light of the emotional extremes of what had just happened. Offensive, even.

The boy, whose name was J'Wan, was ten years old, one counselor told me. In the form's space for "parent or legal guardian," one of the counselors informed me that he was currently living with his aunt. While I was filling out the paperwork, the other counselor, a late-twentysomething white woman, was berating J'Wan for what had just taken place. "That was very dangerous," she said pedantically, as if it hadn't become obvious to him. "No one said you could go down that slide. Why did you do that if you knew you couldn't swim?"

I looked up from the paperwork. "This can happen to anybody," I said. "Really."

J'Wan didn't answer. Being only ten, perhaps he didn't know what he could safely do in the water. Perhaps he relied on adults to make the call. Maybe he did have a sense but wanted to try the slide anyway, its twisting speed and the rush of water. Maybe he didn't realize that the cascade at the bottom of the slide would make it harder for him to surface.

J'Wan looked down, his small shoulders slumped in shame. I was ashamed, too: of the counselor's words; of myself, for having let things happen in the first place; for not getting the rescue buoy under his panicked body; for the fact that J'Wan had been so scared in the first place. He had a right to feel safe.

∴ ∴ ∴

What happened that day on my shift wasn't a "rescue" or a "save," even though that's what it's classified as in lifeguarding language. Instead, I consider the power that put me in the lifeguarding chair in the first place, which has to do, in part, with my ability to swim.

It's true that what happened to J'Wan could have happened to any child or adult unfamiliar with the water. But Black children J'Wan's age—between ten and fourteen years old—are the most likely of any demographic to drown, and almost eight times as likely to drown as their white counterparts the same age. Sixty-four percent of Black children in the United States cannot swim at all. If J'Wan was living with his aunt at the age of ten, I can't help but wonder about his parents, what kind of life they had had, if they were still alive, and what sorts of life circumstances made them unable to care for him.

In our entire exchange, I don't remember J'Wan ever saying anything, save for telling me what phone number to put on the form and his nod when I asked him if he was OK. There was the clamor of the white people all around him: people who were participating, willingly or by default, in the very system that had made him susceptible to drowning in the first place.

J'Wan's struggle in the water was one small window into the history of pools and swimming, a reminder of all the separation and unequalness. Pulling him out of the water that summer was my first taste of the fear that so many parents live with all the time: wanting to keep their child alive when there is seemingly danger everywhere. And for the parents of Black children in particular, there is much in this country to fear.

∴ ∴ ∴

In 2014, just months before I moved to New Orleans, a thirteen-year-old Black boy named Genesis Holmes drowned in his small town of Hollywood, South Carolina. He and his friends were attempting to swim to a small island in the middle of a rural pond, and he'd misjudged how far it was, or perhaps misjudged the depth of the water surrounding it. Maybe he'd felt peer pressure.

"Genesis didn't know how to swim," his mother, Jennifer Holmes, told reporters after his death. "No one in our family knew how. All our life, most of us, honestly, we was told to stay away from the water." When I heard this story, I thought immediately of J'Wan.

Holmes's words conjure up that old racist stereotype that so many have heard, which is that Black people are afraid of water or are incapable of swimming. The former might have a grain of truth to it when you consider all the barriers to swimming in the first place. When it comes to fear of the water, Holmes said: "It's like a family tradition, from generation to the next generation. I taught my children to stay away from the water. If my husband or me had given Genesis swim lessons, he would have made it out."

Hollywood—a town west of Charleston, population just over five thousand—wasn't exactly an easy place to learn to swim in the first place. At the time of Genesis Holmes's drowning, there were no pools serving the public. Jennifer Holmes eventually funneled her grief into civic action, working with the local government to raise three million dollars to build one. She also started the Genesis Foundation, which provides dozens of scholarships for free swim lessons to local kids and adults.

Eventually, Jennifer also learned to swim herself, a thing I imagine must be terrifying in adulthood. In a television interview with ABC4 WCIV, a Charleston news station, Jennifer described entering the water for the first time: "I could feel and imagine what Genesis went through. There was no possible way he could have gotten out. I couldn't move my legs, couldn't move my arms, and I couldn't breathe. . . . To know what Genesis felt, I knew I had to keep going, because many more are going to enter a pool, a pond, a lake, and a river." She saw her learning to swim as a kind of community responsibility, a way of shaping the future.

When Jennifer became comfortable in the water, she got her lifeguard certification. As someone who learned to swim in childhood, I find it hard to imagine how much determination it must have taken to get from nonswimmer to protector of other swimmers in her town. As of 2019, when the story was reported by the local news, Jennifer was taking shifts at the new public pool's lifeguard stand, eyeing the six thousand square feet of water. On camera, she is holding the same kind of rescue buoy I was using the day fifteen years earlier when I shakily pulled J'Wan out of the water.

The Genesis Pool serves not only residents of Hollywood but also, according to the local government's website, "people throughout the Lowcountry region." *Lowcountry*: that part of eastern South Carolina dotted with marsh and swamp, where, like the muggy and insect-laden air, plantation legacy hangs over everything. Where plantations are considered tourist attractions. South Carolina: whose residents elected Strom Thurmond, who tried to prevent the passage of the 1957 Civil Rights Act with the longest filibuster on record. South Carolina: the first state to secede from the Union. South Carolina: along with the rest of the states in the Deep South, one of the poorest states in the nation.

The civic work that folks like Jennifer and her community are doing is both pragmatic and symbolic. It's resistance. It recognizes not just the single circumstance that led to Genesis's drowning but the systemic racism tied to swimming pool access.

After living in New Orleans, my wife got a job in Washington, DC, a city that felt like a liminal space between the South—where I'd grown up, where my roots were—and the North, where I'd gotten my degrees, where Sarah was from. Once we found a place to rent we could afford, it was an easy place to settle into. I loved walking the brick sidewalks of the neighborhood, seeing evidence of the history and cross sections of lives that took place there.

Eighth Street Northeast, the major avenue we lived on, was composed of sturdy brick row houses occupied by renters and home-owners of different ages and races. Kids played in the shared alley behind our houses. Our block had two corner stores, a barbecue joint, and a dry cleaner, all of which were owned by Korean families. Two doors down from our building was a funeral home owned by two older Black men, their 1970s-looking hearse parked in the back. (Once, to our horror, Sarah and I were walking down the alley and found a gurney, a white sheet covering what was unmistakably a dead body.) But gentrification was also the direction here, or maybe the place we'd already arrived. Two blocks up, the price tags on house listings were a million dollars and up. Walking south from Capitol Hill toward Eastern Market, the neighborhood got fancier with every block: stately row houses with stained glass transoms, rose bushes, double strollers parked out front.

This is the route I took to the Rumsey Center, a DC municipal swimming pool that was a thirteen-minute walk from our apartment. It was housed in a utilitarian, squat brick building that had been made more memorable by Aniekan Udofia's dreamy mural: a mythic-looking female swimmer, her neon hair streaming out behind her. The woman looked like a mermaid; her skin was painted electric blue, as if the water itself permeated her body's borders.

Showing your Washington, DC, ID and writing down your zip code got you entry to the building. The pool itself was a modest setup: locker rooms with sometimes-functioning showers (the hot water was a mystery, shutting on and off sporadically); a rectangular pool that was half for laps and half for recreation. The bottom of the pool was scraped and pocked with age. No diving boards or slides. All kinds of people used this pool: babies and old folks, disabled and able-bodied people, swimmers of all races and backgrounds. People were friendly. We shared all the spaces. We greeted one another in the locker rooms and on the pool deck, whether we'd seen each other before or not.

But Sarah, who worked long hours at her new law job, occasionally swam laps at the pool during its most "divided" hour: 6:30 A.M., when the lap lanes, she reported, were mostly filled with triathlete types. These were the people with fancy racing trunks and waterproof headphones and "resistance paddles" strapped to their hands. They were the more upscale, DC version of the early-morning swimmers I'd experienced at the Gentilly pool in New Orleans. These were people who, I often joked, need to impose athletic challenges on themselves. They were likely the people who had access to swim clubs or similar sorts of private pools growing up. Despite making fun of their swimming habits, I couldn't separate myself from them.

Across the last pool lane divide, the open recreation area was filled with the aerobics class ladies, perhaps the pool's most loyal attendees. There was one water-aerobics participant who Sarah reported always being in conversation with, a middle-aged Black woman who used a motorized scooter to get around. She had been coming to the pool for decades, she told Sarah. "Her sister's name is also Sarah. And their mother died last week," Sarah told me. "We ended up in a long conversation about what we thought we wanted to do with our bodies when we die." Sarah paused. "I'm not sure how we got onto this; it just happened." That feeling is one I recognize. There is something about the public pool that can, if you raise your head above the water for long enough, lead to intimate conversation, to unexpected interaction with people whose lives look different from your own.

With my erratic work schedule, I often found myself at the pool at the "off" times, usually midafternoon. During those times, the triathlete types were mostly at their white-collar jobs. The lap lanes were more relaxed; all of us wove back and forth without too much hurry.

There were all sorts of people: white and Black, Asian and Latine, women and men and nonbinary folks, children and the elderly.

In the evenings, when the facility closed to the general public, the DC swim teams also practiced at Rumsey. I learned that the director of the teams, Rodger McCoy, fought to keep the DC public pools open back in 1994, the last time the city tried to trim the budget by closing a number of facilities that served Black populations. McCoy, who grew up in Virginia Beach, didn't learn to swim until the age of twenty because, he is quoted saying in a local newspaper, "Blacks didn't have a place we could learn to swim." McCoy's own first swim class was at the Rumsey pool. He is to thank for keeping the pool open for the new century, and also for a generation of DC residents learning how to swim.

Given Rodger McCoy's labors, and given DC's demographics in general, I still wonder whether this neighborhood pool is just another space that white people are starting to colonize. Or maybe Rumsey, paid for by the city and resident taxes, was simply the thing that worked as intended: a public space, used by all. But what does "public" mean? It's the question I first asked myself in New Orleans. I don't know what will become of the Rumsey swimming pool, what communities it will serve as the city's housing prices keep increasing. I want to say that the pool is for anyone; that it *must* be for everyone for the sake of the public. I wonder whether it's even possible to say this without ignoring the confines of our bodies and the histories they evoke.

Normally, the Rumsey pool was roped off lengthwise: lap lanes on the left, open swim or classes on the right. At certain moments of the day, however, when another aerobics class meets, the pool changed configuration so that the lap lanes are fixed in the widthwise direction. One day, I was swimming during the hour when the change was scheduled to happen. The lifeguard, a young Black woman with a punky, reddish-gold mohawk, motioned me over to the edge of the pool.

"Hey," she said when I surfaced, "can you help me with this?" She handed me one of the hooks at the end of the plastic lane rope, and she pointed to the perpendicular wall.

I kept myself afloat with one hand, dragging the hook behind me. I remembered this drill from early summer mornings in childhood, when we were setting up or taking down the lane ropes for swim-team practice. But I had forgotten how challenging it was to swim dragging one of these things around. When I finally attached the hook to its underwater anchor, I went back for the next rope and the next.

When the guard and I completed the new lane configuration, I went under the water completely for a moment, the way I often did as a child, plunging down until I was touching the bottom of the pool with both feet. I looked up from the bottom of the pool, the slightly cloudy water in a quivering ceiling above me. At one edge of my view, I could make out the edges of everyone else's arms and legs, floating or kicking just beneath the surface, half-obscured by the bubbles that surrounded them. My chest started to tighten from holding my breath too long. I stayed under until I couldn't any longer, and then I hurried toward the air.

WOUND CARE

My mother works as a home health nurse in the 1990s, driving across southeastern Guilford County to visit her patients. In the back of our family's station wagon, she keeps a twenty-gallon Rubbermaid container full of medical supplies: rolls of gauze, medical tape, needles tucked away in tough plastic, a cylinder marked BIOHAZARD, dark bottles of hydrogen peroxide. When my middle sister and I are bored, my mother gives us one of her rubber gloves to blow up into a five-fingered balloon. We bat it around the house, the bloated hand creepily detached from a body. When we get tired of that, my sister swipes a package of unused syringes. She uses hers to perform a cream extraction from the middle of a Hostess cupcake, a procedure that is only moderately successful. I drink juice with mine, shooting it into my mouth one milliliter at a time.

Although my mother's patients are geographically scattered, many of them are located in the rural corner of the county, where we also live. Lots of patients have long, memorable names that feel reminiscent of the old South, like Lulabelle Mae McConnell and Booker T. Washington Pratt. Before the next day's visits, she calls each house to remind people when she'll arrive. "Hi, this is Lindsey. I'm your nurse." A pause. "Lindsey. Yes. The nurse." Her volume increases each time she repeats herself. Many of her patients can't hear very well because they're old. But she is polite and charming on the phone, smiling into the receiver.

She often asks for directions to her patients' houses, making notes on the corner of her wrinkled county map. Sometimes she has to draw in a remote road, one that the mapmakers didn't bother to include: gravel or dirt, sometimes without mailboxes or house numbers, a stretch surrounded by tobacco fields or deep Piedmont woods. Occasionally, a patient's house is without a phone, or the phone's been disconnected because they haven't paid the bill. In these cases, my mom gets in the car and hopes for the best when she arrives.

On her visits, my mother flushes portacaths and inserts catheters, gives shots and changes dressings. When she returns home, her skin smells like rubbing alcohol and rubber gloves. Her dark curls and lab coat, too, carry the scents of other people's houses: cigarette smoke, Pine-Sol, potpourri, fried food.

I eventually learn that she has a nursing specialty: wound care. As a child, the combination of these words strikes me as funny. *Care* is a mandate I hear every day, in all the aphorisms at school: "Care about your neighbor," "Sharing is caring." If you say, "I don't care" to a teacher, it's considered disrespectful. You'll get your name written on the board. But care is also what most of our mothers do, or what others do while our mothers are working: day care, caretake. *Wound*, on the other hand, sounds dramatic and old-fashioned, the stuff of war movies or psalms: "He heals the broken-hearted and binds up their wounds."

A wound, my mother teaches me, is just a cut, though deeper and wider: a rift in the body, something that can't be fixed with a Neosporin smear and a Band-Aid. She has a special ruler for measuring patients' wounds, a transparent sheet marked with series of concentric circles, like tree rings or the ripples from a stone thrown into a pond. The smallest circle is the size of my pinkie nail; the largest, as wide as my head. It's hard to imagine a hole that big in someone's body.

These home health visits are her job, so I'm usually not allowed to go with her. Once in a while, though, if she's just running by someone's house to check something, I will sit in the car, engine still running, in the middle of nowhere, watching her knock on the door of the beat-up farmhouse or split-level ranch, or sometimes a unit in one of the trailer parks. Once, on the eastern edge of Greensboro, she knocks on the door of a public housing project. The concrete walls are tired and stained with mildew, ancient-looking air conditioners churning in the windows. The basketball court and the playground across the street are empty and scattered with litter.

My mother explains to me the difference between Medicare and Medicaid; what dialysis is; why you do compression and elevation; how our circulation works to heal us; that a fever is usually just the body's way of protecting itself. Even in elementary school, I have a basic knowledge and curiosity about most things medical. I'm in and out of doctors' offices all the time myself, too, getting treated for bronchitis and ear infections. Because I'm significantly smaller than all my classmates, my mother takes me to have my hands x-rayed. They determine I'm still growing: I'm just short, like she is.

When I get diagnosed with asthma in the second grade, she teaches me how use my inhaler, which tastes like hairspray. I'm supposed to inhale the medicine on a count of five seconds. Sometimes my mother counts off in French, just to be funny. When I ask her how she knows French, she admits that she was pretty good at it in school. "Your father got a D in French class," she tells me, shaking her head. "It was embarrassing."

In a photo box that my parents keep under their bed, there's one of my mother's nursing school class from the 1970s. In a sea of pointy white hats, I try to pick out her face. Although there are a few men scattered throughout, the crowd is one of women. "Back in my day," she tells me, her tone preachy, "there were two options for most women. You could be a nurse or a teacher. That was pretty much it."

I think she must be exaggerating. Our cousin, Ann, works for the county police. My dad's older sister, who is much older than my mother, even has a doctorate degree: she's a criminal psychologist, visiting prisons and going to court to give her expert opinion on serial killers. But it's still true that most of my teachers are women, and all the nurses I know are, too.

Early mornings, before I wake up, my mother puts on her lab coat and drives off in the family station wagon. Sometimes she is gone longer than she means to be. "He gave me an earful," she always says. People talk for a long time, confide in her. Even as she's taking care of others, the old people are always thinking of her like a daughter. My mother, with her small, five-foot-one frame and perfect skin, looks younger than she is, even after birthing three daughters.

Sometimes the patients give her gifts: sugar cookies, pot holders, dishtowels, strange household items whose uses we never discover and are too embarrassed to ask about. Once, an old man gives her a mason jar full of moonshine, his very own white lightning recipe. She's too polite to refuse it. The jar sits on the back of one of the shelves in the laundry room. My father—who was raised Southern Baptist, even now never having more than a beer here and there—pulls the jar off the shelf one night. He takes a tiny sip. He makes a horrible face, tears springing to his eyes. He pours the moonshine down the sink.

Mr. Pickett, an eccentric old patient who lives down in Julian, hoards magazines. He gives us a huge stack of *National Geographic*, some as old as I am. My sisters and I are always making collages for school, always in need of pictures. I'm transfixed by *National Geographic*, its handsome yellow cover and all the glossy photographs inside. I open one magazine to a picture of a lush gorge in a rainforest. The waterfall is blue with white aeration, and it looks real enough that I reach for it without thinking, half-expecting to feel a cool rush. The moss on the rocks is the greenest green I have ever seen. It almost hurts to look at it.

In my adult life, of course, I will grow suspicious of the magazine—the gauzy distance between the camera's eye and its subjects, as well as its racist history. *National Geographic*, like so much else, is not what I thought it was. But as a child, I fall in love with these pictures, which are a first, imperfect window into the rest of the world, my first signal that much of it looks different from where I live. I sit for hours on our basement carpet, turning through the pages, absorbed by the images' saturated colors. Electric-bodied fish gliding through a coral reef. The gold tiles of a temple.

A group of women stand at the entrance to their village, blue mountains in the background. The country listed is not one I recognize. I look for it on my small plastic globe, turning and turning past oceans and continents, searching. When I glance up from the magazine, I find that the day has nearly disappeared. In the woods behind our house, a profuse orange spreads behind the trees. My mother calls my name, urging me upstairs for dinner.

Distance and movement become something of an obsession in my youth. Just after my eighteenth birthday, I head north. I cross the state line, the Appalachians, and the Ohio River. I weave through Amish country's hills and the ironed-out fields of the glacial till. My first home outside of North Carolina is college, built on the chilly lip of Lake Erie, a landscape so austere and foreign to me that it sometimes feels like another country.

But the students here, who come from places like New York and San Francisco, seem to know everything already. Except accents, apparently. The first day I open my mouth in class, an upperclassman asks me if I'm from Texas. "North Carolina," I say, my face hot with shame. Back home, in my swaggering teenage bravado, I had told everyone that I couldn't leave the South fast enough.

My last year in college marks the beginning of the Great Recession, and jobs for college graduates seem impossible. Meanwhile, I have made a promise to myself that I will live out of the United States when I finish college. When I am awarded a postgraduate fellowship to Asia, the committee places me in rural China, where I will teach English at an agricultural university for two years.

I stay in Beijing for six weeks of language training. The first night I'm there, alone in my dorm room, my heart beats so fast that I lie away all night, confident I'm dying.

Beijing's hecticness and summer congestion doesn't suit me. But I feel a sense of relief when I head west into Shanxi Province, where the landscape seems to break open. On the twelve-hour train ride, I pass through valleys of a dry mountain range, bald rock touching the hot sky. Taigu, the town where I'm posted, is on a loess plateau surrounded by peaks. The coal mines and bauxite plants look like miniature cityscapes against the flatness of the fields: corn and wheat and sorghum, a dusty green and brown sea on both sides of me.

All autumn, women are busy shucking the corn, throwing the cobs onto the houses' flat roofs to dry them out for feed. In the late spring, they wear wide straw hats as they cut the wheat. During the solar term known as Grain in Ear, stalks are cut into smaller pieces and laid out in the middle of the road, where every passing vehicle does the work of threshing. "Waiguoren, waiguoren," the women shout as I ride by on my bike. The translation: "outside" plus "country" plus "person." Foreigner. I blush. Beneath my tires, the wheat makes a hushed sound as I pedal through.

When they placed me in rural Shanxi, members of the fellowship committee back in America said that they thought that the circumstances of my Southern upbringing might be a kind of cultural touchstone: as if I'd recall something in the earth and the people, something that would help me navigate these next two years. But the analogy is much too loose. Nothing prepares me for living in rural China. Each morning, my brain is stuck a kind of bilingual strangeness as I emerge from sleep. And when I finally wake up, it is into dry winds I don't recognize. The thing I miss most when I'm in Shanxi is the air pregnant with rain, the way my hair used to curl tightly whenever a storm was coming.

I do my best to do things the way the locals do. Sometimes Chinese friends come over to my apartment and we'll make *jiaozi*, dumplings we stuff with chives and carrot and pork. We start with the dough, nothing but flour and cold water. ("People ate this in America during the Civil War. It was called hard tack," I joke, already knowing it won't be funny to anyone else.) Wang Yue shows me over and over how to shape each circle of dough so that the filling is secure inside: dampen the edges with water, fold in half, press, flute the edges. Some of my dumplings still burst during boiling, gaping open and floating to the top of the pot.

I begin to discard the cooking liquid when we're finished, but Wang Hui Fang stops me, pouring some into a teacup and pushing it into my hand. "Drink this. It has health benefits," she says to me in Mandarin. The broth isn't exactly delicious, but it's pleasant, mildly earthy. I think of the wheat fields that extend around the edges of campus, a tapestry with light-brown tassels, moving like water without water.

At the agricultural university, there are no textbooks or language materials, no campus bookstore. I don't know what it is I'm offering to the students as a twenty-two-year-old college graduate with little experience. My teaching strategy mostly consists of asking students provocative discussion questions—What makes a good girlfriend or boyfriend? How would you describe the Chinese education system? What's your impression of university life in America?—and having them practice conversing in English with each other and with me. As we talk, I introduce them to vocabulary they aren't familiar with, adjust their grammar in the tricky spots, help with pronunciation of some of the difficult sounds. I open my mouth in an exaggerated way to show them how my tongue and lips are moving. As a group, we practice some sounds together: *ths* with playful tongue flicking through the teeth, and the raised, flat tongue and guttural sound of a dark *L*, a sound that I've always associated with a purplish-blue color: pool, shell, lullaby.

The secretary of the Foreign Affairs Office comes by once a month with my pay slip: membrane thin, the numbers and characters inked by hand. My legal name is nowhere in sight. At the agricultural university, I am told, it is not possible to process anything without a name written in Chinese. Despite my red hair and white skin, I become 罗依琳: Luo Yi Lin, the name that my Chinese teachers in Beijing gave me. Yi Lin is like a sonic diminutive for Elizabeth. Soon it's what everyone calls me. I answer to the name for the next two years, and the Beth of my childhood, the name my mother says she chose for me, disappears for a time.

A few times a year, when I get extended time off from the university, I pull a stack of money out from under my bed and leave town. I travel through China and its borderlands, sleeping in a yurt in Inner Mongolia and going into Xinjiang, where I visit an ancient fortress near the Pakistani, Afghan, and Tajik borders. During the winter break, I leave the country. I fly to Indonesia to visit Sarah, my American girlfriend, whose fellowship posting is in Banda Aceh.

The humidity in Indonesia is womblike, an exaggerated version of the weather I grew up with: a welcome relief from northern China.

Sarah and I travel farther south into Sumatra to backpack in Bukit Lawang, an orangutan preserve straddling a swift river in the rainforest. The Sumatran orangutans have pale auburn hair, almost the same color as my own. I observe their profound faces, their expressions ranging from curious to indifferent, from annoyance to fear. The first female orangutan I see has a baby clinging to her middle. I am obsessed with the baby. It's adorable and perfect, hair like the plush of a child's toy. The mother and I make eye contact for a moment. She purses her lips, as if considering me, and then shifts her gaze to my lunch. I'm eating fried rice and a pineapple spear wrapped in banana leaf.

At the end of the day, we take a bath in a waterfall. Someone in our trekking group passes around a bottle of peppermint soap. Sarah and I stick our heads under the frothing cascade, screeching from the numbing cold torrent.

The long-haired, hippie Sumatran river guide rolls a spliff, which he offers to share with me. I accidentally get so stoned that I become paranoid about my surroundings, afraid of all the weird night sounds in the jungle. But there is a sweet spot before then: sitting with damp hair on a moss-covered rock in the middle of the current, feeling the vibrating energy of the rainforest.

Orangutans, the guide is explaining to me, build a new nest each night, thirty meters or higher above the ground.

I look up at the darkening canopy. By now, that mother and baby must be settled somewhere in those millions of leaves, asleep together in a place I can't see.

∴ ∴ ∴

Back in China, there are times when the landlocked feeling of Taigu begins to wear on me. When the days grow shorter, it augments my sense of isolation. On afternoons when I feel like I am going to lose my mind, all I know to do is to ride my bike toward the mountains, which are often obscured by dust and pollution. The road there is made of packed dirt. I weave through a couple of brick-walled villages and pass piles of coal pellets in the alleys. A few people come out to stare at me riding by.

During Ramadan, when Sarah gets time off from teaching in Indonesia, she travels up to China to see me. We borrow a second bicycle one afternoon so I can take her out to the mountain range. At the first peak, there is a small temple built into one of the outcroppings, and also a staircase built into the slope, shaped like a giant stone dragon. On the other side of Feng Shan, one of the taller peaks, you can see the all the terraced mountains of Shanxi: a failed agricultural experiment, the bleak days of the Great Leap Forward.

When we come down from the summit, we encounter a group of local girls on their bicycles. My guess is that most are nine or ten years old, gauging by their size. They are curious about us, staring and whispering in a dialect I don't recognize. When I speak to them in Mandarin, they giggle in surprise. One of them spots Sarah's digital camera and motions for her to snap their picture. They hug each other in the photo, smiling unselfconsciously in the frame.

Sarah and I get back on our bikes and head toward Taigu. Down the road, we realize the girls are still behind us. They pedal as fast as they can, struggling to keep up. Their bikes out-size them, their small bodies teetering atop the enormous wheels. On the first downhill stretch, their fleet starts to get too close together, and I get nervous.

The girls don't care. They yell out joyfully as they pick up speed. But already I can feel what will happen next. Slow down, I want to yell. Slow down. But I don't say anything.

I look over my shoulder a couple of times. I see the smallest of the girls swerve suddenly before her back wheel comes forward, and she topples over.

We toss our bikes to the side of the road, rushing back toward her. The bike is partially on top of her, the back wheel is still turning its spokes in a horrific slow motion.

The girl is crying hard, but she manages to stand up without any problems. Her jeans are ripped on one knee, the skin underneath scraped. When she raises her hand to touch the underside of her chin, she lets out a scream. Blood pools in the palm of her hand.

I step toward her to look. The gash is ugly, a couple inches across. I can't tell how deep it is. The blood is smeared all around its borders.

It probably looks worse than it is, I try to convince myself. Kids fall off their bikes all the time, I think, remembering my first red Schwinn back in North Carolina: the sting of asphalt, my mother cleaning the pebbles out of my knee. Meanwhile, the other girls are staring at me, waiting to see if this weird *waiguoren* is going to do anything.

I say the word for "paper" to the group, once, twice, three times. One of the kids pulls a tissue packet out of her jacket pocket: everyone carries these, since toilet paper isn't provided at most Chinese bathrooms. I hold the tissues to her chin, compressing. Beyond this, I'm not sure what to do. Bike injuries weren't part of my fellowship training back in America. It's one of those moments where I wish that

I had some real help to offer. I'm even more useless out here than I am in my classroom at the university.

The girls are getting back on their bikes. At first, I think they're going to abandon the scene. But one of the kids motions at Sarah and me, pointing off down the road. I look at her, unsure. She motions at us again. The girls know what we don't. They want us to go with them.

Sarah's bike has a small rack on the back wheel—the kind on which a second rider can balance, if she's careful. The injured girl, who apparently trusts Sarah enough, positions herself sideways on the bike. This whole exchange happens without any words passing between them.

"But where are we going?" Sarah asks me from her makeshift ambulance. I have no idea, I tell her.

Sarah and I trail behind the group: first down the main road, and then turning off into one of the alleys in their village. We pass brick courtyards and anonymous front doors. Finally, we turn the last corner. I see a sign with a green medical cross.

As if intuiting our arrival, a woman in a white lab coat comes out the door. She must have seen us approaching, but I don't know how: the building has no front windows. I brace myself for this woman's surprise, for her to gape at our foreignness. But she pays us no attention. She lifts the injured girl's chin.

I know enough to guess that the girl will probably need stitches, but I don't know how to say so. Instead, I announce, in my still-brand-new language: "Ta diaole." She fell. That's the best I can do. I impart this with great drama, as if I've been waiting my whole life to say it.

The woman in the lab coat nods at me in a no-nonsense way, unmoved by my theatricality. She is still holding the girl's face in her hands. Trying to gauge the wound, she tilts her head and squints a little, her expression like a scientist's but with a softer edge. The girls were right. They found the person to help. I am filled with calm, and then, inexplicably, a longing, something akin to homesickness.

The woman looks at me finally and says thank you in Mandarin. Both of us know I've reached the limit of what I can give. I take a step back, giving them space. The woman, on the other hand, takes the girl by the shoulders, guiding her inside. The back of the woman's lab coat is the last thing I see before they both disappear into the building. I'm reminded of how I pressed my face to the station wagon window, watching as my mother carried her nurse's bag up the steps of someone's home, disappearing through another strange doorway. Day after day, it was her job to tend to the body of any person who needed it, dressing wounds.

The rest of us are still standing outside, not sure what we are supposed to do. One girl drags her sneaker through the dust, as if unimpressed. A few doors down, an older woman emerges from her house carrying a pink plastic tub, the kind people use for dishes or laundry. She looks hard at Sarah and me before she pours out the water into the alley. I can only imagine how this must look to her.

Getting back on our bikes, the girls pedal ahead of Sarah and me, ushering us out of the village and onto the main road. Eventually, they turn around, and we ride off in separate directions. When I turn to look over my shoulder, I see their wobbly vanguard just before they vanish back into the village. The photograph I took of them—earlier, at the face of the mountain—will live on my computer forever, but I'll never know what becomes of any of them. And the girl who fell off her bike, I wonder whether she'll end up with a scar on her chin. Maybe not, if whoever sutures the wound has experienced hands.

In front of me as we ride back to Taigu: dry, tattered fields. The silver outline of a bauxite plant. The low wall of the university is sketched across the horizon. The sun is low and blood colored. My mother is on the other side of the world, in a green pocket of North Carolina countryside. She's twelve hours behind me. Ten thousand miles, give or take, is the gap between us. It's still dark where she is, but I know that soon she'll be waking up for work.

ENCUMBER:
A BRIEF HISTORY

My wife and I put shoes on our baby for the first time. He stands bowlegged in the alley, confused by what to do with his weight. He lifts one foot and touches it down. Lifts the other and falls, smacking the brick and wailing. Like any good primate, he has relied on his toes for balance. But the shoes make him a cartoon, his feet stuck in tar.

Even the sound of *encumber* is bumbling, tripping over its syllables. *Encumber* is transitive, meaning "to weigh down, burden" or "to impede or hamper function or activity."

On our walks in the neighborhood, we pass pairs of teenaged girls on bikes, their limbs in effortless tandem. They whisk past us and away. I remember that sort of lightness, although it feels far away.

I meet my first girlfriend in guitar class when we are both sixteen. Our relationship is secret. On chilly spring nights, I borrow her clothes. My favorite is a yellow sweatshirt with a mountain printed across the chest. Now she has a husband and four children, says she doesn't believe in evolution.

I want to tell her about the orangutans I saw in Indonesia, when I was twenty-two and living abroad. Their expressions are too human, foreheads wrinkled in thought. I want to tell her about the female, the one with the perfect auburn baby slung across her hip.

I'm pushing the stroller when a stranger calls me a *mother*. A word that has never felt right, maybe because I'm not the one who carried him. Or because he has no father. Or because part of me doesn't feel female to begin with. Recently, anything feminine feels too ethereal.

"Elizabeth is a flowery name," the Guitar Teacher tells me. This makes me blush. The Guitar Teacher's name is something too feminine for her. I'm too serious for a teenager, she says. I need to lighten up.

The Guitar Teacher rides a motorcycle on weekends, all black leather and gloves. I ride on the back after a lesson once, clinging to her while the spring blurs green around us. My helmet is too large, leaves my head bobbling. Space helmet. It's meant to be worn by someone else.

The Guitar Teacher lives with the dance teacher, who spends her days teaching us how to fall using our own momentum, without hurting ourselves. It works beautifully for a while.

They have a dog and a pool and a basketball hoop but no kids. The Guitar Teacher says, "I'm not sure a woman can parent and still be committed to art. In the end, someone always loses."

That settles it for me. I decide I'll never have children.

But now I lug the stroller from the street up the steps of our narrow rowhouse. I ache from the labor of lifting my son all day, carrying him from room to room, moving him away from dangers. I'm his main caregiver while my wife exhausts herself at the office. My body is heavier than before, my clothes getting tight. My thinking: fragmented. This is a sleepless year.

His white-noise machine mimics the sound of waves and whales. The blue whale, we learn from one of his books, is the largest animal on earth. Female whales are the heaviest, the extra blubber giving them energy to nurse.

"I'm beached," my wife jokes, lying on her back when she is pregnant. But her arms and legs stay lanky. Before pregnancy, with her short hair and black-rimmed glasses, strangers sometimes called her "sir."

The week before our son arrives, we lumber down the hill, toward the national monuments. I take her picture at the Tidal Basin, the cherry blooms unfolding around her. "Congratulations, Mama," people tell her. "It won't be long now."

Mothers have a special appreciation for the Guitar Teacher. Maybe it's the androgyny. Maybe it's because she calls someone's mother from the school phone every morning: "We've got something for you to hear." She lays down the receiver on the desk so that we can play a song for the mother. For this, she becomes a sort of local celebrity.

The first time the Guitar Teacher reaches down, it's to trace the underside of my foot. I feel my arch traversed by muscles and tendons, that part of me designed to bear my weight upright.

I wear peasant blouses and sheer cottons as a teenager, trying to appear unhindered. Hippie, water nymph, and so on. But all the things I move with are marked by their mass: my books, my velvet-lined guitar case, my old Volvo sedan.

Remember that weight isn't always bad, the dance teacher tells us. It moves your body forward.

"You can never tell anyone about what we have," the Guitar Teacher warns. "No one will understand. I mean, do you get the gravity of this? I could lose my job. Are you listening?"

Encumber, *somewhat formal*: to make someone carry something heavy. A blue whale's heart weighs as much as an automobile.

North Carolina summer, the air is like the inside of someone's mouth. In the front of the Guitar Teacher's Dodge, she edges her hands across my breasts, then down between my legs. She's thirty-seven; I've just turned seventeen. I brace my body for bravery.

When I reach for her, I find that her shorts are damp down the center seam. I draw my hand away instinctually.

She tugs my hand back. "Don't stop," she says.

If not for saltwater's buoyancy, the whale would be crushed by its own weight. Because nothing on land can sustain that kind of mass.

I never tell anyone what happens with the Guitar Teacher. Instead I discipline myself for her approval. I practice fast scales and arpeggios, memorize Paganini's *Romanza*. Once, I try for her attention by giving her the silent treatment.

"Hormones," she calls it.

In Old French, the noun *combre* meant "a defensive obstacle formed by felled trees, with sharpened branches facing the enemy." But what does the enemy carry, exactly?

Away at a summer guitar workshop, I feel an arrow, pain in my back. At some bleached-out Florida hospital, it takes a week of mysterious sickness to pass the kidney stone. In my palm, I hold the pebble with one crystalline spike. Its color is like a window clouded by years of grime.

You? the nurses ask. Meaning I am too young to be carrying this.

Before the stone passes, there are images, a barium contrast, drinking charcoal. "Lie on this table and don't move for an hour while we scan you." The gown is not enough armor. One doctor inserts her big hand, asks for my sexual history. What should I tell her?

The Guitar and dance teachers send me flowers.

Combre also gives us the adjectives *cumbersome* and *cumbrous*, both meaning "awkward" or "difficult to handle." Now that's an understatement: the Guitar Teacher, me, the dance teacher. My body as it leaves the ugly hospital in Florida.

I injure my back from arching in pain, lying in bed for a week. There's a ghost where the stone once was. Someone writes me a Flexeril prescription. The pills make me disassociate, as if my brain were floating too far below my surface. It's like wearing a space helmet.

At music conservatory, on the cold lip of Lake Erie, the snow piles and piles. I meet so many new people, but I'm haunted by the weight of the years that came before.

In deep dives, blue whales can hold their breath for up to ninety minutes.

Is this body even the same body as then? If cells regenerate, making a new self every seven years, by now, at least according to poetry, I should have shifted twice.

But in truth, some cells we carry with us our entire lives. The parts of the eye, for example, or the neurons that control our balance. Whatever is making the baby toddle upright will still be with him when he is my age. Will he remember this?

A whale's plug of earwax can be read like tree rings. Scientists study it to decode the animal's history. They learn that stress hormones peak during sexual maturity but also during periods of migration. Females can transmit bad substances to their young, like pesticides and flame retardants.

Perhaps I resist the term *mother* only because it admits that I'm burdened by responsibility.

In the end, I tell my wife I am fine having a child so long as I don't have to be the one to carry it. I'm panicked by the thought of being so encumbered. Instead, we take something from me to make him, the largest cell in my body. For this superovulation, I pierce my stomach fat with needles. "At risk for overstimulation," the nurse calls me. "You have so many follicles."

Encumber comes from the Old French *encombrer*, which means to block up a current, a river dammed.

My body bloats until I look like something washed up, something in water too long. They say the swelling is temporary. But the truth is that I never go back to the way I was before.

The Guitar Teacher appears on Facebook after years and years of distance. There's no word for this feeling, seeing her face at fiftysomething.

She has a new wife. I see that they got married the same weekend as us. They are growing old hiking in canyons, going on safari, climbing up to Machu Picchu.

Machu Picchu has always been a dream of mine, so seeing her there makes me angry. People don't go to Machu Picchu with a baby.

"Fuck her," my wife says. "She doesn't deserve anything good."

When our son turns one, I'm a month shy of thirty-five. Almost as old as the Guitar Teacher when we met. When I pass a teenager in my neighborhood, I think to myself: *That is a child.*

I'm watching Christine Blasey Ford testify, pained by how her voice wavers. Her long list of credentials and yet I can feel her rendered back to her teenage self, see her pool-messed hair and bathing suit as she's pushed into the room where everything changes.

For a while after that, I think to report the Guitar Teacher. In North Carolina, no statute of limitations means you must shoulder responsibility for your past, no matter how distant. There's no such thing as off the hook.

But what would it take from me to tell this story. To enter that fucked-up current again, my body a new kind of obstacle.

"That notion of holding back," a dictionary muses, "is what informs our verb *encumber*."

When my wife's water breaks around midnight, I carry our things down the steps to the car. The air swells into thunder and downpour on the way to the hospital, too heavy to be contained.

She feels trapped by the hospital gown, insists on laboring naked. Don't touch me, she begs, even though she's alone in her pain.

We have practiced what to do. But in the end, her body can't bear more sensation.

I listen to Christine Blasey Ford's hearing in segments because her story keeps taking me underwater. Her voice wavering and distorted, sometimes tinny like a guitar string. The summer evening she was assaulted, she tells the committee, she had spent the day practicing diving. She wears a navy blue suit now. There are too many people in the room.

It's September when she testifies. We're at the height of infant sleeplessness. I drift like a ghost: downstairs, upstairs. When the baby finally falls asleep to the whale noises, I try to sleep, too.

Another source tells me: a blue whale's mouth is so enormous, a hundred people could fit inside. *Why would a hundred people go inside the mouth?* I wonder. The image is ridiculous.

Dr. Ford wades through the crowd and out of the hearing room, one dark-blue shoulder turning toward the camera. I imagine her descending a flight of stairs, taking a back exit. Warm air hitting her face as she steps out onto the sidewalk.

Up the hill, just ten blocks away, is the house where I live with my family. The upstairs curtains closed. The stroller by the front door.

The baby has my auburn hair, my face inside his face. Even though my wife gave birth, strangers will always assume I was the one to carry him.

My body is thicker now, builds on itself over time. I want to evolve into someone that uses my gravity, knows how to bear any weight.

In the tree outside my son's window, I watch a crow rearrange her feathers in the rain, that bodice with so many dark layers. Glamour and burden and elegance. When I look up again, she's gone.

EAR TRAINING

Given my usual slacker attitude toward parenting, I surprised myself when I registered my nine-month-old baby for a community music class called Music Together! It was a good idea, I reasoned, considering the minimal effort involved. We could walk to the class from our house. I wouldn't have to babysit other people's kids or lead activities. Unlike the library's overcrowded programs or the pool's elusive swim classes that you could never find out about until they were full, I wouldn't have to compete with other Washingtonian parents. DC parents were often the annoying, gunner types who are always asking to be put on a waitlist for everything. Music classes were a low-hanging fruit: cheap and offered on the hour.

The class was my idea, but I remained slightly skeptical. Like any older millennial of the former hipster variety, I am often allergic to cheesiness, especially the cutesy theatricality that seems to be our culture's mode of interacting with kids. With my son, Newman, in my lap, I took one look at the lyrics in the class songbook and wondered whether I could stay committed. "Trot, trot, to Grandma's house, to get a little girl some cherries!" we'd sing, bouncing the kids on our knees, because grandparents' houses apparently still required a nineteenth-century horse and buggy. During "Jack in the Box," with its mousy hand motions and stage whispering, Newman looked up at me, perplexed by my antics, perhaps wondering whether the year of sleep deprivation had finally driven me off a cliff.

But something made me keep showing up on Thursday mornings, parking our stroller with the others and carrying Newman up to the studio. Our circle on the mat was composed of babies who couldn't walk yet to kids almost ready for kindergarten. Then there were the adults: middle-aged nannies, a couple au pairs, two grandmas, one stay-at-home dad, and me: the thirty-four-year-old writer and occasional academic who, in the depressing neoliberal economy, morphed into my kid's main caregiver when he was four months old. (My wife, who gave birth to Newman, had returned to her job as a lawyer.) "Hello to Claire! Hello to Baxter! Hello to Newman! So glad to see you!" we'd begin the class singing, round after round until each person was recognized.

The teacher, Miss Kimmy, was perky and full of vibrato, eyebrows rising expressively. I came home from the first class overwhelmed from her energy alone, feeling like I'd just been in a rehearsal for a DC staging of *The King and I.* But later, when I saw two-year-old Jack pull Miss Kimmy's pitch pipe out from under her sports bra strap, she and I looked at each other and burst out laughing. And as I watched the kids arriving each week, toddlers beelining to hug her even before they'd taken off their coats, I began to appreciate her animation. Behind the facade of the corny curriculum, she was doing something real for the kids.

In our first week, Miss Kimmy explained the Music Together! philosophy: all children are musical; we can encourage musicality by combining movements, play, and stories with sound; and the kids are most engaged when their caregivers participate. The last point meant that none of the adults would be just a spectator. The class's cheesy abandon felt unnatural to me at first, as much of parenting had. Unlike my wife, who seemed unfazed by little-kid culture, I could be timid about any performance of early childhood: its messiness and unpredictability, the exaggerated gestures, the way it sometimes seemed at odds with anything substantial or lasting.

Parenting had certainly changed my life in a visceral way. Before Newman was born, I'd spent a lot of time sitting in front of the computer and around college seminar tables, scribbling in margins, debating language's minutiae. My former jobs teaching poetry involved an abstract gymnastics of the mind. But caring for a baby had humbled me, stripped me back down to rawer elements: those long stretches of shushing my son, carrying him between rooms, cleaning up vomit and poop. After Newman was born, I got so tired that I couldn't read or write much. I could seem to remember only Paul Simon lyrics. "Don't want to end up a cartoon / in a cartoon graveyard," I'd sing, jiggling Newman to sleep, thinking about how much my life had shifted. I was blindsided by how much energy it took to take care of my son, and nothing in my previous life had quite prepared me.

Music class, by extension, also felt like a bodily realm far from the one I'd lived in for most of adulthood. There, we sang and made shapes with our hands. We beat twangy tambourines. We performed cheesy circle dances while trying to sing in languages we didn't speak, everyone looking a bit ridiculous. We tossed bright scarves into the air to visualize pitches' rise and fall, their colors mimicking the timbres of our own voices, everything from Miss Kimmy's coloratura soprano to the stay-at-home dad's off-key bass. I did my best to abandon both my snobbery and my self-consciousness, and I leaned into these other voices. For the first time in years, I started to remember what it felt like to move inside a body of sound.

∴ ∴ ∴

Deep down, I suspect that taking Newman to Music Together! was an attempt to preemptively guide his own musical life, perhaps steering it toward something less troubled than my own. Growing up in the rural South in a family with three daughters, both music and ballet were attempts, at least in part, to socialize us, to turn us into "nice educated ladies." My mother wanted us enriched, but I also suspected the quest was something like upward mobility, subtle reassurance against people thinking we were hicks. I never went to music class when I was Newman's age, but my two older sisters were already taking piano lessons by the time I was a toddler, me listening while I tried to nap upstairs. I started piano in the third grade, which suited me fine, although I cowered at recitals, struggling with nerves. Even then, something about music performance made me disconnect from my real body altogether. I went on to join the school chorus in middle school, comforted by singing in a group. This was followed by my guitar fever as a teenager, which is where the trouble started.

In adolescence, I first began to treat music as not just something that I did, but as an extension of self. My new hungers—for emotional expression, for rigor and recognition, for community, even my queer itch for sex—got redirected and tied up in trying to master classical guitar, an instrument that requires tremendous precision to get a clean sound. Instead of devoting many years to studying, I did the crash-course approach, going from beginner to conservatory level in just three years' time. I took group guitar class with my peers as well as private lessons. I caught the attention of the most esteemed guitar teacher in town.

My relationship with the Guitar Teacher—a socially suave prodigy who struggled with boundaries—was troubled, muddled, too close from the beginning. In private lessons, if I hadn't practiced to her liking, she'd say, "You know, you have a real lazy streak in you." But if I'd been disciplined that week, I was praised. "You are the fiercest girl I know," she'd announce, touching the deep calluses forming on my fingers, grazing them with her teeth as a kind of joke. Things turned vaguely sexual by the time I was a high school junior, although it took a while still for me to name it that. What I didn't understand yet is that boundary crossing is one of the special dangers of the master-apprentice model, a relationship that is founded on a power imbalance.

My neuroticism was at an all-time high when I enrolled in the Oberlin Conservatory of Music at the age of eighteen. I'd quit music school a year later, wanting a clean break from musicianship altogether.

Many years later, when my wife, Sarah, was pregnant with Newman, we mused that we wouldn't put extracurricular pressures on him as he grew up. This included music. "He doesn't need that shit," Sarah insisted. Back in our last semester of college, when we'd first met, Sarah and I bonded over the experience of being serious musicians during adolescence: so serious, in fact, that we both remember what it was like to begin hating ourselves. Sarah, a former pianist who studied at Interlochen every summer, remembered her own tipping point: leaving school for the day and driving around town just to delay getting home and putting in her practice hours. After years of discipline, she suddenly felt trapped, empty, unsure of what the point was. "I had the piano, but no life, no friends," she explained. "I was miserable."

As troubled as my teenage years were, I remember musicianship's highs coming from collective moments, the community aspect. Back in North Carolina, I played in a guitar trio with my two best friends, the three of us alternating who took the bassline, who played middle voice, who was on melody. Although I often trembled behind my instrument playing solo, never feeling quite comfortable with my body or the stringed equipment in front of me, having Kat and Maya's lines interwoven with mine let my ego detach from the act of music making.

This sense of kinship was magnified when I made music with even larger groups. Nothing compares to that oceanic feeling of playing or singing en masse. It's like an ecosystem, each sound register its own biotic stratum: the deep basses like lumbering whales; the middle voices darting like schools of colorful fish, the high-pitched descant like birds gliding atop the whole of creation. Everyone manages to be synchronized, like the lunar push-pull of a tide. It borders on the erotic: this charged, ineffable body that you can hear but never quite put your finger on. Very few things in life can give me a feeling that enormous. And despite my pact with Sarah, maybe it was this particular memory that pulled me to sign my kid up for group music class before he could even walk.

∴ ∴ ∴

Music combined with movement was one point of Newman's class, as much as that is possible with a bunch of tiny humans. With each song, Miss Kimmy encouraged everyone to register music lines in different parts of the body: "Nod your head! Now shrug your shoulders!" Newman was too young to sing or follow movement cues, but he shook bells and babbled at random intervals: a kind of background score against the older toddlers and adults. Other times, he'd clap silently, or crawl like a turtle into the middle of the circle, dazed by the rhythmic movements around him. "Any exposure and participation is good," Miss Kimmy said in her most pedagogical voice. "And yeah, that's backed by research." Whatever fears I have about the culture of musicianship, I suppose I'm still a Kool-Aid drinker when it comes to general music education, the studies that suggest it helps our brains with everything later on: decision-making, empathy, math, coordination. Early exposure to music, it's thought, might literally change the shape of the brain.

The Music Together! curriculum is based on childhood development research, but, as I learned from Newman's class's book, it's also
an offshoot of Dalcroze Eurhythmics, a music theory approach that
involves movement, listening, and vocalization to strengthen "intuitive" musicality. Dalcroze was a turn-of-the-century Swiss composer
and professor, dissatisfied with abstract, technical, in-your-head
approaches to teaching music. The methods were not making his students better musicians, he thought. With his conservatory pupils as
test subjects, Dalcroze developed a new system by which musicians
responded to a score's pitches and rhythm using their bodies directly.
This series of "games," as Dalcroze called them, targeted discrete
musical skills and could be used for children and adults alike.

At Music Together!, we played "sing and stop," a variation of a
Dalcroze game. For a song in 6/8 time—an energetic waltz—we sang
one pitch for three beats and spun around in a circle, then kept our
bodies and voices still for the next three. Newman wasn't walking
yet, so I'd pick him up for the locomotive parts. Miss Kimmy sang a
counterpoint melody in a minor key, pausing only to give us movement instructions: "spin and stop," then "walk and stop," and so on.
This was a way for the kids to practice moving with the beat but
against the melodic line. Dalcroze's games are a sneaky but painless
mode of introducing basic concepts in music theory. As I held Newman on my chest and weaved him through the group, I begin to feel
the contours of musical lines. Miss Kimmy 's voice was a flurry of
eighth notes above our slower, rhythmic bass. I saw our voices charted
on an imaginary board, sort of like a music theory classroom in the
back of my mind.

When I arrived at Oberlin Conservatory of Music in the fall of 2003,
Dalcroze's influence was all over the curriculum. There was even a
separate Dalcroze Eurhythmics course for upperclassmen, although
it wasn't a core class for performance majors. Our heavy course load
required private lessons and ensembles, several music histories, sup-
plementary piano, four levels of music theory, and four levels of aural
skills. During orientation, in the cavernous recital hall where we gathered for course placement tests, the professor playing piano turned his

back to us and asked us to name the intervals, hitting all notes in the chord together instead of separating them the way my teacher back in Greensboro had. The pitches and their overtones mushed together in my ear. I froze in my panic, not being able to name what I was hearing. Although I managed to test out of Introductory Music Theory, I got placed in Aural Skills I, what musicians colloquially refer to as introductory "ear training." Ear training is meant to teach you how to identify pitches, chords, melodies, and rhythms by listening alone. It targets the very weaknesses that Dalcroze claimed in his students, the ones who couldn't connect what was written on the score to the actual playing.

Ear training's other major component is developing something called "audiation," that mysterious experience of being able to hear music in your brain even when there is no real-life sound. It's a kind of visualization, but in the ear and body instead of the mind's eye. ("Audiation," I read in Newman's songbook's introduction, "is also what is happening when you can't get a song out of your head.") At music conservatory, we transformed our audiations by sight-singing. We learned how to look at a score and use our voices to mimic the sounds we heard in our head, using correct pitches and in the right time signature. Singing itself isn't the skill being practiced; rather, it's just a way of marking what the score is doing. Dalcroze believed that singing and musical cognition were one and the same: "The mere thinking of a tune arouses in the throat the muscular movements necessary for its vocal emission." Thanks to him and some of the theorists who came after, all kinds of musicians learn how to sight-sing in music school.

Ear-training class at Oberlin was rigorous but also surprisingly communal, a nice change from the lone hours I spent in the practice rooms. Two mornings a week, my harpsichordist roommate and I rolled out of bed and shuffled into Professor Miyake's classroom. There were twelve of us. The first weeks were embarrassing for everyone, save the voice majors. If you're not used to singing solo, or if you have a not-great voice, being called on at random to sight-sing music lines is a vulnerable, public experience. Imagine the dream where you're naked in front of class, except the nakedness is your voice.

While sight-singing, each student also conducted with their right arm in the time signature. Combining these elements of voice, motion, and reading the score is a kind of game, not unlike the play-ful challenges often asked of children: Can you pat your head and rub your stomach at the same time? Now say the alphabet? Dalcroze believed that, in an ideal education, all musical concepts should be introduced through the body. This is perhaps why his approaches are used not just for older students but also for little kids like the ones in Newman's class, the ones who don't read music.

Most conservatory students dread ear-training classes, seeing them as a silly institutional hoop to jump through. For me, it was differ-ent. There was a deeper trust forming between all of us in that space, an intimacy that comes from watching people uncalculated and silly and vulnerable in their voices and bodies. You never see much of this in musicians' polished performances, which are choreographed from the moment they walk onstage until they bow. In ear training, my classmates and I got used to singing and conducting in front of one another, imperfect (and even ugly) as we worked out the struggle of the coordination. Our singing, good or bad, became the lingua franca of the classroom.

My own self-consciousness began to recede to the background as I became part of this group practice. Once, after Professor Miyake called on me to sight-sing, she praised me. "Do you hear how attuned she is to phrasing?" she asked the other students. "This is the musical-ity we're after."

Attuned is the exact word: focused on the movements of my body, the score, and the sounds I made, I sometimes achieved a feeling of synthesis, forgetting about performance. This experience was tran-scendent, a feeling I rarely had when I played my instrument alone, no matter how hard I tried. Even in my best moments with solo gui-tar, I was usually still caught up in the trickiness of technique, the occasional buzz or wrong note. I never got used to the lonely, exposed feeling of being the only person making sound in the room.

The somatic memories began to surface slowly, some sixteen years later, as I sat cross-legged in the Music Together! circle with my baby, listening to people work through their rhythmic challenges. As Miss Kimmy introduced another corny song—this one about a cat named

"MEL-lis-sa AG-nes JANE" and a dog "CHRIS-to-pher AL-ex JAMES"—I noticed adults struggle to clap on the strong beats while they sang, giggling because they kept coming in one note too early. Amalia's nanny was tapping her foot at random intervals. The stay-at-home dad had given up altogether. The "extra" beat in each measure, Miss Kimmy explained, was throwing everyone off: the song was written 7/8 instead of standard four-beat divisions. Ironically, the older toddlers seem to have no problem clapping, leading me to wonder how adults had blunted their rhythmic sense over time. Too many obligatory "Star-Spangled Banners" and all those pop songs on the radio, maybe?

Complex rhythms were my favorite when I was a music student, the unexpected patterns alighting my nervous system. I remember feeling something open inside me while playing Benjamin Verdery's guitar ensemble piece *Scenes from Ellis Island*, which uses a rhythm called a cow's tail for how it narrows: three measures of 6/4 followed by three measures each of 5/4, 4/4, 3/4, and 2/2. Playing the piece required a concentration so complete that I'd had no choice but to muscle memorize the rhythm, let my body take over the experience. It's not surprising to me that Dalcroze believed rhythm was music's most transformative agent, "coordinating all the spiritual and corporal movements of the individual." In the recital hall, repeating this rhythm with a vanguard of other guitarists, I got goose bumps.

But such highs never seemed to last long. In solo study, where most of the emphasis is if you're in music school, a kind of mechanical monotony hindered whatever realm I tried to reach. It was a conundrum: on the one hand, to have so much passion for music as to want to devote my whole education to it; on the other hand, "devotion" requiring the pursuit of technical perfection, endless slur studies and études and required hours of "butt in the chair," as professionals sometimes called it. In the conservatory practice rooms, I'd sometimes catch myself staring hollowly at my image in the mirror—why were there mirrors at all?—and realize I'd been zoning out for five minutes. My heart pounded, and for a second, it was hard to remember what I was doing there in the first place.

In Newman's music class, holding his little hands and clapping them to the beat, if I could get past the songs' cheesy lyrics and theatricality, I sometimes found myself overcome with a different emotion, a wave of grief. I can't think back to my musical adolescence without remembering an existential sort of sadness, and also a sense that I would never be good enough as a guitarist to achieve what I was after. In Newman's Music Together! songbook, the introduction gently acknowledges that music—even music for toddlers—can open up old wounds in adults. "Not every parent feels comfortable in class at first. You may have grown up with no music in your life," it says, "or you may have had a difficult time with music or music lessons." *Well, that is one way of putting it,* I think to myself. And then, a gentle suggestion: "We invite you to try and experience music as if it were new to you."

Yes, I thought to myself. This is a hunger I've always had. And perhaps taking Newman to music class was less about his needs than my own, me reaching for something from my previous life. It was much too early to predict what my kid's relationship to music would be. Maybe he wouldn't care for it at all. But I felt a twinge of anxiety when I knew that the opposite was possible. I thought of how he listened intently as I sang to him before he fell asleep, how he wouldn't give the song up until his eyes closed completely. Down the road, it's possible he will care about music so much that it becomes his main devotion, his whole body like an ear.

After I dropped out of music school, I enrolled in the college division of Oberlin and found myself drawn to other art forms: writing, which was new to me, along with dance, something I'd done throughout childhood. Not far from the Oberlin Conservatory sat Warner Center, the Victorian-era gymnasium that had become the college's home for dance. Perhaps seeking that somatic wholeness I'd felt in ear-training courses, I took modern dance in Warner's cavernous upstairs studio, a space that had been the college's basketball court in the early twentieth century. During warm-up exercises, lying belly-up on the cool floorboards, I looked past the railings of the old running track and up into the wooden rafters. This room was a cathedral to me, a place where we moved through our teacher's sequences week after week, sweating and breathing hard in the company of others. When I took the college's choreography course, I made my dances in this empty space late at night, the high-ceilinged quiet willing me to create.

Dance culture at Oberlin had an avant-garde quality, often more concerned with experimentation than accuracy. Some of my professors had studied and performed with dancers from the Judson Church in Greenwich Village, a generation who believed in a more inclusive approach to dance and who incorporated other art forms rather than teasing them apart.

My sophomore year, there was a buzz on campus about which students might be chosen for an upcoming residency with Meredith Monk, the queen of interdisciplinary art forms. Before she came to Oberlin, I didn't know much about Monk, the singer-composer-dancer-choreographer-filmmaker who started her career by making unclassifiable, site-specific pieces.

"I work between the cracks," Meredith Monk once said, "where the voice starts dancing, where the body starts singing, where the theater becomes cinema." The students who got picked for the Monk class would be people who could work in more than one discipline: musicians who had studied filmmaking, painters who sang, or, in my case, an ex-musician studying dance and writing. When the class list was finally posted, I was excited to find my name among eleven others.

Meredith Monk arrived on campus that winter like someone from another era: a tiny, exuberant woman in her late sixties who dressed in long black tunics and wore her hair in two braided pigtails. Though hosted by the dance department, Meredith was most famous for her voice and music compositions: bizarre, hypnotic songs that layered repeated phrases or modules of sound, lyrics eschewed in favor of a nonlinguistic vocables. It's like listening to Gregorian chant, opera, synth-pop, and a cappella folk songs from an imaginary country all at once. At the concert she gave when she arrived, I sat in the balcony of the chapel, watching her in bird's-eye view, her small figure at the end of a mammoth Steinway. The piano, it seemed, was mostly there for layering sound, a scrolling landscape where her vocals could roam. Meredith's voice was like a separate body altogether: light but not tentative, what whispered and yodeled and glided from between phrases.

Meredith's classes were held in Warner's upstairs studio, her flexible soprano seeming to bounce off the rafters as she led us through vocalizations, acrobatics for the mouth and throat. Meredith explained that she, too, had studied Dalcroze Eurhythmics in childhood, and much of her work married the voice and the body. But unlike my previous training, Meredith's exercises weren't about becoming more technically proficient musicians. They were about becoming different musicians altogether. What was a musician, even?

"Now I want you to take this vocal score," Meredith instructed, "and create, say, a little folk-type dance that has strong beats. That's going to be your percussion." We gave each other looks at first, but she was serious. If anyone ever made a parody of liberal arts college, I'm pretty sure "create a little folk dance" was party of the storyline.

But by the time Meredith went back to New York, our group had bonded over the shared vulnerability of making odd compositions together: pieces where musicians and sculptors were dancing, where the dancers were singing. The class had created a subculture, a floating island that surfaced on early Wednesday and Friday mornings when we met in the studio. For the first time, I was making music that wasn't directed by someone else's notes on a staff, music that wasn't following conventional Western rules for melody, had no discernible tonal center.

Our final evening-length performance had a surreal, "exquisite corpse" quality, created by all of us, rejecting the notion of one subject or unified vision. My main contribution to the performance was a dance piece that included "trained" and nontrained dancers, twenty-four helium balloons, a classmate attached to the ceiling by bungee cable, and an electronic score created by another classmate. The piece was probably the strangest thing I'd ever made. In the final scene of our performance, my classmate, Tatyana—who ended up a well-known choreographer in New York City after college—staged the entire group moving across the room in a flocklike formation, speaking in a rhythmic unison. We spoke five syllables while we ran forward, four syllables as we swung our bodies to the left, three syllables as we turned to face the person beside us, two syllables as we jumped in different directions. The rhythm reminded me of the cow's tail from my guitar ensemble days, the feeling intensifying as the units grew smaller, our heartbeats closer together. The show sold out every night, its unclassifiable strangeness receiving attention in nearby Cleveland, even though we were just students doing all this for class credit.

I sometimes wonder what parallel universe we were living in, spending so many hours of our time creating something like this. Unlike my ear-training courses in the conservatory—or Dalcroze's games, even—Monk's class wasn't necessarily designed to refine a more discreet skill, like playing an instrument. Even Miss Kimmy was able to qualify her methods in this respect. So, what were we learning here? What was the point?

Sixteen years later, when I look back at that semester of college, it seems that mostly what my classmates and I were doing was playing. Not as in instruments or as in rehearsing for something else. I don't even mean theater. I mean the kind of imaginative stuff that has intrinsic motivation, what we often associate with children.

Flipping through the book for Newman's Music Together! class, I couldn't help but notice that the guidelines for the curriculum sounded suspiciously like some of the stuff from my Oberlin years. "In music play," the text reads, "the child teaches herself about the music of her culture by experimenting with the information she has gathered from her music environment. Her music play may take place simultaneously with motor or other forms of play, or it may take place alone. She may sing parts of familiar songs or create her own short songs; she may recite familiar chants or make up new ones about her play objects or experiences; and she may also experiment with different kinds of rhythmic movement." If I had to translate this, I'd say, "The children are trying out nonverbal mediums, which have the ability to move us in ways we don't quite understand."

The connoisseur in me wanted to claim there were a million degrees of separation between what I'd done in college and the stuff in Newman's class: the cheesy lyrics, people singing out of tune, babies wandering off to the corners of the studio. Little Baxter scratching his butt while he sang. Me placing the instruments Newman had chewed on in the bucket labeled "soggy." But my body told me something else. This experience connected me to my communal musical past, memories from the Monk residency popping up we strolled home from music class. The tacky songs of Music Together! became earworms, audiating for hours inside my brain after we'd left the arts center. When my wife and I collapsed onto bed at night, that parental exhaustion deeper than any I'd known, the melodies were still with me.

Once, while Newman was napping, I pulled off the bookshelf my copy of Deborah Jowitt's edited collection of Meredith Monk's writings and interviews. A red discount sticker from Oberlin's indie bookstore was still stuck to its spine. I paused on a diary entry from the 1980s, back when Meredith was staging her opera *Quarry*. She writes about one of the performer's kids entering her creative process: "Lanny's four-year-old daughter, Hannah Pearl, comes to rehearsal. When I am in bed [playing a child], she is next to me. She 'helps' Pablo tuck me in after my dance. I love having her in rehearsal— another reality bumping up against the work. I watch her movement/ posture for inspiration. . . . The rehearsal has an easygoing discipline about it. Everyone participates in the investigation."

Well, OK, sure: in an ideal world. *Meredith never had any kids herself,* I thought to myself as I collapsed on the couch. She didn't exhaust herself to the point of mental cloudiness by taking care of Hannah Pearl all day before the rehearsal. But I was still curious about Meredith seeing this toddler as part of the creation—a kind of muse, even. Another reality bumping up against the work.

I thought of all the creative spaces I'd been in where a child doesn't belong: the ear-training class, the instrumental practice room. The concert hall. The table in the poetry workshop. The literary reading where everyone but the poet must be absolutely quiet. Kids were considered a nuisance, a distraction from art making, almost everywhere I'd been. Even now, in the room where I try to write this, I'm struggling not to let my attention drift to Newman, who is downstairs with my wife, screeching at the top of his lungs. Another reality bumping up against the work.

Since I'd become a parent, creativity often felt partitioned off from the rest of my life, my day-to-day so noisy and unchoreographed. But if I got myself into the Meredith Monk mindset, the divisions between what is art and what isn't began to seem more artificial— maybe even antithetical—to creating.

I tried to picture how Meredith would respond to Music Together!, what might occur to her as she entered our circle on the mat. She would watch the kids clapping and moving clumsily in the circle dance, listening to Miss Kimmy's soprano and Baxter's grandmother doing her harmonizing. In my mind, I saw her running between the scarves as they flew through the air. I imagined her being interested in some of the weird instruments on the floor, thinking about which ones she could use in future pieces. Instinct tells me that Meredith would probably feel less self-conscious than I have about the campiness, the performativity. I imagine that she'd commit herself fully to this world of play. When it comes to creation, could Miss Kimmy's classroom be just another way of getting at the real thing? And what is it, exactly, that has kept me from seeing it that way?

∴ ∴ ∴

Newman and I had been going to Music Together! for only a few months when the COVID-19 pandemic hit with full force. My wife came home from the office with all her equipment and never went back. I kept Newman home from music class. I tried to imagine our music circle full of holes, our line-and-circle dances with socially appropriate distances in between each body. This was before we began to understand that the virus could be transmitted through aerosols, that the act of singing together could be a superspreading event.

Eventually, the arts center closed down. That Thursday window when I normally took Newman to music class shut for good, forgotten and blurred into the rest of our days. The Music Together! songbook was smushed at the bottom of the diaper bag. I'd come around to some of the songs from class, but I couldn't quite muster the will to sing them without the community of voices around us.

By the time everything shut down, Newman was almost eleven months old. He'd begun to walk. His first word arrived soon after, a hard, surprising syllable: *cat*. His babbling became more operatic. I watched as he suddenly became sensitive to household sounds that struck him as scary or sad: minor intervals in the washing machine's spin cycle, low bass notes when our fridge compressor hummed. At home, he'd point to my old pitch pipe, a relic from my former musical life, demanding I get it off the shelf. Within a few months, he'd learn to blow into a couple of the holes simultaneously, the rough clash of pitches making him cry. "Why do you keep doing this if you hate it so much?" I asked him, a question that certainly applied to both his parents at different point in their own musical lives.

As case numbers swelled, posts from Meredith Monk's professional pages began to show up frequently in my social media accounts. The tone of the writings was too entrepreneurial to be written by Meredith herself; someone from her foundation must have been in charge of the advertisements for "Zoom singing workshops" and Vimeo links to Meredith's works. I watched a few clips from her 1989 film *Book of Days*, set in Europe at the start of the Black Death, which I hadn't seen since college. The images from the film felt mythic and elusive to me back then, but now they were almost too close to our current experience: a pile of plague-claimed bodies in the cobbled street; a red blot on the map of the walled city, representing illness spreading through the community; groups of Christian mobsters, dressed in white, blaming Jews for the plague. The film terrified me, felt more relevant than ever. "My work is about cycles about human experience," Meredith claimed, always interested in speaking to our time and place by referencing another, searching for the common thread.

If it weren't for watching Newman's accelerated growth—using new words, suddenly being able to climb into a chair or screw a jar lid, bringing me his shoes when he wanted to go outside—I might've lost my sense of time altogether. Cooped up during those early pandemic months, I began to feel like I had right after Newman was born: at home all the time, bone tired from caregiving, struggling to think clearly. In the afternoons, I tagged alongside Newman as he toddled down the sidewalk, delighted by his new mobility.

Cleaning up after dinner one night, I listened to Meredith Monk give an interview in which she describes writing music furiously during lockdown, holed up in the same bare-bones Manhattan loft she's had since the 1960s. She was alone there except for her forty-year-old tortoise, Neutron. "The music is just flowing out of me," Meredith says, the phone making her voice sound far away. I felt jealous, thinking of quarantine's isolation without the constant demands of caregiving. But on the other hand, Meredith admits, "I just feel this wave of sadness coming over me about the suffering out there." I felt this as I watched the death toll, a red line rising on the chart.

Early mornings, my family went outside, one of us pushing Newman in the stroller, the neighborhood as quiet as a film set. The pandemic erased the city's congestion. I saw Newman attuned to the small sounds around him. A bird twittering. A squirrel rustling the leaves above, fluttery percussion. The slow crescendo as a car approached us: the pitch rising as it came closer—a Doppler shift—and lowering as the car disappeared ahead. We walked, jogged, stopped at traffic lights, jogged again. The sounds became their own reality. Divorced from my usual sense of time, I felt as though we were inside some bizarre minimalist composition, the three of us the only performers. Silent houses stood at the periphery, full of people we couldn't see. What did the world mean, I wondered, without coming close to other people?

Since I hadn't followed Meredith Monk's career very closely since leaving Oberlin, there was a lot of catching up to do. Her most recent full-length work—debuted at Brooklyn Academy of Music in 2018, and then on the road in 2019 and early 2020—was called *Cellular Songs*. "A cell is a miraculous prototype of cooperation," Meredith explained. "My piece is about the possibility of human cooperation." I watched a performance online, finding it to be absolutely bare bones: no frills, no narrative threads, no instrumentation, just a cappella voices. There is none of the absurdist excess you might find in some of her early theater. The five women wear white tunics and white pants, as if blank canvases, erased of characterization. They begin to sing with one another quietly, the syllables *nyo-me-nyo-me-nyo-me* on a loop, creating a small wavering. The women stand facing one another in easy geometric formations: sometimes a rhombus, other times, circles.

Two women add a layer of high, ethereal-sounding harmony, a descant that teeters between the main pitch and a half-step below, what sounds like a scale trying to finish itself but instead keeps knocking inside its own kinetic loop. *Nyo-me-nyo-me-nyo-me* sounds, at first, almost humorous, like a kind of Teletubby gibberish, maybe even some ridiculous game from Newman's music class. But the tiny sounds create a kinetic rush as they layer and build. It made me remember, too, the Monk residency at Oberlin, our voices clustered in Tatyana's performance piece as the group moved in unison.

Meredith and the four other women stop singing on occasion, the sudden tacitness seeming louder than the chorus itself. In the silences, they shift geometrical formation, everyone taking a step backward, widening the shape. Immediately I was able to envision this virus, how it spread exponentially, entering so many bodies. The women begin to sway at a glacial speed, their torsos bowing toward one another. It's like looking at cells under the microscope, their bodies like cilia: those small hairs on the cell's perimeter, waving rhythmically. Suddenly everything makes sense—the busy, kinetic-feeling, small sounds; the geometric formations; the small movements they make in tandem. The performers transform themselves into energy on a microscopic level. They are no longer individual bodies, but more like organelles in a single unit. It felt strangely moving to watch this in a time of pandemic, when public health officials asked us to think about our action as collective. When we stayed home, at least in part, to increase everyone's chances of survival.

There's nothing sentimental in *Cellular Songs*. The music and movement is elemental, zero excess. But even with science being the inspiration for the piece, the way the elements come together is anything but clinical. Something moved through me as I watched, something that connected to me to a bigger feeling—something like a common thread of humanity, as grandiose as that might sound. I realized, too, that I was experiencing the alchemy of performance before the pandemic. I had just heard a story of the community choir in Washington state, where one person with COVID-19 managed to infect 87 percent of the choir's members. There was a good reason Newman's class was canceled. The act of making music together, which often means sharing the same air, might be the closest you can get to other humans. And suddenly, it was that very closeness that signaled danger.

Group performances, the bedrock of Meredith's career, were off-limits for the time being. Instead, Meredith was at home, creating and exploring what came next. "One morning I woke up," Meredith stated in a recent interview about creating in the time of COVID-19, "and thought, hats off to this virus. I mean, one brilliant organism. It's adaptable, it moves quickly." Even in the face of pandemic, with all the deaths and restrictions, she was trying to lean into awe. "One thing I've learned over the years is resilience," she said. "I just take it step by step and try to work with the limitations."

"Work with the limitations." When I heard that, I paused. In my whole history of being a creative person, this idea rarely presented itself: not from the Guitar Teacher or the conservatory faculty at

Oberlin, not the dance teachers or the people I studied from in graduate school, or the people who hired me to teach poetry. But the limitations have always been there, even if it has taken becoming a parent to begin to see them clearly. To finally understand how we are dependent on one another for pretty much everything. If any creative space has acknowledged limitation, it's probably Miss Kimmy's class, where it was OK to clap on the wrong beat, to sing off-key, to let your kid wander off into the corner. Come as you are, Music Together! seemed to say, because you have no other choice, but also because you will be enough.

I never wanted to raise a child like this, I thought, isolated months later at home during the pandemic, without any community. At the park, Newman ran toward other small children, and I steered him away, fearing exposure. Instead of "socializing" him, I was doing the opposite: convincing him to leave others alone. While my wife worked long hours, I chased our child, picked him up, fed him, read to him, changed his diaper, fed him again, cleaned his hands and face, put him down for a nap, chased him again. I kept him from hurting himself, and he brimmed over with new toddler anger, sobbing on a loop until I sang "The Itsy Bitsy Spider," the rhythm and movement resetting his brain. Singing had suddenly become important to him. "A-tan," he said when I got to the end of the song, his new sound for *again*.

Even as my kid grew more expressive, more human every day, the monotony of caretaking in isolation often felt like it was closing in on me. I worried that I had lost the things that made me more than just someone's parent. Even when my wife was with Newman and I holed up to write for an hour or two, I often found my mind bleached of language, my body feeling like one of those pandemic-emptied auditoriums. No poems came to me. Anything I was working on before the pandemic felt irrelevant to this new life, which was mostly about surviving and minimizing damage to others. Some days, it was like hitting the same note over and over again, waiting to see if the sound changed. *Work with the limitations*, I remembered Meredith Monk saying. On good days, I leaned into the mantra, hopeful that I was always on the edge of something I didn't understand, something that might change me for the better.

A final scene: We've been home for seven months on the rainy October morning that I feel compelled, out of curiosity or instinct, to show Newman my guitar for the first time. He is eighteen months old, rambunctious and obsessed with the mechanics of everything. He doesn't have much language yet, though he can suddenly count to ten: his routine as we walk down the stairs, like we're practicing scales. I bring out the guitar case and undo the brass buckles, Newman's attention sharpening. The familiar spruce scent wafts up like a genie released from a bottle.

Newman puts his palm to the spruce soundboard. I pluck the low E string, that bedrock of the instrument's range, and feel my body remember something I can't unlearn. I try to read Newman's shifting expression as the first sound floats toward him. He holds his hand up to the dark sound hole, like someone feeling for a source of heat.

Now my body alights with its own thorny history: the memory of learning each note, fret by fret. The shapes and timbres of the pieces I learned, how they shaped me. The terror of performing solo, jumping through the technical hoops, bald and exposed. The cold practice rooms in Ohio. The sanctity of playing alongside others, the hugeness we made together.

Newman taps all six strings at once, discovering that direct force makes a sound. I imitate him, tapping three times. He taps again, waits for me to answer. Hitting the guitar makes it sound rustic and angular, like one of the weird folk instruments Meredith Monk might use in an opera. We spend a few minutes playing this way: call-and-response, the bony ghost of an E chord rising between us.

I have spent so much time like this: creating little games to show Newman something he might not know, small ways of passing our long days. I know we might spend years playing like this, that it's part of the promise I made when I decided to raise a child. I imagine these games getting more complex over time, until there's a day that he no longer needs me to play. That time still feels so far away, and yet, I can already see Newman having his own ideas and desires, his babyhood nearly gone. Watching him each day is like watching a live performance, the shape and sounds of everything vanishing as quickly as they appear.

Newman loses interest in the guitar after a few minutes, preferring his devilish climbing over the couch cushions and compulsively clicking our cat's laser pointer, its red eye flickering on the ceiling. I almost feel relieved when I get bored, too, and lay the guitar down again. I admire its structural beauty from a distance. A few minutes later, I'm putting the guitar back into its case when Newman snatches a wooden coaster from the table, somehow managing to drop it directly onto the guitar. There's a thwack where it hits the soundboard. I freeze in terror, my old protective instincts firing up. The worst is true: I see a hairline crack on the soundboard.

How could I have let this happen, I think, staring at that tiny split in the wood. The small opening is like an eye into some new interior. Another reality bumping up against the work. Or thrown against the work, quite literally. The parent I've become just shrugs her shoulders. He's eighteen months old. He acts completely on instinct. I should've been watching him more closely, I guess. Even then, I'm not sure I could have changed the outcome.

But this moment is already over. Newman barely registers the drama he's just created, is going on to his next reality. He is pulling his little body up onto the windowsill, eager to see the approaching garbage truck, its maniacal beeping coming closer and closer. It's a strange, relentless sort of music. I close the guitar case and hurry over to the window, helping him up, both of us eager to see the source of what he hears.

SOME MOTHERS

One mother dresses like a cave person for Bible camp, makes the room darker by covering the ceiling with garbage bags.

Another mother lets her kids run wild while she smokes with her friends by the pool, wears a bikini and green visor that makes her look like a poker dealer.

David's mother, briefly an actress in New York, leads the drama club at school. She gives everyone a song from a musical. Mine is "Castle on a Cloud" from *Les Misérables*. It's sung by a French girl who doesn't have parents.

My sisters and I are always pretending we're orphans for some reason. Annie. Anne of Green Gables. Dorothy. Pollyanna. Mary from *The Secret Garden*. Their mothers died in fires or from scarlet fever or in childbirth. These daughters have to go live elsewhere, always arriving by train.

In reality, our mother is alive in the next room, slicing a cantaloupe and putting it in a Tupperware.

Allison's mother is always busy with her hot-glue gun, attaching beads to everything. My own mother is not interested in crafts. "Who has the time for that," she says. "Also, what's the point?"

My mother brings home flu shots from the clinic where she works and gives them to the family. Sometimes we play dress-up with her nursing uniform from the 1970s, those unimaginable years before we were born.

My mother teaches me how to sew on a button and sew up a hole. How to tell if you need to go to the doctor or just stay home and wait it out. How to read the bass clef and the treble clef. My mother helps me memorize my multiplication tables so well that I have never forgotten them.

One mother is the school principal, so everyone is scared of her, but I have seen her barefoot and in shorts.

One mother turns out to be our friend's grandmother instead. She makes people look more beautiful, braids hair for a living.

Another mother, whose hair is growing thin, styles her hair like she's walking directly into a gust of wind.

∴ ∴ ∴

The first mother was made of rib. The first mother was made of corn. The first mother fell from the sky, but two swans caught her. The first mother became a mother because her brother slapped her with a fish and got her pregnant.

In Chinese, the character for *mother* is made from a woman with her legs crossed and a horse beside her. The horse is not part of the mother's story. It's just the sound of the horse that's important. *Ma*, which means horse, sounds like *mama*.

In China, my coworker's wife must stay home for weeks after their baby is born. "Sitting the month," they call it: 坐月子. She isn't allowed to wash her hair.

The character for *good* shows a woman with her legs crossed but also a baby beside her.

My mother's hip bones are so narrow that they had to cut her open to get the three of us out. On her belly, a light scar stretches out like the rail of a train track.

When we're kids, Erin's mother swings a pencil on a string above our arms, which is supposed to tell you if you'll have a boy or a girl when you grow up. Erin's pencil swings one way, saying she'll have a boy. My pencil keeps changing direction.

"Who knows?" says Erin's mother, and I wonder whether this means I won't be a mother at all.

Erin's boy is born when we are in our twenties.

In college, a friend's mother is the first to die. Breast cancer. When our friend returns to school a week later, she walks differently, as if there were an invisible veil trailing behind her.

In graduate school, none of the women teaching me has any children. "Who has time," one says, "to both mother and be a writer?"

My mother nursed me for years. My mother rocked me to sleep in the rocking chair. My mother put love notes in my lunch box.

My mother erased my handwriting on my homework and made me write my answers again. "It's hard to read what you wrote," she insisted. "I think maybe you should try again."

My graduate school classmate, whose mother is an immigrant and works in a factory, writes a poem I can't forget. "Who is the most important person in your life?" the poem begins.

The refrain: "Your mother, your mother, your mother."

An older mother told me that becoming a mother would make me a better person. She was trying to encourage me.

In reality, the baby revealed some parts of myself that were not better. For example, the part of me that still wishes I could lock myself in a room for hours and not be bothered or asked for anything. The part of me that wants to not be awake at 5 A.M. The part of me that needs to be left alone.

Also: the part of me that worries all the time, imagines drownings and getting hit by cars, the baby who stops breathing in his sleep for no reason.

After they retrieved my eggs, my abdomen was bruised for weeks. "It was hard to get to your ovaries," they tell me. "They're sort of hidden behind your other organs."

Never once had I imagined where my ovaries were. Although I did imagine the eggs inside them from time to time: pearls with little question marks on their faces.

Sometimes my mother seems more worried about my baby than she is about me. I say, "Please be my mother." She gets angry, doesn't speak to me for weeks.

Whenever I fight with her, I think about how her own mother, Frances, has been dead since 1980. She got a brain tumor in her early sixties. My mother cared for her while she was dying: the confusion, the projectile vomiting. She mothered her own mother.

My mother has already outlived the age of her own mother.

David emails me from Colorado to say his mother has early onset Alzheimer's. She is in a facility in our hometown somewhere. As the oldest, he is the one responsible. His father left her years ago.

I remember old stories I heard from other kids about her fits of rage. The way she let sheep wander her yard, then the house itself. We thought she was just eccentric, but now I wonder.

My mother was only twenty-five when she became the only mother left. "I never learned how to mother adults," she tells me. This is her version of an apology, I guess.

It's hard for me to sleep with the baby monitor on. I keep staring at the bloated ghost of his body, whitewashed by the light of the shitty camera. What if something gets him in the night?

My wife takes my photo for the back of my book, the one about to be published. My last author photos are from when I was twenty-five years old, and we agree they can't be used anymore. "But I don't want to look like a dorky mother," I say to her. We take about one hundred photos in the back alley while the baby sleeps strapped to her chest.

We haven't slept in months. All the mothers we know "sleep train" their babies around this time, swear by the method.

But my mother shakes her head. "Rule number one of parenting," she says. "Don't leave your kid crying alone in a room."

My mother teaches me that it's better if you just give up and let the baby come into bed with you. Put your mattress on the floor, she says. "Everyone will sleep better," she says. And she is right. We do this until he becomes a toddler.

"Don't tell the pediatrician," she warns me. "There are things they don't need to know."

My mother doesn't understand why I don't call myself mommy or mom. "No one else can have those names," she tells me. "They are the most special."

On some level, she thinks I may be rejecting her. My wife goes by ZaZa. I go by BeBe. I want to unyoke myself from gender. Plus, it's confusing if my wife and I are called versions of the same name.

It doesn't matter what name I go by, I tell my mother. The results are the same.

In the backyard, my son names three squirrels: Baby Squirrel, ZaZa Squirrel, BeBe Squirrel. Our son thinks *mother* is a character in a book or a song, usually in the form of a duck.

I try to write about my son, but I worry it is turning me into someone I don't want to be. He takes up all the space in my brain. At night, I talk to my wife about the things my son said during the day, the strange metaphysical utterances.

Today it was "You have ocean water in your belly."

I look at him, perplexed. He has been to the ocean twice—Brunswick County, North Carolina, the beaches of my own childhood—but learned to like it only the second time, screaming with joy each time a wave came in.

Like many parents, I don't quite understand where he came from.

We move back to Oberlin just after he turns two, in part to try for a life that's less chaotic. At the day-care drop-off, two mothers tell me I look awesome in my vest and oxfords, which is not the uniform of most mothers. All day I hold onto their words.

One mother teaches literature in French. One mother is my department chair. One mother is pregnant again.

In a young mother's apartment above the coffee shop, we drink hot things and talk about how difficult it is to plan for your child when you don't know whether your contract is getting renewed or where you'll be working next year.

They talk about how difficult it is to be pregnant. The mothers look at me for confirmation, not realizing I've never carried a baby. I have to explain to them how things went in the years before I knew them.

I feel like a mother because I carry a diaper and wipes and a snack everywhere I go. I feel like a mother because my body hurts from wrangling my toddler. I get diagnosed with arthritis of the knees at thirty-six years old. I use a heating pad and an ice pack at the end of the day.

"I'm done with kids," one of the mothers says, sipping her tea. "I had one. I'm not going through that again."

∴ ∴ ∴

My child pedals his tricycle through the leaves. He learns how to make coffee. My child puts his stuffed octopus to bed.

My mother sends my son a tractor, a singing giraffe, a Halloween card. My mother sends my son a book about the alphabet. A is for alligator. B for boat.

He has another alphabet book that says L is for lesbian. N is for non-binary. It cracks us up when he starts to say these things out loud.

B is for BeBe, he says.

My mother and I share two of our three names: Lindsey and Rogers. Only Elizabeth belongs to me alone. Rogers I share with my child. In that way, our family might be matriarchal.

But on the birth certificate, my wife is listed as mother. I am listed as "father/other parent." My son looks just like me, except his eyes are blue like my father's, while mine are an amberish green.

Maybe I don't feel like a mother because there is no father. The either-or choices don't fit.

In the picture we have of the sperm donor, I see my son's eyebrows, his big earlobes. Otherwise, he doesn't resemble him at all.

It's not a lie: he has no father.

My child struggles with *you* and *I*: when to use *them*, who is who. But before this, he barely spoke at all. I took him to a speech therapist, whom I had to correct: I don't go by that name, I said.

When the speech therapist said the word *mommy* to him, he turned to look behind him, seeing no one.

In the early morning, my child crawls into my bed, the toddler heft of him a kind of messy miracle. I hold onto him, knowing this version of him won't last.

We contemplate a second child, even knowing all that we know. We know our window is limited. We're aging fast.

The years are hurtling past us. Things hurt. Also, how can we put ourselves through the hardest parts again: the trauma of birth, the sleeplessness that makes us ill.

My child wants to write our names on the bathtub. He learns to spell *Rogers* even before he learns how to ask a question, before he understands what parents are.

We are his parents: Sarah, Elizabeth. We buy a heavy bike and attach a child's seat to the back. He yells from the bike: "White house! Gray house! Blue house!" He tells the air his full name: Newman. Christopher. Rogers. Two of three names he shares with us.

What he calls me, BeBe, is my favorite of all my names. Better than Beth or Elizabeth.

Sometimes I think I should have gone by it all along.

I pedal him around town all autumn, until the snow starts to fall. And even when I'm riding solo, everyone I pass knows what the small seat behind me means.

ACKNOWLEDGMENTS

While all events in this collection are true, names of the people involved have been changed.

Some earlier versions of essays have previously appeared in journals and anthologies: "A Bearing" and "Encumber: A Brief History" in *The Rumpus*; "Miss Southeast" in *The Journal*; "Dyke Litany" and "Shame" in the *Cincinnati Review*; "One Person Means Alone" in *The Best American Nonrequired Reading 2017*, *The Best American Travel Writing 2017*, *LitHub*, and the *Missouri Review*; "Public Swim": in *Prairie Schooner*; "Wound Care" in the *Hong Kong Review*; and "Ear Training" in *West Branch*. Thank you to the editors who selected these essays and the editorial staff that brought them into the world.

The Kenyon Review Fellowship first provided me the support to begin teaching myself to write essays a decade ago. Thank you to the DC Council on the Arts as well for its fellowship assistance.

For their eyes and ears at various stages of writing and creating this collection, I would like to thank Janet McAdams, Lisa Ampleman, Anne Beatty, and Lynn Powell. Thank you to Marisa Siegel for her editorial expertise and for the vision to bring this collection into the world.

Thank you to everyone at Northwestern University Press for bringing this book to readers.

And thank you to my family: especially my rock star wife, Sarah Newman, for her love and support.